THE BEAUTIFUL GAME REIMAGINED: WOMEN'S SOCCER IN BRAZIL

THE BEAUTIFUL GAME REIMAGINED: WOMEN'S SOCCER IN BRAZIL

EDITORS:
LÍVIA GONÇALVES MAGALHÃES,
TIAGO FERNANDES MARANHÃO, AND
BERNARDO BUARQUE DE HOLLANDA

First published in 2025
as part of Sports & Society Book Imprint
Common Ground Research Networks

University of Illinois Research Park
2001 South First St, Suite 201 L
Champaign, IL 61820 USA

Library of Congress Cataloging-in-Publication Data

Names: Magalhães, Lívia Gonçalves, editor. | Maranhão, Tiago Fernandes, editor. | Hollanda, Bernardo Borges Buarque de, 1974- editor.
Title: The beautiful game reimagined : women's soccer in Brazil / Editors: Lívia Gonçalves Magalhães, Tiago Fernandes Maranhão, and Bernardo Buarque de Hollanda.
Description: Champaign, IL : Common Ground Research Networks, 2025. | Summary: "This collection reimagines Brazilian football by spotlighting women's football as the future of the sport. The anthology brings together innovative academic research to explore the evolving role of women in the game. With a diverse range of interdisciplinary approaches, the essays draw on oral histories, digitized archives, digital humanities, and more to illuminate the untold stories of female athletes and marginalized communities in football"-- Provided by publisher.
Identifiers: LCCN 2024057292 (print) | LCCN 2024057293 (ebook) | ISBN 9781966214038 (hardback) | ISBN 9781966214045 (paperback) | ISBN 9781966214052 (adobe pdf)
Subjects: LCSH: Soccer for women--Brazil. | Women soccer players--Brazil. | Soccer--Brazil. | Sex discrimination in sports--Brazil--History.
Classification: LCC GV944.5 .B43 2025 (print) | LCC GV944.5 (ebook) | DDC 796.334082--dc23/eng/20250124
LC record available at https://lccn.loc.gov/2024057292
LC ebook record available at https://lccn.loc.gov/2024057293

ISBN: 978-1-966214-03-8 (HBK)
ISBN: 978-1-966214-04-5 (PBK)
ISBN: 978-1-966214-05-2 (pdf)
DOI: 10.18848/ 978-1-966214-05-2/CGP

Cover Design: Phillip Kalantzis Cope

TABLE OF CONTENTS

EDITORS AND CONTRIBUTORS

About the Editors

Bernardo Buarque de Hollanda

Bernardo Buarque de Hollanda holds a PhD in the social history of culture from the Pontifical Catholic University of Rio de Janeiro (PUC-Rio). He is currently associate professor at the School of Social Sciences and researcher at the Center for Research and Documentation on Brazilian Contemporary History at the Getulio Vargas Foundation (FGV/CPDOC).

Lívia Gonçalves Magalhães

Lívia Gonçalves Magalhães is professor at the Institute of History at the Fluminense Federal University (UFF). She has a master's in Latin American studies (UNSAM, Argentina, 2008), a PhD in social history (UFF, Brazil, 2013), and a postdoctorate in history at Unimontes/Brazil (Capes Scholarship 2014–2016) and at the University of Paris-Est Marne-la-Vallée (Capes Scholarship December 2017–March 2018). She has published *Soccer Stories* (2010) and *With the Cup in Hands* (2014) and is the owner of the research grant "Jovem Cientista do Nosso Estado" FAPEJ (Brazil) between 2023 and 2025.

Tiago Fernandes Maranhão

Tiago Fernandes Maranhão is assistant professor at Loyola University New Orleans. Before earning a PhD and an MA in history from Vanderbilt University, he worked as a college professor in Brazil for several years. After concluding his doctorate, he worked as a Mellon Foundation postdoctoral faculty fellow at Tougaloo College (Mississippi) and as a lecturer at the University of Michigan. He also earned a master's degree in political science from the University of Lisbon and a bachelor's degree in history from the Federal University of Pernambuco.

About the Contributors

Aira Bonfim Fernandes

Aira Bonfim Fernandes has a master's degree in history from FGV CPDOC–Rio de Janeiro, Brazil, with research on the initiation of Brazilian women into football in the early twentieth century. She was co-curator of the exhibitions Rainhas de Copas (2023), Contra-Ataque! The Women of Football (2019), and Football and the Olympics (2016), all at the Football Museum, in São Paulo. She is the author of the book *Futebol feminine no Brasil: entre festas, circus e subúrbios—uma história social (1915–1941)*, launched in 2023.

Brenda Elsey

Brenda Elsey is an American historian studying the history of popular culture and politics in twentieth-century Latin America, in addition to gender, social theory, sports and Pan-Americanism. Dr. Elsey co-edited the 2017 volume *Football and the Boundaries of History* and is the author of the *Futbolera: A History of Women and Sports in Latin America*. She has been the co-director of the Latin American and Caribbean Studies program at Hofstra University since 2008 and directed the Women's Studies program from 2009 to 2013. She is currently chairperson of the Advisory Board for Hofstra's Center for Civic Engagement.

Carmen Rial

Carmen Rial is full professor at the Universidade Federal de Santa Catarina (UFSC), in Brazil, since 1982. Additionally, she holds the position of chair at the National Institute of Science and Technology for Brazilian Football Studies. Rial has an extensive body of published work that covers various subjects, including globalization, emigration and displacements, consumerism and waste, documentary film, and football. Her research delves into themes of inequality, power, gender, and national identities.

Carolina Moraes

Carolina Moraes is a sociologist and has a master's degree in culture and society from the Federal University of Bahia. She has experience in network coordination

(Brazilian Football and Culture Network and Street Football Network) and has been conducting research and publications with the topics: football (soccer), culture, gender, and supporter groups. She is known for her performance in initiatives for training, mobilization, and knowledge production. Currently, she is master advisor at the Latin American Faculty of Social Sciences.

Caroline Almeida

Caroline Almeida is postdoctoral researcher in anthropology at the Universidade Federal de Pernambuco. She holds a PhD and a master's degree in social anthropology from the Universidade Federal de Santa Catarina. Additionally, she is one of the coordinators of the Research Line focusing on Women's, Indigenous, Paralympic, and LGBTQIA+ Football at the Brazilian Football Studies Institute for Science and Technology (INCT—Estudos do Futebol Brasileiro). Her research interests span the fields of sports anthropology, waste anthropology, globalization, and gender studies.

Daniela Araújo

Daniela Araújo has a PhD at post-graduation program in politics, history and cultural heritage at Fundação Getúlio Vargas (FGV-CPDOC). She is a scholarship holder at CAPES and is a journalist and has a master's in communication from the graduate program in communication at Universidade Federal Fluminense (UFF-Rio de Janeiro).

David Wood

David Wood is emeritus professor of Latin American studies at the University of Sheffield, where until 2021 he carried out teaching and research on the cultural production of many countries in the region. He has focused on socio-cultural elements of football in Latin America for over 20 years and has published more than 50 books, chapters, and articles, including *Football and Literature in South America* (Routledge, 2017).

Fernanda Haag

Fernanda Haag is a PhD candidate in social history at the University of São Paulo (USP). She researches Brazilian football through the lens of gender and labor relations. She is a university professor and the author of the book *História e Historiografia do Brasil República*. She is a member of Stadium: Grupo de Pesquisa em História do Esporte e das Práticas Lúdicas, a research group from University of Santa Maria (UFSM). Additionally, she writes a weekly column called "Elas por Ela" about women's football for the newspaper *Brasil de Fato*.

Gustavo Fernandes

Gustavo Fernandes is an undergraduate student of the Department of Journalism of the State University of Rio de Janeiro. He holds a complementary learning scholarship to intern at the Laboratory of Studies in Media and Sport (LEME-Uerj).

Leda Maria da Costa

Leda Maria da Costa is assistant professor of the Undergraduate and Graduate School of Social Communication at the State University of Rio de Janeiro. She is chief editor of *Esporte e Sociedade* journal of the Department of History at Federal Fluminense University (UFF). She is also a researcher of the Laboratory of Studies in Media and Sport (LEME-Uerj).

Luiza Aguiar

Luiza Aguiar is professor at Centro Federal de Educação Tecnológica de Minas Gerais and at the professional master's program in education and teaching at Universidade Federal de Minas Gerais. She is a physical education teacher and has a master's degree in leisure studies and PhD in human movement sciences. Her research deals with football, supporters, leisure, and school physical education, focused, above all, on gender and sexuality discussions.

Mariane da Silva Pisani

Mariane da Silva Pisani has a PhD in social anthropology and is professor at the Department of Social Sciences and the Graduate Program in Anthropology (PPGAnt) at the Federal University of Piauí (UFPI). She can be reached at marianepisani@gmail.com or at https://orcid.org/0000-0001-6925-4912.

Marina Mattos

Marina Mattos is psychologist and professor at the State University of Minas Gerais. She has a master's in social psychology at UERJ and a PhD in social sciences at PUC-SP. She holds a postdoctorate in leisure studies at the UFMG. She is a researcher at Study Group on Football and Torcidas (GEFuT/UFMG), at the Study and Research Group in Social Psychology of Sports (GEPSE/UFMG), and in the Sport, Culture and Society Working Group of the CLACSO. She dedicates herself to studies about soccer and subjectivity production.

Nathália Fernandes Pessanha

Nathália Fernandes Pessanha is a PhD student in history at the Fluminense Federal University in Rio de Janeiro. She develops research on women and soccer, with emphasis on the women's prohibition on soccer in Brazil. Gender studies, history of the body, and social history are her theoretical basis. She is currently writing in a column for the "História da Ditadura" website. She was awarded with the scholarship from the International Centre of Sport Studies (CIES/Switzerland) in 2021/2022.

Renata Maria Beltrão Lacerda

Renata Maria Beltrão Lacerda holds a master's degree in museology from the University of São Paulo (2023). Since 2019, she is the coordinator of the communication and marketing department at the Museu do Futebol (Football Museum) and the Museu da Língua Portuguesa (Museum of the Portuguese Language), both located in São Paulo. She is also a journalist and a specialist in public management.

Ronaldo George Helal

Ronaldo George Helal is full professor of the Undergraduate and Graduate School of Social Communication at the State University of Rio de Janeiro. He is a researcher at the National Council for Scientific and Technological Development (CNPq), at the Rio de Janeiro State Research Support Foundation (Faperj), and at the Scientific, Technical and Artistic Production Incentive

Program (Prociência/Uerj). He is also the coordinator of the Laboratory of Studies in Media and Sport (LEME-Uerj).

Rosana da Câmara Teixeira

Rosana da Câmara Teixeira has a bachelor's degree in social sciences and PhD in anthropology. She is an associate professor and researcher at the Institute of Education of the Universidade Federal Fluminense (UFF). She is member of the Laboratory of Education and Cultural Heritage. She has developed postdoctoral studies in social anthropology at the Museu Nacional (UFRJ—Rio de Janeiro, Brazil).

Silvana Goellner

Silvana Goellner is retired professor at Federal University of Rio Grande do Sul (UFRGS—Brazil) and currently visiting professor at Federal University of Pelotas (UFPel—Brazil). She holds a PhD in education and postdoctorate in sports (Portugal) and is vice-coordinator of the Study Group on Sport, Culture and History (GRECCO) and a member of the Women in Football Study Group (GEMF). She is also a researcher and activist in women's football, has published several books and article about women's football in Brazil, and is a columnist for Portal Ludopédio.

FOREWORD

Brenda Elsey

The study of history can provide alternatives, "usable pasts," to the present, while deepening our understanding of the contemporary moment. Cultural traditions undergird gender, racial, and national identity, so the way we tell their history is a choice with important consequences. Brazilian football culture has become infamous, globally, through international tournaments, marketing, and iconic players. Foundational to that image is a vast network of clubs, fans, and sports journalists. Women participated in all aspects of football since its earliest iterations, facing stark sexism. Over the past decade, women footballers and their allies have created a transnational social movement demanding gender equity. Scholars, swimming in the same currents, have undertaken important research into women's sport.

The work in this volume refines our picture of the significance of women's football, what it has meant for participants, and the social struggles that take place around it. Sweeping narratives on football have typically neglected women altogether and rarely examined gender politics of the sport. This has been a detriment to our understanding of gender and intersectional inequalities of race, class, abilities, and region. These essays highlight the persistence of women in football and demonstrate crooked lines of progress in gender equity. The research in this volume contextualizes women's sports within the growth of education, labor agitation during the period of the "social question," and the expansion of modern media.

Girls and women's formal introduction to sport was often through physical education programs. The expanding educational curriculum of the state and Catholic schools codified gender ideologies for generations of students. Across Latin America, state crafters hoped these programs would create ideal citizens, a nation of healthy soldiers, workers, wives, and mothers. The curriculum taught students that boys' superiority and heterosexuality were immutable facts, as was girls' purpose to become mothers and wives. Physical education teachers promoted gentler activities for girls, such as calisthenics, which would preserve their health for pregnancy and desirability on the marriage market. Sports associated with elite and European customs, such as tennis, were deemed acceptable for girls who could access them. The more popular football became in Brazil, particularly among Black and working-class men, the stronger restrictions on women players became. The essays included here join prior scholarship in exploring resistance to the draconian ban on football, among other sports, imposed on women between the 1940s and the 1970s. Women challenged men's monopoly on public space, cultural capital, and state resources in football.

Feminist theory has informed and inspired the academic work on women's sport. However, many champions of women's football have not identified as feminist, or at least they did not leave evidence of such allegiances. Whether they occupied a formal place in feminist movements, women such as Cléo de Galsan, who wrote about women's football in the 1920s, clearly challenged the patriarchy. Not just playing, but consuming, writing, and promoting women's sports was deeply disruptive. When feminist organization and grassroots movements support the cause of women's football, it has been a significant benefit to women athletes. Feminist journalists protested the prohibition on women's football in the 1940s, players refused to give up the game they loved, and grassroots organizations marched in the 1980s to allow women back on the pitch. In more recent years, feminist framings of sexual assault and intimate partner violence have brought real change, even to mainstream media, such as the magazine *Placar*. This progress, as with feminist struggles more broadly, has prompted strong push-back. The 2018 assassination of queer, Black, feminist Marielle Franco is a terrifying reminder of the dangers of activism, particularly when advocating for multiple (intersectional) causes.

Academic research on football contributes to theoretical problems in the social science that transcend sports. The scholarship in this anthology grapples with the question, if implicitly, "How are identity and structure reflected in physical practice?" The issue of embodiment has been important to seemingly adjacent fields, such as philosophy and biology. A healthy dialogue between these fields can inform the contemporary struggles for LGBTQ+ rights and the inclusion of transgender athletes in football. There are few spaces more segregated in Brazilian society than sports, which have helped to define sex binaries. How will performance and participation of women, nonbinary, and trans athletes reshape ideas of gender? These are not abstract questions, but instead pressing concerns for policy and human rights.

The essays in this volume are illustrative of the interdisciplinary methods that serve the study of women's football. Studies of marginalized communities cannot rely on the same documentary base as those focused on powerful actors and mainstream subjects. Oral histories provide and confirm some of the basic facts, but also become ways of understanding athletes' own interpretations of their experiences. Other essays mine newspapers extensively, aided by the digitization of many Brazilian historical newspapers. Authors included here pieced together stories, biographies, and narrative shifts, often working like detectives. Still others have relied on digital humanities and statistics, participant observation, and textual analysis.

The crucible of corruption and misogyny in global football governance, of which Brazil has played a major role, has generated a dismal landscape for women's football. Yet, women fans and players have responded and successfully held leaders accountable. Their actions have been inspired by heterogeneous feminist organizations, some of which identify as part of #NiUnaMenos. Athletes, many of whom are working class, women of color, or queer, may finally feel that the feminist movement is intersectional enough to represent them. From its incipient focus on femicide in Argentina, #NiUnaMenos expanded popular conceptions of gendered violence, advocated for reproductive rights, as well as combatted sexual harassment, and media bias. These issues are central to athletes, professionals and amateurs alike. The #NiUnaMenos collective organized a general strike of women in 2016, as well as massive street demonstrations in Argentina, Bolivia, Brazil, Chile, El Salvador, Guatemala, Mexico, Paraguay, Peru, Puerto Rico, and Uruguay. It was in this moment that many women players went on strike and demanded greater influence in football clubs.

Solidarity across countries has proven a crucial tool in women's sports. Across the Americas, groups of women fans have demanded safer stadiums, the formation of gender commissions, and changes in the management of teams. It is crucial to note the overlap between feminist and antiprivatization efforts within sports clubs. In the early twentieth century, soccer clubs in Latin America, unlike in Europe, formed as mutually owned civic associations. This structure meant that clubs developed a democratic structure that became sites of community engagement, although with reduced rights for women. In the 1980s and 1990s, however, clubs fell into serious debt because of high overhead costs, a downturn in attendance, corruption, and the export of top talent to Europe. Thus, the finances of clubs have meant that their status as "member-owned" is under constant threat. Corruption within clubs, but also at the federation and confederation levels, has been a major obstacle to improving the conditions of women's football. From absconding funds meant for the development of women's football to supporting abusive coaches, men with unchecked power have made it difficult for women to thrive in football. Labyrinthine bureaucracies, bribes, and embezzlement have worked to shield these men from accountability.

As with any important work, this anthology lays out tantalizing possibilities for further research. The history of racial minorities, and their regional identities, in football sports demands sustained attention. New revenue streams, sponsorships, and social media communities have changed traditional ways that football creates communities and generates wealth. The ways in which these new modes of consuming and playing football will shape the women's game pose new challenges. Nonetheless, if this anthology is any indication, women's football scholars, players, and supporters will be ready to tackle them together.

Introduction: Toward a Historiography of Brazilian Football in the Twenty-First Century: The Time and Place of Women[1]

Tiago Fernandes Maranhão, Bernardo Buarque, and Lívia Magalhães

This collection aims to be a contribution to the social studies of Brazilian football, by presenting an emerging approach to academic production on the subject in the last decade, when a research agenda took hold in the field of sports historiography. It is common knowledge and practice to date the inaugural entry of football into the Brazilian social sciences since the early 1980s, thanks to the field of anthropology and the initiative of a group of anthropologists from the National Museum in Rio de Janeiro, under the leadership of Roberto DaMatta (1982).

The establishment of football as a legitimate scientific subject in Brazil can be traced back to the last four decades, a period in which authors and works, themes and clippings, research methods and techniques, and working groups and research laboratories have shaped an area of expertise in the country's academia. The legitimization of a subject that was initially viewed with intellectual prejudice and of less theoretical relevance, a perception whose resilience has still not completely waned, has allowed publications to grow, both quantitatively and qualitatively. In fact, in more recent times, its development and expansion, its consolidation and deepening in the wake of mega-sporting events (the 2007 Pan-American Games and the 2016 Olympics), as well as the crisis of a dramatic political situation, have led to a critical review, diversification, and polarization of a series of perspectives on the football phenomenon in contemporary times.

One of the topics that has come to the fore in recent years, as a result of the accumulation of research carried out by different generations within the scope of postgraduate studies, coincidentally, between the 1980s and 2020s, when master's

[1] This study was funded by FAPERJ—Carlos Chagas Foundation Assistance to State Research in Rio de Janeiro. Process SEI E-26/201.354/2022.

and doctoral programs took root and spread nationwide, has been the historicity of women's football in Brazil. Its emphasis was on diachronic aspects of female participation, but also synchronic, with anthropological and sociological emphases.

In fact, the invisibility of women in the practices and representations of sport, especially football, is one of the most eloquent silences that strikes us when we evaluate the books, articles, and chapters produced by scholars in history and the social sciences over the last four decades, with occasional exceptions, recent discoveries, and surprises found here and there in the midst of this retrospective look by researchers.

In part, this realization about the historiographical gaps, the erasure of women's presence and the obfuscation of their history in sporting life and the football system goes hand in hand with a broader investigative turn in social theory and cultural studies today. Undoubtedly, this is a national and international reflection of a critical deconstruction movement, led by many female voices and hands, hearts and minds, questioning the very episteme that reifies and naturalizes sexual dichotomies and gendered binary positions. Far from being confined to yet another new specialty, gender studies have shown the breadth of their scope, with countless interfaces and transversalities, with unexpected intersections and unexpected scientific findings (Daflon and Campos, 2022).

The transversal nature of gender studies (would it be a "new wave," a century after the Suffragettes? would it be a "feminist explosion" in the middle of the 21st century?) (Hollanda, 2018), makes it possible for it to spread across the most diverse flanks of social realities and through different shortcuts and angles, gaps and fields of research. Of course, the questioning of a canon and the questioning of established time frames are also manifested among football historians and social scientists, in a field of collective life in which the ethos of masculinity, the cisgender standard, and heteronormative virility (Bandeira, 2016) have always been worshipped, with male hegemony becoming naturalized in a more imperceptible way.

Since the narratives of origin, the omnipresence, omniscience, and omnipotence of male practitioners and managers who neglect and make it impossible for them to coexist with women, purposely or tacitly, subtly or openly, have been the keynote of sports relations in their different institutional spheres and hierarchical positions.

As suggested above, the change brought about by the process of restoring women's place in the world of football is not an epistemological exclusivity of the humanities and social sciences. It has a strong dialogue with historical transformations and demands made by feminist movements in public life and in the intellectual milieu of the twenty-first century, in Brazil and beyond. The demands for gender equality, in the midst of various identity agendas for affirmation, revision and reversal of a historical framework of male domination (Bourdieu, 2010) and submission, and asymmetry and subalternity, are also mirrored in football, albeit in a nonmechanical or reflexive way.

Thus, there are deductive and inductive, external and internal or, as it were, concave and convex ways of understanding the mirroring relationships between football and society. Through them, in a two-way street, a context is circumscribed for rethinking, empowering, and repairing the asymmetrical gender relations that are constitutive of the sports field in contemporary times.

One index of the relationship between academic work and the issues at stake in contemporary society is expressed in the stance of the players involved in the sporting environment. Since the 2010s, these actors have progressively engaged in mobilizing to change the *status quo*, which for decades has remained silent and complacent with the institutional structures of football power. *Pari passu* with the dissertations and theses defended in the last decade, there has been a series of demands from athletes and other professional women in the field. They are female journalists, reporters, announcers, coaches, fans, referees, managers, and administrators.

This pushes institutions (broadcasters, clubs, football federations, and confederations) toward destabilizing dissent, with inevitable tensions and conflicts that are necessary, although not yet sufficient, to agree new attitudes and implement the minimum and most basic isonomic and equitable rights, paying attention to the norms and customs that surround the 'macho,' sexist, and misogynistic mentality and morality on and off the pitch.

In this sense, this book was conceived as a way of bringing together these studies produced over the last decade, of arranging them and making them known to an audience abroad, perhaps already exhausted by the weakened and anachronistic metaphor of the "country of football." The high-performance men's football team, despite winning the Confederations Cup (2005, 2009, and 2013) as well as the unprecedented triumphs in two Olympic Games (2016 and 2020), has faced years of criticism, particularly in the World Cup, where it has not secured any trophies since 2002. As the title of this collection suggests, perhaps only women today are capable of updating the aura of the virtuosos of football technique, a wishful thinking, a promise of things to come that the work looks forward to in the present.

In the meantime, this materialization proposes a certain organicity to the thriving intellectual production by women, and about women themselves, since two of the organizers of this collection are men who are also interested in the subject, in universities in Brazil and elsewhere. Academic work, but also committed words, the task is as much about blurring arbitrary boundaries and mitigating their resilient discriminations as it is about immersing research subjects and objects in an agenda that has, in turn, reshaped the very idea of "football."

Mutatis mutandis, this category has also shown itself to be changeable, with the shift from the initial epistemological horizontality, which sought to give isonomy to bodily practices in the midst of the blinding supremacy of spectacularized professional football, to contemporary political diversity, whose recognition of the role of women is one of the vindicating facets of this ongoing mutation (Damo, 2018). While anthropologist Arlei Damo captures this transit in relation to his own original formulation of the constitutive plurality of football, it is his professional colleague Wagner Xavier de Camargo (2018, 2020) who advances this understanding of the polyphony of "multiple footballs," among which the gender dimensions stand out and without which their intersectionalities cannot be understood, be it the performance of women related to class and race, or the inscription of dissonance made up of the proactiveness of *gay* collectives and LGBT+ leagues in this sport.

Tracing the incidence and the signs of concealment implies, from the outset, a historical observation that says less about the gender differentiation of the "object" and more about the, so to speak, "subjects" of the investigation. Having said that, if we started this text by mentioning the agreed date for the introduction of football in the Academy, the 1980s, with DaMatta at the forefront, a new look at the genesis of a national football field identifies pioneering women researchers who, in various fields of knowledge and from different backgrounds, turned their attention to investigating this phenomenon as early as the 1970s. The examples go first to Janet Lever, a Brazilian-American sociologist who came to Brazil at the beginning of the 1970s to do her PhD at Yale, with a fascinating, albeit dated, fieldwork on the place of football in Brazilian society, under the impact of winning the World Cup in Mexico.

Another noteworthy academic pioneer, contemporary to Janet Lever's work, went unnoticed for decades. We are referring to Mario do Carmo L. de Oliveira Fernandéz's master's degree, defended in the Literature Department at PUC-Rio and transformed into a book in 1974, with the title *Futebol, fenômeno linguístico—análise linguística da imprensa esportiva* (Football, a linguistic phenomenon—a linguistic analysis of the sports press). The examples of these beginnings of university production by women in the 1970s culminate with the name of anthropologist Simoni Guedes, who in 1977 defended her thesis and became a master at the National Museum, thanks to her dissertation "*Futebol brasileiro, instituição zero*" (Brazilian football, zero institution), published in book form as a posthumous tribute in 2023.

Simoni Guedes became a better-known name because, in addition to a kind of fierce militancy in this area of study, she belonged to the group of anthropologists who took part in DaMatta's essay collection "Universo do futebol: esporte e sociedade" (Football universe: sport and society) (1982). Unlike her male colleagues, as Pablo Alabarces rightly noted in a celebratory lecture in 2018, the anthropologist was not only the only woman in the group, but also the author with an actual previous dissertation on the subject.

Therefore, only Guedes had actually done ethnography, while the rest of her colleagues produced interpretative essays that, although seminal, were based on distant observations, book references, and secondary sources. A young woman in the 1970s, Simoni Guedes went into the field, immersed herself in a hegemonically male environment at the time and developed her ethnographic work, which resulted in the anthological chapter: "*Subúrbio—celeiro de craques*" (Suburbia—barn of stars). She did this, it has to be said, without any kind of self-glorifying heroism, since in her testimonies about this period, Guedes always showed herself to be devoid of romanticism, she did not cultivate self-worship, she did not claim a "perspectivism" or "speaking from authority" and neither did she allow her disciples to mythologize her.

We could list more names of "subject" researchers. The field of physical education, in this sense, is a forerunner, as it has a longer tradition of studies linking sport and gender. This is the case of Professor Heloísa Helena Baldy dos Reis, herself a footballer with Guarani Football Club in 1983, whose experiences on the pitch made her aware of a research agenda around the discourses and violent behaviors experienced in football.

As a researcher, her work focused on the problem of transgressive and violent acts by fans in stadiums, the same ones who in her football experience offended and cursed the players. As a woman, she was involved in public debates with sporting authorities and leaders of organized supporter groups, the overwhelming majority of whom were men with traditional and conservative values.

If the football-violence dyad has been at the heart of her academic output, Heloísa Reis recently reflected on women's practice in the chapter "*Projetos de vida, mulheres e futebol*" (Life projects, women and football) (2020). In the text written in partnership with Osmar Souza Junior (2013), her doctoral student, the author turns to the trajectory and memory of former female players who gained prominence in this sport, such as Marta, Elane, Nildinha and Aline, with the reconstruction of biographical narratives capable of making sense of professional performance, media visibility, and recognition achieved in the professional environment. The chapter is not confined to the memoirs of the "retirees," but also looks at the challenges of the profession among the aspiring players, by following athletes at the start of their careers in the Santos youth teams, as well as producing empirical sources and oral sources, through interviews with players from three clubs taking part in the *Campeonato Paulista* (São Paulo Championship).

Back in the social sciences, in the 1990s, there were still women researchers who tackled the subject of football, especially in the sub-area of organized supporter groups, where, from an investigative point of view, men also hegemonized until very recently. Alongside Simoni, it is worth mentioning another anthropologist, Rosana da Câmara Teixeira, author of Chapter 10 in this volume, who in the mid-1990s boldly embarked on ethnographic research with members of organized supporter groups in Rio de Janeiro. Her anthropological aim was to gain a less stigmatizing understanding of the fan ethos, known for its sexism and masculinity, which is as virile and aggressive as it is homophobic and intolerant.

Her dissertation, rewarded with the publication of a book, unfolded into a perennial research agenda that in recent years has expanded into ethnographies and interviews with female fans, participants in the internal life of organized supporter groups, and in certain situations tensioning and re-signifying the dominant values of these groups. Proof of this was the initiative taken by supporters to promote the event "Women in the stands: resistance and empowerment," which in 2017 brought together around 300 female fans from all over the country at the Football Museum, for a collective discussion around their common demands in the spaces restricted by the men who control these associations.

A list of other pioneering women's experiences in this field of research could lengthen the list, without preventing forgetfulness or omissions, so we have restricted ourselves here to a few cases that are considered exemplary. Within the specific scope of the history of women's football in Brazil, it is also worth pointing out a unique feature of this entry and these beginnings. If it has already been said that universities, under certain theoretical weights and intellectual traditions, viewed the scientific study of football with skepticism, having placed it in a marginal position for a considerable time, we have observed that this vacuum provided shelter in other spaces peripheral to the Academy, but porous to the introduction of football topics.

One of them was museums, as Luiz Henrique de Toledo (2023) described in his last article, with their exhibition spaces, but also their archives, capable of becoming reference centers that were more open to the new historiographical objects that were projected from France in the 1970s onward.

In Brazil, at the same time, the Museum of Image and Sound (MIS) was the museum responsible for recording sound and creating the first collection of audio-visual documents about Brazilian football between the 1960s and 1980s. This happened both at the MIS in Rio de Janeiro, from 1967 onward, and at the museum of the same name in São Paulo, between 1981 and 1984, both of which were public facilities that welcomed and legitimized the practice and the assembly of their historical collections (Rajão and Hollanda, 2021), a persuasive demonstration of the sport's lateral but prominent place in society, culture, and the arts in general.

In equal measure, it can be said that the twenty-first century is witnessing the decantation of the art–architecture complex (Foster, 2017), with the *boom* of a leisure and entertainment industry focused on themed museums and the interactive consumption of their more or less futuristic technological and exhibition elements. This led to the conception of a Football Museum for the first time in the country, which came to fruition in 2008, located on the premises of the traditional *Pacaembu* public stadium. In addition to the collections of interviews inspired by the MIS, five years after the opening of the São Paulo museum, the management team and a group of research staff started the project entitled "Visibility for women's football," a proposal that over the course of a decade (2013–2023) will take on a life of its own inside the museum.

In fact, the review of the curatorial principles that created the concept and exhibition of football in its museal journey is gradually becoming aware of the importance of this conceptual shift and the inclusion of women in this narrative. As will be seen more closely in this book, in Chapter 12 by museologist Renata Maria Beltrão Lacerda, over the course of a decade, the search for women's traces in football, whether as players or fans, has become a mission and a challenge for those involved. One of its products is the exhibition "COUNTERATTACK! The Football's Women" and another consisted of the inscription of athletes like Sissi, honored today in the "Baroque Angels" room, which initially featured only men.

We identify and propose the centrality of this museum for the purposes of our argument, based on the understanding that this set of actions and initiatives, although not directly related in cause and consequence, creates "elective affinities" and inspires greater conditions, in turn, for what has been growth and affirmation in the wake of football studies since then. Of particular note in the museum's fifteen-year history is the quadrennial organization of the International Symposium on Football Studies, which began in 2010 in the context of the World Cup in South Africa and will continue until 2022 with the FIFA World Cup in Qatar.

More than just one of many such events, this symposium has managed to become a central reference point, capable of giving cohesion and a sense of unity to football teaching, research, and extension in society. In it, women's protagonism is a trend and a concrete fact that stands out when you look at the increase in the incidence of women presenting their research, giving talks, and mediating debates on equal terms with men.

Let us also remember that the museum's inauguration in 2008 followed the start of the so-called mega-sporting events in Brazil (2007–2016) by one year, with the Pan-American Games and the Olympic Games, both in Rio de Janeiro. The "Visibility for Women's Football" movement, launched in 2013, preceded the men's FIFA World Cup by a year, which took place in the country in 2014, a fact that drew attention to the similar women's editions in 2015 (Canada),[2] in 2019 (France), and in 2023 (Australia-New Zealand),[3] with growing mobilization in the museum, with appeal in the sporting world and, consequently, with the awakening of interest in society. If Brazil's bid to host the 2027 FIFA World Cup is successful, the practice's opportunities and legitimization will tend to increase its potential for recognition.

One of the bridges between this museum and the university throughout this period was the curator Silvana Vilodre Goellner, a full professor at the Federal University of Rio Grande do Sul (UFRGS), who is now retired and who signs the afterword to this book. Goellner's background is in physical education and from an early age, she turned her attention to investigating gender relations and sport

2. The seventh, eighth, and ninth editions, respectively. Before that, officially, we had the first in China (1991); the second in Sweden (1995); the third and fourth in the United States (1999 and 2003); the fifth again in China (2007); and the sixth in Germany (2011). Regarding its beginnings, the French magazine *So Foot* did a great report on two precursor experiences of Women's World Cups, the first in 1970 in Italy and the second in 1971 in Mexico, following the Men's World Cup held in the same country. See: https://www.sofoot.com/articles/1970-et-1971-ces-premieres-coupes-du-monde-feminine-que-tout-le-monde-a-oublie. In Brazil, Leda Costa covered the context of the 1970s and the emergence of women's football competitions at international level (Costa, 2020).

3. Despite the fact that we are in the ninth edition of the competition, a BBC report shows abuse suffered by athletes playing in the World Cup in New Zealand and Australia. According to the British broadcaster, one in five footballers at the World Cup suffered some form of discrimination or received threatening messages on social media. See: https://www.bbc.com/sport/football/67686209

(Goellner, 2003, 2013), paying special attention to the discourse of journalistic coverage and historical sources. By turning to the sport of football, at the invitation of the museum, she led and qualified a new generation of researchers in Rio Grande do Sul, as well as establishing national and international networks that boosted research and activism around the fight for space and the transformation of dominant values in football.

Without confining herself to the university and academic sphere, since collaborating on the project "Visibility for women's football," the professor has circulated among the protagonists of the subject, players and former footballers, managers, judges, and coaches, in order to build a propositional and incisive platform for questioning the *standard of* power of institutions such as the São Paulo Football Federation (FPF) and the Brazilian Football Confederation (CBF). With the CBF and the FPF, private entities, and with the federal government's National Football Secretariat, she has even provided consultancy, in dialogue with former footballer and current sports manager Aline Pellegrino, and collaborated in working groups, always with a critical stance and a greater commitment to the cause and the banner of what she calls "women in football."

In academic terms, her intellectual production and mentoring work remained active and intense. Collecting testimonies, for example, led her not only to set up an interview database for the Centro de Memória do Esporte—Ceme (Sports Memory Center) at UFRGS, but also to publish articles and books, among which we highlight "The pioneers of football ask for passage: to know in order to recognise" (2020). This work was done in partnership with Juliana Ribeiro Cabral, former captain of the Brazilian national football team and Olympic medalist in Athens 2004, and is dedicated to compiling the life stories of a series of women who began playing for the national team when it was formed in the 1980s, ranging from the characters Ketty and Meg to Helena Pacheco and Dilma Mendes, including Soró and Ita Maia.

As we said above, the picture sketched out is just a suggestion of a way to understand this scenario of the development of the practice and study of women's football. This is because we could mention other avenues parallel to those of the museum, if we think about the career of Cláudia Samuel Kessler, an anthropologist from the state of Rio Grande do Sul, who introduced the subject of women's football in her *stricto sensu* master's degree in social sciences as early as 2008. Her doctorate, defended in 2015 under the supervision of Arlei Damo, explores the subject as early as 2011, the year before the museum's visibility project. Her research sheds light on the conditions for training footballers in Brazil, from an ethnographic perspective compared to the United States, a country in which *soccer* has been given more space, hosted World Cups and created the means for winning performances in international competitions, winning four World Cups out of nine.

However, even though the Brazilian women's national team has yet to win any significant titles, a type of collection that instills a dominant professional viewpoint, to the detriment of gratuitousness and playfulness, as if there were only one way of gauging the positivity of sporting performance by winning trophies, the field of idolatry is still filled in the footballing imagination when we consider the case of Marta Vieira da Silva, the athlete from Alagoas who has won the annual FIFA award for several consecutive years.

This player was the target of the combined interests of the two researchers mentioned above, Silvana Goellner and Cláudia Kessler, in the chapter "Brazil is *hexa*: Marta's sporting career" (2020). The authors include the athlete in an agenda typical of the field of football studies, which articulates the configuration of the idol in sport, the "empress" Sissi or "queen" Marta, based on media narratives of social ascension, overcoming obstacles, and the internationalization of her career, given her performance in world competitions and her circulation in clubs abroad, from Sweden to the United States.

The above reference to the discourse and framing of journalism, whether in print or on digital platforms, reminds us of alternative experiences to the traditional media. The strengthening of women's football has also come about through the creation of specific spaces to publicize it, as happened with the "*Dibradoras*" channel (https://dibradoras.com.br/), which was created in 2015 with the explicit purpose of giving women a leading role in sport, particularly football.

The role of Luciane de Castro (Lú Castro) and a team of journalists and former players is highlighted on this virtual site and then spreads, with activist work on publications and dissemination in recognized social institutions, such as the various SESC units in São Paulo, which also includes the mediation of researcher Aira Bonfim, author of Chapter 2 in this book. The proactiveness of the "*Dibradoras*" marks a move into the networks, but also an innovation in the way sports is covered, with the monitoring of different competitive spheres. These range from regional club competitions to daily reports on the Brazilian championship and, of these, coverage of the women's national team training sessions at Granja Comary, the headquarters and main training center of Brazil national team.

In any case, the presence of women in *mainstream* sports coverage has led researchers to understand the implications of these *staff* changes within sports journalism, something that is very noticeable to those who watch television channels dedicated to sports. In his post-doctorate, historian Leonardo Pacheco (2020) approached the subject from the specific angle of voiceover and the narrating voice, with an emphasis on the linguistic aspects of intonation and rhythm as well as the socialization of female journalists in the broadcasting booths, a traditionally male space of sociability and power.

This collective mobilization around the promotion of women has been the keynote not only of the repercussions of the media but also of scientific production. Therefore, rather than individualizing the names of researchers who are prominent in this process, it is worth highlighting the group efforts of the networks that articulate the potential for development in the area. This should include the crucial role of Professor David Wood, from the University of Sheffield, one of the contributors to this collection, a Latin Americanist whose project to support the development of women's football on a South American scale enabled a series of continental meetings in the cities of Buenos Aires, Medellín, Rio de Janeiro, and São Paulo between 2016 and 2019.

Entitled "A level playing field? The practice and representation of women's and girl's football in South America," the proposal brought together players and researchers from different universities and institutions in Argentina, Brazil, and Colombia. The integration lasted over a four-year period and led to a series of intergenerational contacts, thanks to the auspices and financial support of the UK's *Arts and Humanities Research Council.*

The articulation in favor of practice and scientific reflection manifests itself not only in these seminars, but also through collections, an effort to which our book intends to add, with its panorama now aimed at familiarizing foreign readers. Before announcing this contribution, however, we recognize the remarkable growth in publications and highlight two works that we consider to be excellent in bringing together the research carried out in the country, reflecting the state of the art and the thematic flanks explored to date.

The first work is suggestively entitled "*As mulheres no universo do futebol brasileiro*" (Women in the universe of Brazilian football), organized in 2020 by Cláudia Kessler, Leda Costa, and Mariane Pisani, the last two of whom are also present in this book and are unavoidable references in the field. The title of the book is in itself an allusion to and a provocative dialogue with the collective organized by Roberto DaMatta, whose "burden" as an inaugural bibliographical landmark, as Toledo (2023) suggests, has become a repeated and worn-out truism in the literature on the subject. In our opinion, this reification, which has been repeated so much, has ended up disregarding antecedents, such as the female researchers from the Academy, as we have listed above, as well as ignoring the context that surrounds him and his peers from São Paulo, such as professors José Sebastião Witter and José Carlos Sebe Bom Meihy, with their book *Futebol e cultura: coletânea de estudos* (*Football and Culture: A Collection of Studies*) (1982), which for a long time went unnoticed on white clouds.

In this provocation toward a new foundation for football bibliography, whose foreword by Simoni Guedes—the only female author on the 1982 "Universo" team—is its most eloquent indication, the volume organized by Cláudia, Leda, and Mariane contains eighteen chapters signed by a total of twenty-one male and female authors, in an overview capable of taking into account the current Brazilian research framework. It is no coincidence that the book begins with the contribution of a male researcher, Fábio Franzini, who, in the mid-2000s, published an article on the subject entitled: "Is football a 'male thing'? A small sketch for a history of women in the country of football."

Divided into three main parts, the book was grouped around the axes of history, resistance, and professionalization. To this end, it covers a constellation of subjects, agents, and regions, ranging from the clubs to the fans, from Bahia to Rio Grande do Sul, from the players to the referees, from journalism to feminism, among other sections of this new and different "universe." This one intends to stop being a parallel universe, and it is now pushing the 'Dammatian' orbit forty years on.

Another work similar to the one proposed here was organized recently by Jorge Knijnik and Soraya Barreto Januário, entitled *Futebol das mulheres no Brasil: emancipação, resistências e equidade* (Women's football in Brazil: emancipation, resistance and equity) (2022). Spread over almost five hundred pages, the sixteen chapters also set out to present a panel of current or recently carried out research in the country on the subject.

An apparent detail does not go unnoticed and concerns the terminology embedded in a subtle change in the preposition of the book's title. If those involved in the field opted at one point for the expression "women's football" (*futebol de mulheres*), instead of the qualifier "ladies' football" (*futebol feminino*), in Jorge's and Soraya's book, the proposition becomes even more affirmative: it is about "women's football," denoting their greater capacity to take over and appropriate the practice.

In any case, in terms of structure, the four parts outline a thematic division with an emphasis on history, the media, and the players on the pitch and in the stands. Their latitudes are even broader, from the presence of women in futsal to the image of women in suburban football. At first glance, they follow the same thread as the structure of Cláudia, Leda, and Mariane's book. However, there is also a widening of the scope of their fronts. This includes the field of education, since the organizers, unlike the social scientists, are closer to educational experiences in schools and the work of physical education teachers in the classroom.

Having done this and looked for a common denominator in this research, we are now in a position to approach the proposal that guides this book. The presentation could, of course, expand its scope to include an interlocution with the international historiography on women's football, which we have bypassed and will only point out briefly below, given the length of this introduction and its non-exhaustive purpose, since intellectual production on the subject has grown and become increasingly large and more substantial.

Let us just say that, as historians, the organizers of this volume are inspired by two seminal works. The first is of French-speaking origin and was written by Professor Laurence Prudhomme-Poncet, from the University of Lyon 1. The French researcher, back in 2003, twenty years ago, dedicated herself to a diachronic view of French women's football in her book *Histoire du football féminin au XXe siècle*. This is an exemplary publication for anyone looking for a research parameter linked to the social history and political history of women's football at the national level in a European country.

Another book, published more recently, comes from the English-speaking world and is entitled *Futbolera: A History of Women and Sports in Latin America* (2019). It was written by Brenda Elsey, the author of this book's preface, and Joshua Nadel, two Americans who work in the field of Latin American studies in their home country and who have carried out thought-provoking research on football in the region. One of the virtues of their approach is that they have overcome the traditional paradigm of the nation in their research.

Research on a transnational scale is undoubtedly a challenge for new researchers to overcome the recurring tautology that reduces football to the contours of national identity. Furthermore, it is worth emphasizing that Brenda and Joshua do not just focus on a single sport, which is a kind of vice originating from the vast majority of historians and social scientists, whose blinders only see the phenomenon of football, with it being framed among dozens of other sports.

Along with the references produced in France and the United States, and why not mention England and the doctoral thesis by Mark Biram, from the University of Bristol, after ethnography with the "santistas da Vila sirens?" (2021), another international source that we have, which is still unexplored in Brazil and which could enhance the agenda of studies on women's football, is the *Football Observatory*. This body is of Swiss origin and is part of the *International Center for Sport Studies* (CIES), a center founded in 1995 that in recent years has provided a consistent series of indicators for monitoring female athletes and leagues, through a wealth of statistics and data mining (Hollanda, 2021).

As a cause and consequence of the so-called "globalisation" (Figols, 2016), this research center has specialized in creating tools to monitor professional football worldwide. It produces quantitative data on demographics, performance, and the football transfer market on a weekly, monthly, half-yearly, and an annual basis.

Their reports and analyses, under the responsibility of three geographers (Poli et al., 2021), also offer rankings by country with figures on the international circulation of male and female players, which even allows comparisons with the current men's framework. This is because Brazil usually tops these rankings among men, with an average migratory flow of more than a thousand expatriate footballers a year. On the other hand, Brazilian women, *pé-de-obra* (foot-labor) are currently in the ninth place in this ranking, without reaching the hundredth mark. This does not prevent a considerable degree of internationalization and significant emigration by our female athletes, who have recorded club mobility abroad since 1980, when the practice was legalized in the country.

As we know, the pioneering experience was that of midfielder Lúcia Feitosa, from the famous Rio team *Radar* (Almeida, 2013), who played for the Brazilian national team and competed in the Mundialito in Italy in 1986, being signed by an Italian club at the end of the competition in the host country. The 1990s also saw international experiences for Brazilian women, such as strikers Michael Jackson and Roseli, who played not only in Italy, but also in Japan and the United States. In the 2000s, the flow continues to move our stars, like Sissi, Katia Silena, and Pretinha who, along with the destinations already mentioned, go on to play in Spain and France, Scandinavia, and even in faraway South Korea.

The visibility of these players reached its peak with the international prestige of Martha and Formiga, but it also became routine with the departures of goalkeeper Andrea and center-back Rosana, defender Juliana, and defender Tamires from different Brazilian teams in the first decade of the twenty-first century. The 2010s saw the continuation of this process of spreading the *pé-de-obra* (foot-labor) to different continents and regions of the globe, such as Érika (USA) and Debi Zanotti (China), Aline Pellegrino (Russia) and Debinha (Norway), and Bia Zaneratto (South Korea) and Geyse (England).

With that said, we would like to say that the initiative for this book derives from this dual inspiration, that is, from what has already been done and what still needs to be done. In this sort of middle ground between the past and the future, we have put together this collection. In summary, the structure can be seen as divided into two main parts, using a fundamental anthropological concept: diachrony and synchrony.

The first concerns historical aspects of the development, discontinuities and intermediate, and free and/or borderline zones of action in women's football (Rajão, 2018). This first part covers socio-cultural aspects of the practice and representation of women in football and its stadiums. There are six chapters, written by seven authors, two of which are dedicated to the acts of supporting and cheering by women in the Brazilian stands, in a time gap of long duration. The first, by Daniela Araújo, referring to the first decades of the twentieth century, and the second, by Nathália Pessanha, in chronological sequence with the first, spanning the 1940s and the second-half of the last century until it expanded to the present time.

The first part also provides a diachronic perspective on the work of women in the field, through three chapters. These are written by Aira Bonfim, Caroline Almeida, and Carmen Rial, the latter an anthropologist of fundamental importance in researching the subject and in training a new generation of researchers, and Fernanda Haag, respectively. The division spans three time periods, namely: the pre-prohibition period (1915–1941); the almost four decades of prohibition (1941–1979); and the period following the liberation and freedom of the practice, covering the next forty years until professionalization in contemporary times (1983–2013).

The fifth chapter looks at the participation of Brazilian women in FIFA World Cups since they were organized in China at the end of the 1980s. Leda Costa makes use of a classic approach on the agenda of media scholars. This consists of investigating the valuations of female performance in light of the media discourses of the sporting press. This mechanism has structured the field of sports studies in the country and now applies to the journalists' view of the nation, when represented by the performance of women.

The second part is what we call synchronic, as it deals with contemporary divides that are dear to the interrelations between football and gender. There are seven more chapters, signed by a total of seven female authors and one male author. The division does not prevent the existence of bridges between the two parts, but let us see: in this second block, two manuscripts also focus on women fans, this time with a more specific focus, namely women's demands within the country's organized supporter groups, in ethnographic experiences in Bahia and Rio de Janeiro, as revealed by the fieldwork and interviews carried out by Carolina Moraes and Rosana Teixeira.

On the subject of football and the media, we have David Wood's research. He is the only male contributor to the volume and his importance in creating a network has already been emphasized here. He focuses on the imagery and textual frameworks of the sports magazine *Placar*, emphasizing the way in which women have traditionally been represented, not to say stereotyped, in the periodical. Seen as objects, the images of women were, as a rule, passive and sensual, with the aim of fulfilling the supposed sexual desires and fantasies of its male consumer-readers, alongside the consumption of football news.

A unique feature of the second part of the collection is the existence of chapters that take stock of academic production on women's football, a retrospective and overview that is essential in shaping the quantitative and qualitative contours of a scientific field (Toledo, 2021). While researchers Luiza Aguiar and Marina Mattos, both with degrees in physical education, focus on a *quantitative* survey of four decades of publications on football, anthropologist Mariane Pisane provides a quantitative overview combined with a qualitative assessment of the dissertations and theses defended in Brazil over the last ten years. In this way, she maps out the main lines of force in this emerging scenario of growth in research on women at the postgraduate level in the social sciences.

Another unique feature of this second part is the text by historian Lívia Gonçalves, who presents the challenges of implementing and teaching about football in the classroom and the pedagogical practices related to gender propaedeutics and the potential for fostering sports feminism.

Last but not least, museologist Renata Maria Beltrão Lacerda, who holds a master's degree in her field from the University of São Paulo (USP), explores what she calls a "small feminist revolution" in the museum field, by reconstructing the experience of reviewing and renewing the exhibition and curatorial criteria at the Football Museum, the importance and centrality of which we have emphasized throughout this Introduction.

After this long but necessary introduction, we proceed to the reading and enjoyment part of this collection, the fruit of an endeavor that began in 2022, when two of the organizers, Bernardo and Tiago, met in the context of an international sports colloquium. After two years of many exchanges and correspondences, to which was added the partnership of a third organizer, Lívia, here is the result we have reached as a trio and thanks to the dozens of collaborators.

We realize that if the work is not complete, a sign of the strength and vitality of women on the pitch in recent years, it is capable of providing foreign readers, who are demanding, curious, and interested in Brazilian football, with a representative selection of the best literature on the subject. If temporariness and contingency are the cornerstones of scientific work, this is our starting touch for women to roll the ball and dominate the game.

BIBLIOGRAPHY

ALATAS, Syed Farid; SINHA, Vineeta. "*Eurocentrismo, androcentrismo e teoria sociológica*" (Eurocentrism, Androcentrism and Sociological Theory). In: **Labemus Blog**. Niterói: 2019, pp. 1–16.

ALMEIDA, Caroline Soares de. ***Boas de bola**: um estudo sobre ser jogador de futebol no Esporte Clube Radar durante a década de 1980* (Good with the Ball: A Study of Being a Footballer at Radar Sports Clube During the 1980s). Florianópolis: Master's dissertation in Anthropology/UFSC, 2013.

BANDEIRA, Gustavo. 2016. ***Do Olímpico à Arena**: elitização, racismo e heterossexismo no currículo de masculinidade dos torcedores de estádio* (From the Olympic Stadium to the Arena: Elitisation, Racism and Heterosexism in the Masculinity Curriculum of Stadium Fans). Porto Alegre: Doctoral Thesis in Education/UFRGS, 2017.

BIRAM, Mark Daniel. "*As sereias da vila na terra do Rei: uma etnografia do Santos FC feminino*" (The Mermaids of the Village in the Land of the King: An Ethnography of Santos FC women). In: **Revista Movimento**. Porto Alegre: v. 27, 2021, pp. 1–17.

BOURDIEU, Pierre. ***A dominação masculina*** (Male domination). Rio de Janeiro: Bertrand Brasil, 2010.

CAMARGO, Wagner Xavier de. *"Dimensões de gênero e os múltiplos futebóis no Brasil"* (Gender dimensions and the multiple footballs in Brazil). In: GIGLIO, Sérgio Settani; PRONI, Marcelo Weishaupt (Orgs.). ***O futebol nas ciências humanas no Brasil*** **(Football in the human sciences in Brazil)**. Campinas: Editora Unicamp, 2020.

CASTRO, Lu; RICCA, Darcio. ***Futebol feminista***: *ensaios* (Feminist Football: Essays). Rio de Janeiro: Football Books, 2020.

CHAN-VIANNA, Alexandre Jackson. ***Meninas que jogam bola***: *identidades e projetos das praticantes de esportes coletivos de confronto no lazer* (Girls Who Play Ball: Identities and Projects of Women Who Play Team Sports for Leisure). Rio de Janeiro: PhD Thesis in Physical Education/Gama Filho, 2010.

CONNELL, Raewyn. *"O Império e a criação de uma ciência social"* (Empire and the Creation of a Social Science). In: **Revista Contemporânea**. v. 2, n. 2, 2012, pp. 309–336.

COSTA, Leda. *"Década de 1970: o impulso globalizante e desobediente do futebol feminino*" (The 1970s: The Globalising and Disobedient Impulse of Women's Football). In: LOURENÇO, Marco; ANDREUCCI, Raul; FIGOLS, Victor (Orgs.). ***Uma década de Ludopédio***: *dez textos da história da Arquibancada* (A Decade of Ludopédio: Ten Texts of the History of the Stands). São Paulo: Editora Ludopédio, 2020, pp. 43–56.

DAFLON, Verônica Toste; CAMPOS, Luna Ribeiro (Orgs.). ***Pioneiras da sociologia***: *mulheres intelectuais nos séculos XVIII e XIX* (Pioneers of Sociology: Women Intellectuals in the 18th and 19th Centuries). Niterói: Ed. UFF, 2022.

DAMATTA, Roberto. (Org.). ***Universo do futebol***: *esporte e sociedade* (Football Universe: Sport and Society). Rio de Janeiro: Edições Pinakotheke, 1982.

DAMO, Arlei. *"Futebóis – da horizontalidade epistemológica à diversidade política"* (Football— from Epistemological Horizontality to Political Diversity). In: **Revista Fulia**. Belo Horizonte: v. 3, n. 3, Sep–Dec, 2018, pp. 37–66.

DAMO, Arlei; KESSLER, Cláudia. "*A partir do legado de Simoni: um olhar crítico sobre gênero e futebol no Brasil"* (From Simoni's Legacy: A Critical look at Gender and Football in Brazil). In: HELAL, Ronaldo; COSTA, Leda (Orgs.). **Sport and Society**: the Contribution of Simoni Guedes. Rio de Janeiro: Apris, 2022.

DUNNING, Eric; MAGUIRE, Joseph. "*As relações entre os sexos no esporte*" (Gender Relations in Sport). In: **Revista Estudos Feministas**. Florianópolis: v. 2, 1997, pp. 321–348.

ELSEY, Brenda; NADEL, Joshua. **Futbolera**: A History of Women and Sports in Latin America. Austin: University of Texas Press, 2019.

FERNANDÉZ, Maria do Carmo Leite de Oliveira. ***Futebol, fenômeno linguístico***: *análise linguística da imprensa esportiva* (Football, a Linguistic Phenomenon: Linguistic Analysis of the Sporting Press). Rio de Janeiro: PUC Ed. Documentário, 1974.

FOSTER, Hal. ***O complexo arte-arquitetura*** (The Art-Architecture Complex). São Paulo: Cosac Naify Publishing House, 2017.

FRANZINI, Fábio. *"Futebol é coisa pra macho? Pequeno esboço para uma história das mulheres no país do futebol"* (Is Football a Male Thing? A Small Sketch for a History of Women in the Country of Football). In: **Revista Brasileira de História**. São Paulo: vol. 25, n. 50, 2005, pp. 315–328.

FIGOLS, Victor de Leonardo. ***FC Barcelona***: *entre o regional e o global* (FC Barcelona: Between the Regional and the Global). São Paulo: Master's dissertation in History/Unifesp, 2016.

GOELLNER, Silvana. ***Bela, maternal e feminina***: *imagens da mulher na Revista Educação Physica* (Beautiful, Maternal and Feminine: Images of Women in the Magazine Educação Physica). Ijuí: Editora Unijuí, 2003.

GOELLNER, Silvana. "*Gênero e esporte na historiografia brasileira: balanços e potencialidades*" (Gender and Sport in Brazilian historiography: Balances and Potential). In: **Revista Tempo**. Niterói: vol. 19, n. 34, 2013, pp. 46–54.

GOELLNER, Silvana; CABRAL, Juliana Ribeiro (Orgs.). ***As pioneiras do futebol pedem passagem***: *conhecer para reconhecer* (The Pioneers of Football Ask for Passage: Know in Order to Recognise). São Paulo: Editora Ludopédio, 2022.

GOELLNER, Silvana; KNIJNIK, Jorge (Orgs.). *"Dossiê Futebol e mulheres: performances"* (Dossier Football and Women: Performances). In: **Revista Fulia**. Belo Horizonte: UFMG, vol. 8, n. 3, 2023.

GUEDES, Simoni Lahud. ***Futebol brasileiro, instituição zero*** (Brazilian Football, Zero institution). São Paulo: Editora Ludopédio, 2023.

HOLLANDA, Heloísa Buarque de (Org.). ***Explosão feminista***: *arte, cultura, política e universidade.* (Feminist Explosion: Art, Culture, Politics and the University.) São Paulo: Companhia das Letras, 2018.

HOLLANDA, Bernardo Buarque de. "*Entre a pesquisa acadêmica, a difusão científica e o mercado futebolístico: ciência de dados no estudo do futebol—o caso suíço do Football Observatory*" (Between Academic Research, Scientific

Dissemination and the Football Market: Data Science in the Study of Football—the Swiss Case of the Football Observatory). In: **Revista Fulia**. Belo Horizonte: UFMG, vol. 6, n. 1, 2021, pp. 50–87.

HOLLANDA, Bernardo Buarque de; ALVES, Carolina Gonçalves; JOSIOWICS, Alejandra (Orgs.). ***Mulheres escritoras***: *arquivos literários e feminismos na América Latina.* (Women Writers: Literary Archives and Feminisms in Latin America). Rio de Janeiro: FGV Editora, 2023.

JACOBS, Barbara. ***The Dick, Kerr's Ladies***: *The Factory Girls Who Took on the World.* London: Robinson, 2004.

JANUÁRIO, Soraya Barreto; KNIJNIK, Jorge (Orgs.). ***Futebol das mulheres no Brasil***: *emancipação, resistências e equidade* (Women's Football in Brazil: Emancipation, Resistance And equity). Recife: Ed. UFPE, 2022.

KESSLER, Cláudia S. ***Mais que barbies e ogras***: *uma etnografia do futebol de mulheres no Brasil e nos Estados Unidos* (More than Barbies and Ogras: An Ethnography of Women's Football in Brazil and the United States). Porto Alegre: PhD Thesis in Anthropology/UFRGS, 2015.

KESSLER, Cláudia S. (Org.). ***Mulheres na área***: *gênero, diversidade e inserções no futebol.* (Women in the Field: Gender, Diversity and Insertions in Football). Porto Alegre: Ed. UFRGS, 2016.

KESSLER, Cláudia S.; GOELLNER, Silvana Vilodre. "*O Brasil é hexa: a trajetória esportiva de Marta*" (Brazil Is Hexa: Marta's Sporting Career). In: GIGLIO, Sérgio Settani; PRONI, Marcelo Weishaupt (Orgs.). **Football in the Human Sciences in Brazil**. Campinas: Editora Unicamp, 2020.

KESSLER, Cláudia S.; COSTA, Leda; PISANI, Mariane (Orgs.). ***As mulheres no universo do futebol brasileiro*** (Women in the Universe of Brazilian Football). Santa Maria: Ed. UFSM, 2020.

LEITÃO, Eliane Vasconcellos. ***A mulher na língua do povo*** (Women in the Language of the People). Rio de Janeiro: Achiame, 1981.

LEVER, Janet. ***A loucura do futebol*** (The Madness of Football). Rio de Janeiro: Record, 1983.

MANSFIELD, Louise; CAUDWELL, Jayne; WHEATON, Belinda; WATSON, Beccy (Eds.). **The Palgrave Handbook of Feminism and Sport, Leisure and Physical Education**. London: Palgrave Macmillan, 2018.

MORAES, Enny Vieira. ***As mulheres também são boas de bola****: histórias de vida de jogadoras baianas (1970–1990)* (Women Are Also Good with the Ball: Life Stories of Bahian Women Footballers (1970-–1990)). São Paulo: PhD Thesis in History/PUC-SP, 2012.

PACHECO, Leonardo Turchi. *"A palavra e a voz no futebol: apontamentos sobre mulheres e narração esportiva"* (The Word and the Voice in Football: Notes on Women and Sports Narration). In: GIGLIO, Sérgio Settani; PRONI, Marcelo Weishaupt (Orgs.). **O futebol nas ciências humanas no Brasil** (Football in the Human Sciences in Brazil). Campinas: Editora Unicamp, 2020.

PISANI, Mariane da Silva. ***Poderosas do Foz****: trajetórias, migrações e profissionalização de mulheres que praticam futebol* (The Powerful Women of Foz: Trajectories, Migrations and Professionalisation of Women Who Play Football.) Florianópolis: Master's dissertation in Anthropology/UFSC, 2012.

POLI, Raffaele; RAVENEL, Loïc; BESSON, Roger. "The Demographic Evolution of the Principal Women's Football League (2017–2021)." In: **CIES Football Observatory Monthly Report**. Neuchâtel: n. 66, June 2021, pp. 01–05.

PRUDHOMME-PONCET, Laurence. ***Histoire du football féminin au XXe siècle*** (History of Women's Football in the 20th Century.) Paris: L'Harmattan, 2003.

RAJÃO, Raphael. "*Futebol de mulheres em tempos de proibição: o caso das partidas Vespasiano x Oficina (1968)*" (Women's Football in Times of Prohibition: The Case of the Vespasiano x Oficina matches (1968)). In: **Revista Mosaico**. Rio de Janeiro: vol. 9, n. 14, 2018, pp. 48–69.

RAJÃO, Raphael; HOLLANDA, Bernardo Buarque de. "*Museus de fronteira e a musealização do futebol: o lugar da memória futebolística no campo museal brasileiro (anos 1960–1990)*" (Border Museums and the Musealisation of Football: the Place of Football Memory in the Brazilian Museum Field (1960s–1990s)). In: **Revista Museologia e Patrimônio**. Rio de Janeiro: vol. 14, n. 1, 2021, pp. 121–147.

REIS, Heloísa Helena Baldy dos; SOUZA JUNIOR, Osmar Moreira de. *"Projetos de vida, mulheres e futebol"* (Life Projects, Women and Football). In: GIGLIO, Sérgio Settani; PRONI, Marcelo Weishaupt (Orgs.). ***O futebol nas ciências humanas no Brasil**.* (Football in the Human Sciences in Brazil). Campinas: Editora Unicamp, 2020.

RITCHER, Ana Cristina; BASSANI, Jaison José (Orgs.). ***Memórias do futebol****: infâncias em jogo* (Football Memories: Childhoods at Stake). São Paulo: APGIQ, 2019.

SILVA, Giovana Capucim e. ***Narrativas sobre o futebol feminino na imprensa paulista****: entre a proibição e a regulamentação (1965–1983)* (Narratives About Women's Football in the São Paulo Press: Between Prohibition and Regulation (1965–1983)). São Paulo: Master's dissertation in Social History/USP, 2015.

SOUZA JUNIOR, Osmar Moreira de. ***Futebol como projeto profissional de mulheres****: interpretações da busca pela legitimidade* (Football as a Professional Project for Women: Interpretations of the Search for Legitimacy). Campinas: PhD Thesis in Physical Education/FEF-Unicamp, 2013.

TEIXEIRA, Rosana da Câmara. ***Os perigos da paixão****: visitando jovens torcidas cariocas* (The Dangers of Passion: Visiting Young Fans in Rio de Janeiro.) São Paulo: Annablume, 2004.

TOLEDO, Luiz Henrique de. "*Balanços bibliográficos e ciclos randômicos: o caso dos futebóis na antropologia brasileira*" (Bibliographic Balances and Random Cycles: the Case of Football in Brazilian Anthropology). In: **BIB**—Revista Brasileira de Informação Bibliográfica em Ciências Sociais. São Paulo: n. 94, 2021, pp. 1–32.

TOLEDO, Luiz Henrique de. "*Universos em emoção: a propósito de uma exposição de arte, seu catálogo e a coletânea de estudos socioantropológicos sobre futebol*" (Universes in Emotion: About an Art Exhibition, Its Catalogue and the Collection of Socio-Anthropological Studies on Football). In: **Mana**: Estudos de Antropologia Social. Rio de Janeiro: n. 29(3), 2023, pp. 1–34.

TOLEDO, Luiz Henrique de; CAMARGO, Wagner Xavier. "*Futebol dos futebóis: dissolvendo valências simbólicas de gênero e sexualidade por dentro do futebol*" (The Football of Footballs: Dissolving Symbolic Valences of Gender and Sexuality Within Football). In: **Revista Fulia**. Belo Horizonte: UFMG, v. 3, n. 3, Sep–Dec 2018, pp. 93–107.

VOTRE, Sebastião; MOURÃO, Ludmila. "Women's Football in Brazil: Progress and Problems." In: **Soccer and Society**. v. 4, n. 2, 2003, pp. 254–267.

WITTER, José Sebastião; MEIHY, José Sebe Bom. ***Futebol e cultura****: coletânea de estudos* (Football and Culture: A Collection of Studies). São Paulo: Official Press, 1982.

Links Cited and Consulted

BBC
https://www.bbc.com/sport/football/67686209
Dibradoras
https://dibradoras.com.br/
So Foot Magazine
https://www.sofoot.com/articles/1970-et-1971-ces-premieres-coupes-du-monde-feminine-que-tout-le-monde-a-oublie

PART I

Socio-Historical Aspects of Women's Football Practice

CHAPTER 1

A New Decade for the "Bello Sexo": Female Participation in the Stands during the Consolidation of Soccer in Brazil

Daniela Araújo

To understand the importance and development of female participation in soccer and in the stands, we begin our analysis with the period of introduction and consolidation we have of modern sports in Brazil. To this end, we analyzed the narratives about women football fans present in the periodicals *Jornal do Brasil*, *O Paiz*, and *Vida Sportiva: hebdomadário sportivo e mundano*, available in the Hemeroteca Digital of the National Library, between the 1910s and 1920s.

In this way, we can observe the presence and role of women within soccer fans, in the sporting context and in Brazilian society in general. As Leonardo Affonso de Miranda Pereira states in his thesis "Footballmania: A Social History of Soccer in Rio de Janeiro (1902–1938)," defended in 1998, "it [the history of soccer] appears as a rich means of analyzing the possibilities of dialogue and clashes between groups" (p. 6).

Throughout the twentieth century, soccer and its fans were therefore an important lens through which to examine gender relations and the social issues of each era and each historical community from a specific angle. According to Pinheiro, "the ways of cheering thus differ at each moment in society and dialog with its customs and transformations" (2014, p. 2).

Between 1889 and the end of the 1920s, Brazil experienced the so-called First Republic. This period saw major changes in the shape of modern Brazilian society. It is important to note that this was a period of introduction and consolidation of soccer in Brazil, when the Brazilian economy was beginning its industrial process—especially the textile and food industries—and was still based on agricultural production, notably the export of coffee. According to José Miguel Arias Neto (2003), "the coffee-industry binomial" (p. 195), despite having deeper roots, characterizes the process of national economic development. The policy of issuing paper money and the boom in coffee exports created favorable conditions for industrial development in the country.

Indeed, urban growth also intensified, especially in the Federal Capital, Rio de Janeiro, and in São Paulo (NETO, 2003), especially with innovations in the means of transportation, through streetcar lines (animal-drawn and later electric), investment in shops and the establishment of manufacturing, albeit rudimentary. According to Humberto Fernandes Machado:

> In this context, innovative habits were emerging. The elites, especially women, began to flock to Rua do Ouvidor, where the heart of Carioca society beat, as it was there that the stores were located, displaying the latest European fashions. Men's clothes followed the rigor of English fashion, while women delighted in the ornaments found in the stores of French merchants. (Machado, 1999, p. 92)

The myth of the introduction of soccer in Brazil is that it was brought from England by Charles Miller, a student from São Paulo, in 1894 and, despite its amateurism, it was followed by a "very well-educated elite, as one might expect in the case of a sport fed by rich people" (Guterman, 2009, p. 229). Soccer, therefore, arrived in Brazil in principle as another fad of European modernity incorporated into the culture of the Brazilian elites, with their concern for imitating customs and standards of civility.

In this context, English sport arrived in Brazil, mainly in Rio de Janeiro and São Paulo, through the sons of an economic elite who sent their heirs in the certainty of a good European education. Thus, football took on the appearance of an elite sport, "another face of the famous British imperialism," impacting on the modern habits of the new century (Pereira, 1998, p. 18). At the beginning of the 1900s, football clubs and teams were springing up in the capital of Rio with great enthusiasm from their founders and practitioners, but without any major press coverage.

During this period, turf, like rowing, was the popularized sport that deserved the attention of journalists and readers (Mascarenhas, 1999; Pereira, 1998). Although this attention and intense sporting activity did not, in fact, represent a notoriety for sports journalism in the period. At the beginning of the twentieth century, the press turned its attention to political discussions caused by the still heated division in the periodicals between republicans and defenders of the old imperial regime (Sodré, 1998).

> [...] the city of Rio de Janeiro experienced, from 1850 onwards and more intensely in the period spanning the first three decades of republican life, a rich sporting activity, characterized by the introduction and multiplication of new sports and the proliferation of civil associations created for this purpose. (Mascarenhas, 1999, p. 18)

In fact, when soccer was introduced in Brazil, it found a fertile sporting field. This sporting fever, to use the creative and contextually expressive term, since it refers to the period marked by the Spanish Flu/Fever, coined by Gilmar Mascarenhas (1999), occurred as a result of the modern changes in Brazilian urban life, especially in the capital of the Republic, Rio de Janeiro. Even in the colonial period, little is known about sporting practices, with only a few mentions of hunting, horseback riding, and the occasional bullfight.

At the beginning of the twentieth century, adherence to sports and leisure gained momentum in society. New habits for caring for the body and for entertainment emerged and expanded in the city of Rio de Janeiro. The Latin motto of a healthy mind in a healthy body, attributed to the Roman poet Juvenal, was incorporated into the daily lives of men and women in the Republican capital. This gave rise to the figure of the sportman and, later, specifically in Brazil, fans (Melo, 2012). Victor Andrade de Melo states:

> Sportmen, as those involved in sports in the most diverse roles (whether as public, manager, coach or practitioner) were called in England, will over time receive new denominations: for competitors, the use of the term athlete will become commonplace; the public will be called fans, aficionados, torcedor (in the case of Brazil), among others. (Melo, 2012, p. 24)

Although "often ignored by soccer historiography in Brazil, which tends to focus its analysis on the high seductive capacity of soccer and its easy assimilation" (Mascarenhas, 1999, pp. 28–29), the sporting space already consolidated by rowing, turf, and cycling is fundamental to the rapid popularization of soccer, which brings in its form of cheering characteristics that are reminiscent of the modalities of its predecessors. Soccer arrived in Rio de Janeiro, along with swimming, cycling, and athletics, already inspired by the models built by bullfighting, rowing, and turf (Melo, 2012), both in the organization of the event and in the behavior expected of its spectators.

In the first decades of the nineteenth century, bullfighting was a popular sport in Brazil. With the sport being used as entertainment, not only on festive dates, notably Catholic festivities, arenas were built with ticket sales and differentiated values based on the comfort of the stands (Melo, 2012). According to Victor Andrade de Melo (2012), bullfights alternated between periods of popularity and great disinterest, mainly due to the disorderly acts of the spectators present. The public, once they had paid for a show and bet money on it, saw themselves as entitled to demand higher quality and so caused fights and destruction of the arena's structures.

Over the course of the twentieth century, bullfighting was replaced by horse racing (turfe). Although it still attracted a large audience, bullfighting suffered from the economic situation and the structural and social changes in the city of Rio de Janeiro. With the air of modernity coming to the urbanized capital, activities that referred to the countryside lost popularity (Melo, 2012). The landmark of this change in the status of the most popular sport, according to Victor Andrade Melo (2007), was the creation of the Club de Corridas in 1849.

Turf racing arrived on the scene in Rio in the early decades of the nineteenth century "as yet another civilizing activity" (Mascarenhas, 1999, p. 28) promoted by the elites and the English colony. From 1850 onward, the races began to gain notoriety, including in the newspapers. The inauguration event of the Derby Club, located where the Mario Filho Stadium—Maracanã—was later built, was attended by around 8,000 people, for example. Victor Melo (2012) states that "its inauguration seems to have been one of the great social events of the year" (p. 30). In fact, the Derby Club's success in terms of attendance, credited mainly to the good organization of sporting events and its privileged location, also reflects the growth of turf as the sport of expression in the period.

Another indication of the importance of turf in Brazilian society, especially in the capital, Rio de Janeiro, is the association of the sport with a practice of economic speculation, the Encilhamento. The reference to the starting point of the horses in the races refers to the policy of issuing capital and shares in companies, which existed practically only on paper (Neto, 2003; Sevcenko, 1998).

The space where the turf races were held bore the characteristics of social distinction based on the price of the tickets, the most expensive of which, aimed at the elite, gave access to more comfortable seats. Turf racing inaugurated a practice that is relevant to the way people cheer for soccer: membership of sports clubs. This practice allowed members of high society to have privileges and their wives and daughters to attend the clubs.

> Normally the stands were divided into four sectors: the general public, individuals from the middle or lower classes; members, members of the elite; authorities and special guests, where members had relative transit; and a special sector for the press, considered to be of great importance for publicizing events and attracting audiences. (Melo, 2012, p. 32)

It was also with the consolidation of turf that we saw more active public participation in the stands, even though the contortions of the fans were due to the amounts bet, a fundamental element for the popularity of the races, according to Melo (2012). However, there is no denying the popularity of the sport and its impact on the culture of cheering that was yet to come in soccer. Although the most active fans are credited to the culture of betting money, turf still attracted a large audience and the attention of the sports columns of the newspapers in the 1910s. For example, in the April 30, 1915 edition of *Jornal do Brasil*, in which the Sport column urges supporters of the horse Buenos Aires to take part in the Grand Prix (Figure 2.1).

With the gradual change in social behavior, we can see a greater female presence in public spaces. Victor Andrade de Melo (2007) states that "turf was one of the valves for female social participation, since it was considered to be aristocratic

Figure 2.1: *Jornal do Brasil* urging fans to attend the turf competition in 1915.

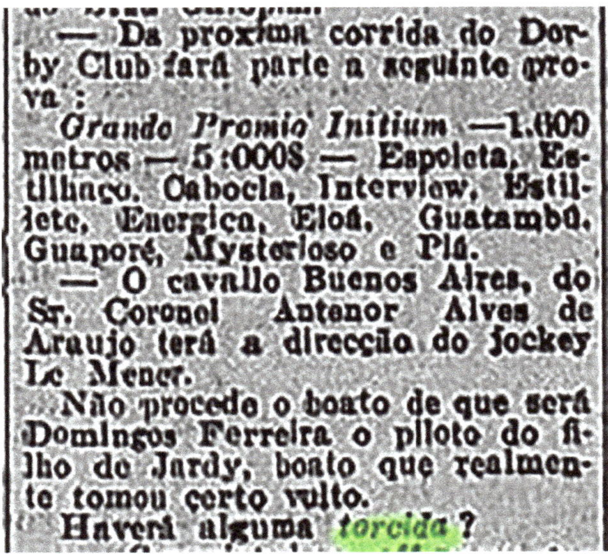

— Da proxima corrida do Derby Club fará parte a seguinte prova:

Grande Premio Initium — 1.600 metros — 5:000$ — Espoleta, Estilhaço, Cabocla, Interview, Estillete, Energica, Eloá, Guatambú, Guaporé, Mysterioso e Plá.

— O cavallo Buenos Aires, do Sr. Coronel Antenor Alves de Araujo terá a direcção do jockey Le Mener.

Não procede o boato de que será Domingos Ferreira o piloto do filho de Jardy, boato que realmente tomou certo vulto.

Haverá alguma *torcida*?

and family-oriented" (p. 130). In fact, the female public accompanied their fathers and husbands, members of the clubs, to the turf events and this was a time for socializing. There was even a specific fashion for the women of Rio's elite to parade in the grandstands of the racecourses, wearing hats, the latest dresses, and jewelry that often made reference to horse racing (Pacheco apud. Melo, 2007).

> We can't ignore the fact that the presence of women in the meadows was also seen as another way of introducing women to the "cream of society," making them known to some "good match," predisposing them to a good marriage. For single women, it was even a chance to flirt, something that challenged the traditional social structure. (Melo, 2007, p. 131)

The turf, therefore, is possibly the first social space that allows men and women to meet and flirt at sporting events. It is worth noting that this behavior is a notorious change in Brazilian society. At this time, universal suffrage, following the popularization of Stuart Mill's works, began to be discussed more vehemently in Brazil. Active female participation in social political life is still a point of great disagreement, with the concept of women's main mission being to educate and care for their families (Marques, 2019).

Rowing, in turn, eliminated betting and reformulated a series of sporting concepts and practices. Privileged by the Pereira Passos reform (1902–1906), the sport became an important social event, gathering huge crowds in the coves and by the sea.

This was mainly due to a change in social behavior, with more frequent visits to the beach, medical recommendations for bathing in the sea, with the popularization of hygienist theory, and the beautification of the city's waterfront (Mascarenhas, 1999). For Victor Andrade de Melo:

> In the transition between the 19th and 20th centuries, rowing was already more structured, with many clubs that not only promoted frequent activities but also sought an organization in the form of a federation, with a view to establishing unique rules and boosting its presence in the new scenario of the city and the country. It was at this point that one of the elements that marks contemporary sports practice began to emerge in Brazil, including and fundamentally with regard to public participation: club identification. (Melo, 2012, pp. 38–39)

It is important to note that rowing laid the foundations for cheering as we know it in soccer, not only with club identification, but also with rivalry between teams;

the incorporation of the social distinction of the grandstand, through the value of the tickets for the pavilions; greater participation of women in the halls of the teams and in the grandstands (Melo, 2012). As early as August 26, 1912, the *Jornal do Brasil* showed us signs of this female participation in rowing competitions:

> O Aspecto do Cais
>
> There was no memorable competition in the opening regatta of the season, dedicated by Natação to Mr. General Julio Roca, Plenipotentiary Minister of the Argentine Republic in Brazil.
>
> However, the long quay was home to thick circles of people, some leaning over the rail, others on their tiptoes to get a better look at the garrisons, who were speeding towards the finish line.
>
> On top of this multicolored, undulating mass of people, several rows of flags and foliage swung down as fixed decorations.
>
> The number of people who had traveled to Botafogo to watch the regattas was considerable on the road and in the gardens along that stretch of Avenida Beira-Mar.
>
> Families were predominantly out for a stroll and the varied hues of the women's costumes gave the place a beautiful appearance. (*Jornal do Brasil*, issue 239, August 26, 1912. Our emphasis)

Rowing was consolidated at the turn of the century and became one of the symbols of the modernity that Rio de Janeiro was trying to achieve. The population of the new capital of the Republic was made up mostly of Blacks, former slaves migrating from the coffee plantations of the Paraíba Valley or already living in the capital, who clustered mainly around the port region in search of work. This population lived in unsanitary tenements, which led to a series of endemic diseases that ravaged the city every year, according to the authorities. The image of Rio de Janeiro, especially to foreigners, was of a dirty, deleterious, and unattractive city, despite its port being the third most important in the world.

In order to change Rio de Janeiro's appearance and reputation as a "foreigner's tomb" (Sevcenko, 1998, p. 22), structural and sanitation reforms were carried out in the port and downtown. The engineer and urban planner, Pereira Passos, was in charge of reforming the city, widening streets to increase traffic flow, tearing down the mansions in the center, and enhancing the beachfront.

Therefore, rowing also delayed the overtaking of soccer as the most popular sport due to its strong appeal in the constitution of a healthier life by the sea and also the incentive produced by Pereira Passos' reforms (Mascarenhas, 1999). In this sense, we can initially justify the emergence of the main soccer teams linked to the rowing clubs and the rivalries born out of maritime competitions that also developed on the soccer field.

With regard to the presence of women in rowing competitions, we can see a greater occupation of public spaces by women, especially during leisure time. Not just the idea of following sporting activities, rowing has enabled a new form of social interaction. Victor Melo (2007) states:

> In Rowing, one really notices a small direct participation of women. As leaders, some sportswomen even held the position of social or grandstand director. These were not the most important positions in the clubs and regattas, but it has to be said that, in any case, a new step had been taken. It should be noted that previously there hadn't even been a term to describe women involved in sport, such as sportman, used to describe male fans. If a new term found its way into newspapers and magazines, this could be an indicator that there was a new sensibility about women's roles. (Melo, 2007, pp. 137–138)

In other words, rowing laid the most solid foundations for the introduction of soccer. It is even possible to see the involvement of women in the stands, with prominent roles in the way the public watches the event. Thus, we can say that the presence of women in popular sports is not new or exclusive to soccer. The change in women's social behavior, based on the growing discussions about equality, suffrage, and education for women, has also reverberated in their performance in the sports field.

With this brief summary of the sports scene when soccer arrived in Brazil, we can see that the consolidation of this sport in the country came about more easily not only because of its power to fascinate, its degree of unpredictability, and its inspiration of social justice, as Roberto DaMatta (1994) points out. The sporting environment was already prepared to receive the European novelty and society also craved the icons of modernity of the time.

"Vida Sportiva" and "Mundana": Weekly Magazines, Female Participation, and the Development of the Sports Press

Between 1910 and 1914, Brazil, which had been proclaimed a Republic since 1889 and was governed by Marshal Hermes da Fonseca, experienced a series of political, urban, and behavioral transformations that marked modernity in the country. One of the first measures of the Republican government was to open up the economy to foreign capital and rush to industrialize and modernize the country (Sevcenko, 1998). These and other changes resulting from the Second Industrial Revolution, or Scientific-Technological Revolution, had a direct impact on social behavior. Nicolau Sevcenko, in *História da vida privada no Brasil*—volume 03, states that:

> In fact, in no previous period have so many people been involved so completely and so quickly in a dramatic process of transformation of their daily habits, their convictions, their modes of perception and even their instinctive reflexes. Not just in Brazil, but in the world as a whole. (Sevcenko, 1998, pp. 7–8).

In fact, during the time frame of this chapter, we can observe major changes in social behavior and in the narratives about them. Major historical events, in addition to the First World War (1914–1918), had a direct impact on the daily life of Brazilian society, especially in Rio de Janeiro, such as the Revolta da Chibata (1910) and the Spanish Flu (1918–1919). At the outset, it is worth noting that both represent two major problems that the government and society's elite tried to suppress from the city's image: the legacy of a slave economy, with a growing Black population living in the port area, and Rio de Janeiro's unhealthy conditions.

To this end, the transformations of Pereira Passos' urban and sanitary reforms were orchestrated. In other words, it was at the turn of the nineteenth to the twentieth centuries that we saw a change in public spaces in Rio de Janeiro. This social context is fundamental for understanding the communication production of the period (Barbosa, 2013). In addition, the height of the Belle Époque in Rio de Janeiro also reverberated in social behavior, especially among Rio's elite. They sought to get closer to the European ideal of modernity, especially the French, not only in terms of urban architecture. As a result, there was a social construction of new practices considered good taste and refinement in the upper classes, directly impacting on female participation in society and its representations (Voks, 2012).

The speed of change in the new century also had an impact on the process of communication. "The entire First Republic (1889–1930) saw the beginning of the implementation of modern mass communication in the country" (Barbosa, 2013, p. 236). In other words, this period saw an expansion of the public and the consolidation of new communication technologies, such as the use of the telegraph to transmit messages over long distances and the use of photographic images as a contribution to the reality narrated by the periodicals (Barbosa, 2013).

During the 1910s, we can see a growing number of photography professionals in the city of Rio de Janeiro, as well as publications that used this imagery to expand the reading possibilities of their audience. Technological advances, made possible by the opening up of Brazil's economy and the transformations brought about by the scientific–technological revolution, also had an impact on the way readers observed the world around them. It is important to note that this work does not cover the history of photography and reading in Rio de Janeiro, but these facts lead to a new subsidy for social behavior and the development of narratives pertinent to the periodicals of the time.

For Marialva Barbosa (2013), it was with the expansion of technologies in the twentieth century that the "modern observer" emerged (p. 227), i.e. the reader began to be able to decode the message through photography, reading, and orality, expanding the reading capacity of individuals. The photographic resource not only expands the individual's reading possibilities, but also contributes to broadening the audience reached. Photographs are independent of the reader's literacy in order to be understood. Even if they lack pertinent information about the event depicted, looking at the printed image already gives the viewer the message to be conveyed. Written text, therefore, becomes an accessory in certain printed productions, such as photo captions. As stated by Marialva Barbosa (2013), photographers have replaced the recording of moments that previously could only be done through written reports. Consequently, it could only be decoded by a select and literate audience.

During the 1910s, "soccer started to become a subject of great journalistic interest" (Silva, 2006, p. 35). In addition, it was during this decade that soccer began its transition from a sport representing the nobility to the most popular sport in the country (Pereira, 1998). The popularization of the sport that represented the modernity desired by the elite also began during the period when the press was transformed into mass communication. Voks (2012) states that the social transformations that took place at the beginning of the twentieth century had an impact on the press. It grew and lost its artisanal character, becoming a set of profit-driven communication companies, therefore, aiming to increase its consumer readership.

In this period, we see the emergence of a weekly magazine focused exclusively on sports, leisure, and social life. The weekly magazine *Vida Sportiva: hebdomadário sportivo e mundano* circulated in Rio de Janeiro between 1917

Figure 2.2: Photo caption of the A. A. Palmeiras match and its fans.

Source: Revista *Vida Sportiva:* hebdomadário sportivo e mundado. Issue 60, October 12, 1918.)

and 1922 and, according to the catalog file of the Brazilian Historical and Geographical Institute (IHGB),[1] published by Guimarães & C. Despite its short circulation time, the period shows us the growing importance of sports journalism until it reached its apex in the consolidation process with the creation of *Jornal dos Sports* in 1931, which we will see in the next chapters. In addition, the weekly magazine also hints at the development of women and their correlation with sports participation. As early as the first issue of *Vida Sportiva*, we can see

1. For more information, consult the cataloguing form available on the website of the Brazilian Historical and Geographical Institute (IHGB) via the link: Para maiores informações, consultar a ficha catalográfica disponível no site do Instituto Histórico e Geográfico Brasileiro (IHGB) através do link: https://www.ihgb.org.br/pesquisa/hemeroteca/periodicos/item/102250-vida-sportiva-hebdomadario-illustrado,-sportivo-e-mundano.html.

that the publication tended to target both male and female audiences with soap operas and news about the behavior of mademoiselles, fashion, flirtations, and dances that took place during the week.

The illustrated weekly *Vida Sportiva*, which appeared with the option of buying a single issue or a six-monthly or annual subscription, with headquarters at Avenida Mem de Sá n. 149 and 151, published its first issue on August 25, 1917. More than just a weekly informative publication, *Vida Sportiva*, like the illustrated

Figure 2.3: Advertisement page of the first issue of *Vida Sportiva* magazine.

magazines of the time, was also a "product intended for sale and consumption" (Voks, 2012, p. 179). In addition, the publication's first editions included advertisements for medicines, hair products, women's clothing stores, and photography courses. Therefore, the text and images projected in the periodical should attract and please the paying public, those in privileged socio-economic conditions, with a view to the profitability of the media company and its advertisers.

The hebdomadário *Vida Sportiva*, more than a sports publication, is a narrative construction about social behavior and reproduces the development of the press in the early years of the First Republic. Its photos, illustrations, cartoons, and texts represent the ideal of modernity that the elite, especially in Rio, wanted to achieve. However, it is important to note that, like a game of mirrors, the reflected image can cause an optical illusion in the observer. Since the representations constructed by the magazine show the desires of a literate elite who consume the publication and the products advertised, they hide social realities with which the elite do not wish to share the same space, whether in publications or in the urban city.

The weekly magazine played a fundamental role in the communication scenario of the time, linking images of everyday life with the political and cultural projects of the intellectual elites (Barbosa, 2013). Therefore, the popularization of soccer was also part of a political and cultural process by the literate elites to expand their audience using photographic resources, thus, transmitting to a greater number of individuals the modern behaviors that should be replicated throughout society. It therefore creates a memory of the present in which social, economic, and urban transformations have taken place at an accelerated pace. Modernity and the development of an economy geared toward consumption marked a new behavioral pattern in the country that was increasingly instigated by illustrated magazines and cultural processes, through music and dance, the spread of sports and, later, cinema (Sevcenko, 1998).

At the beginning of the twentieth century, photography was an important factor in the popularization of periodicals in social life. Marialva Barbosa points out that the use of images is a resource widely used in publications of the period and transforms the reader into an observer. In addition, photography became an instrument for consolidating a visual memory of a period of accelerated technological, economic, social, and communication changes. Therefore, photography, according to Ana Mauad:

> It is a message, which is processed over time, whose constituent units are cultural, but assume differentiated symbolic functions, according to both the context in which the message is conveyed and the place they occupy within the message itself. (Mauad, 1996, p. 7)

More than just an instrument for constructing a memory, a portrait of reality, photography became an important element in the popularization of periodicals in the twentieth century and, consequently, the sports and social behaviors they portrayed. Thus, the use of images contributed to the transformation of periodicals restricted to a select literate public into a mass press, here synonymous with a widely circulated press, and of the public into readers and observers of the construction of the memory of their contemporary reality.

It is therefore possible to infer that the use of photography, especially caption photos of sports competitions, was essential for the consolidation of sport and the sports narrative. Ana Mauad (1996) states that photography is a portrait established by society to represent a reality. "Without ever forgetting that every document is a monument, if photography informs, it also shapes a certain worldview" (p. 8).

Vida Sportiva is a sports and world publication, so it portrays the development of society through its sporting events or clubs and associations. There are also fashion sections and soap operas on its pages. The use of photographs, cartoons, and caricatures brings the reader closer to the journalistic narrative. For the female audience, specifically, it is possible to see a characterization of behavior and appropriate clothing for young women who frequent the leisure spaces of the city of Rio de Janeiro. It is important to note that, as a magazine that sought above all to sell its copies and increase advertising in its spaces, the construction of the female imaginary is a White woman, from the elite, whose behavior is docile and gentle. The "ilustríssimas" and "gentilíssimas" did not represent Black women in Rio de Janeiro society. The poor and Black population was part of a colonial slave memory and should be hidden from the French-inspired urban modernity of the Republic.

The weekly magazine and the photo captions in the periodicals of the decade also contributed to the transformation of soccer into a sport beyond the elite. The sport of football became a shared code, a point of contact for various social groups, in which the centrality of attention was commonly associated with the sportmen. "The game proved capable of articulating differences and identities, whether racial, regional or national" (Pereira, 1998, p. 5). Given that the use of images does not require knowledge of letters, soccer began to portray its era, attract new readers, and expand its capacity to enchant. According to Marialva Barbosa (2013):

> In the major centers there was a common media territory characterized by the creation of new modes of communication based on the proliferation of periodicals whose main strategy was to win over the public, in a long process that would lead to the formation of a mass society. (Barbosa, 2013, p. 245)

In other words, as a social political instrument, soccer builds its image on the figure of the young nobleman living in the southern zone of Rio de Janeiro. They have their memory preserved in the history of soccer in Brazil as its precursors. However, their portraits also reinforce the stories that should be erased from the memory of the soccer field. As part of a project of social adaptation to the new acceptable urban behaviors, the women present in the stands were also frequently portrayed in the illustrated magazine in order to identify and characterize modern female behavior. The elite, white woman began to circulate in the city's public spaces. Soccer and leisure venues become central to the social life of upper-class women. These are the places that allow them to be present and to socialize with individuals of the opposite sex.

It is worth highlighting the editorial of the first edition, in which we can see the editors' intention to portray the dynamics of social and sporting life through the discourse of modernity. Journalism became the shaper of reality, the verisimilar portrait of truth and current affairs (Barbosa, 2013). It was through publications, such as the weekly *Vida Sportiva* that the memory of soccer began to be constructed through the popularization of the sport, transforming readers into mass consumers of printed periodicals and characterizing acceptable behavior in sporting environments, as well as class distinctions.

It is worth noting that in the 1910s, despite the fact that soccer began to attract the Black and more popular classes to practice and cheer, the portrait of the social stratum associated with the sport corresponds to the image of the nobility. The public and private spheres, the enjoyment of social life, were the privilege of an elite that restricted the lower classes. Soccer, therefore, also presents this point of tension. It increasingly attracts the attention of the lower classes, while its representation remains an elitist environment.

> Sporting Life
>
> In an environment like this, where the taste and enthusiasm for sport is growing daily, the appearance of an illustrated, sporting and worldly weekly like Vida Sportiva was indispensable.
>
> **We say sporting and worldly because they are so closely linked. They complete each other, and one cannot exist without the other.**
>
> Theophile Gautier said: "the human face is a soft wax, easy to modify at will" and Delphina de Girardin also said, with great common sense, that **"a woman's first duty is to be beautiful."**
>
> The plasticity of muscle is truly admirable and it's curious that today's man hasn't been able to take advantage of it, letting the human plant vegetate instead of flourishing in its vigor and grace.

> Dickens immortalized the portrait of the institute that forced its disciples to psalmody litanies with words in pr, in order to make a small mouth!
>
> The Greeks, who knew everything, or who guessed everything they didn't know, took physical education much further than any modern nation.
>
> They played the discus, the ball, the sword; they threw the arrow and knew very well the art of preparing a handful of men to face millions; their runners announced the victory of Marathona almost as quickly as the telegraph; they won naval battles by rowing and got fighters as beautiful as the marbles of Phidias.
>
> Fashion, on the other hand, does not consist, as many might think, only of clothing, but also of the way we live, the way we spend our lives, our occupations and our distractions.
>
> The day of a worldly woman today, despite often being as frivolously employed as that of yesteryear, is nothing like that of that time.
>
> **It's no longer the intimate meetings that take up hours; in the morning it's churches, in the afternoon it's the Avenue, shopping, footing it, etc., in the evening it's the cinema, concert or theater.**
>
> **Our era is the triumph of outdoor life: races, sports of all kinds absorb and attract our gentle patricians.**
>
> All the sections are in the hands of competent people and as there is a place under the sun for everyone, Vida Sportiva counts on the benevolence of its distinguished colleagues in the press of this capital and of the very respectable public, to achieve this desideratum (*Vida Sportiva*, issue 01, August 25, 1917. Our emphasis)

In it we can see that sporting events are also treated as major social events in urban and newly modern life. Sport and worldly life are inseparable in the fashions of the period. Leisure activities, parties, and even carnival balls are held in the halls of sports clubs. It is also in this environment that high society can be recognized, and its members introduced to each other in order to unite in marriages or political and economic alliances. The sports arena, as well as the theater and later the cinema, is the space for shaping the body physically and socially, in other words, disciplining the body (Foucault, 2014) both through their presence in public spaces and through the narratives in their publications.

Another aspect highlighted in the first edition is the presence of women in sporting and worldly life. Women's participation in public spaces in Brazilian society during this period was strongly associated with leisure time. The presence of girls in the stands was constantly celebrated for embellishing the event or for characterizing the environment as family friendly.

According to Aira Bonfim (2019), "In other words, the presence of women in sports environments at the time corroborated the designation of attributes such as 'wealth', 'family', as well as the feeling of social 'adequacy' in the stands and spaces of sociability in sport." The woman shifts her social locus from the private to the public, but still carries in her characteristics the familiar, docile, and subservient character exalted in the caregivers of the family and home in the previous period.

However, it is important to point out that the portrait of urban life and the leisure offered by sport also represents the movement to increase the presence of women in Rio's urbanized society. The act of going to a place to practice or watch a sport may seem insignificant to an inattentive observer, but it represents the beginning of a movement of emancipation, especially for elite women. It is

Figure 2.4: Photograph of a woman illustrates the editorial of the first issue of *Vida Sportiva*

Source: *Vida Sportiva*, issue 01, August 25, 1917.

important to note that the female experience, the becoming a woman described by Simone de Beauvoir in *The Second Sex*, in 1949, is tensioned by a set of powers, such as class and race.

The women in the crowd are representatives of Rio de Janeiro's elite, characterized by the term's mademoiselle, madame, gentilissima, and patrician. As we can see in the excerpt above and in the photograph of Mlle. Lydia Cardoso de Oliveira (Figure 2.4), described as "the very kind daughter of Minister Cardoso de Oliveira, a figure of high importance in Brazilian diplomacy" (Vida Sportiva, issue 1, August 25, 1917, p. 3).

It is clear to see that the representation of this female elite also shows us the development of female participation in Brazilian society. As *Vida Sportiva* magazine states in the editorial of its first edition, transcribed above, "it's no longer the intimate meetings that absorb the hours." Women no longer participate only in private spaces, but also in the public environments of urban life.

This interaction between men and women in the city's public spaces also led to a change in love relationships. Arranged marriages began to give way to the habit of flirting. This new behavior in the relationship between the sexes can be seen several times in the Frivolidades section of the magazine *Vida Sportiva*, a column of social notes from the sports stands and the mundane life of Rio de Janeiro.

In the June 15, 1918 edition, the column stated:

> Do you want to know the truth, Mlle. N.V.C.?
>
> Well. Don't put too much faith in him. He's a very fickle boy, a flirt only on occasion. Just Sunday, we saw him flirting with an American fan during the America vs. São Christóvão match.
>
> C.B. worries too much about the other one, the beautiful tricolor fan. She's his golden idol. So, mlle., get rid of her…. (*Vida Sportiva*, issue 43, June 15, 1918, p. 18)

It is worth noting that until the middle of the previous century, women, especially those from the elite, were educated to be "good" housewives without being allowed to circulate widely in public spaces. In addition, marriages were arranged according to the convenience of the alliances desired by their parents (Melo, 2007). Therefore, the act of flirting and arousing the interest of young people for dating and marriage is a change, albeit a slow one, in the sociability between men and women.

The dynamics caused by this affront to "the traditional social structure" (Melo, 2007, p. 131), despite causing strangeness in the more traditional individuals of Brazilian society, are narrated positively and with a certain lightness in the pages of *Vida Sportiva*. The Frivolidades column was the space to narrate the meetings and mismatches of potential high-society couples, preserving their identities by only naming the initials of their names. As we can see in issue 43, of June 15, 1918, of *Vida Sportiva*, in which the young H.S.G., "a charming profile of the São Paulo elite," turned all her attention to cheering on her team in a match in the Rio-São Paulo competition, and failed to notice the admiration of the "nice young man" from society who showed impatience and despair at being ignored by "mademoiselle."

It is common to see female fans characterized by "sweet," "kind," "graceful maiden," "mademoiselle," "beautiful sex," among other adjectives that give beauty and docility to the sports arena. In addition, these adjectives, like the beauty contest, "Which fan is the most beautiful?" promoted by the magazine in 1918, which rewarded the first and second place winners with photos printed large in the publication, corroborate the normativity of female behavior requiring male approval. In other words, the narratives about the presence of women in stadiums also reinforce the social behavior of female subservience to male interests.

> Deeply impressed by the beauty of that silhouette, we climbed up with great difficulty to the stands and caught a glimpse of the enchanting figure of Mlle. L.P., the gentle supporter of the 1910 champions. The Ipanema air made her blush and look more beautiful. Mlle. L. didn't say a word: she was as if mute, such was her dejection.
>
> We could see the silhouette of Mlle. Maia, whose sadness was visible and contagious. contagious. And the afternoon fell slowly…
>
> It was the end of a day full of excitement and joy for the fans of the tricolor, full of misfortune and sadness for the fans of the alvi-negro (*Vida Sportiva*, issue 50, July 27, 1918).

However, despite sometimes serving the interests and gaze of men, the female element in the stands should not be seen as secondary. Just as at the beginning of the century, women began to demand greater participation in social activities, such as studying and voting, women's presence in the stands should not be seen as passive.

The fans are portrayed as "parochial," "distracted" by focusing their attention only on the match, "nervous," "enrage."[2] In the October 5, 1918 edition of *Vida Sportiva*, in the Frivolidades column, "violent arguments" between fans of Botafogo and Fluminense were reported. An alvinegro fan, indignant at the defeat, gesticulated and shouted at the tricolor fan that her team had only won because the referee had been bought off. In the July 13, 1918 issue, the hebdomadário recounts how a fan from Rio de Janeiro gesticulated with her "pink umbrella" when "the crowd was too big" without worrying about whether she might disturb or injure another spectator in the stands. The illustrated magazine also contributed to the characterization and development of female soccer fans by publishing a questionnaire on female profiles in its Confidencial column in 1919.

Figure 2.5: Confidential column with the characteristics of a Flamengo fan. (*Vida Sportiva*, November 29, 1919.)

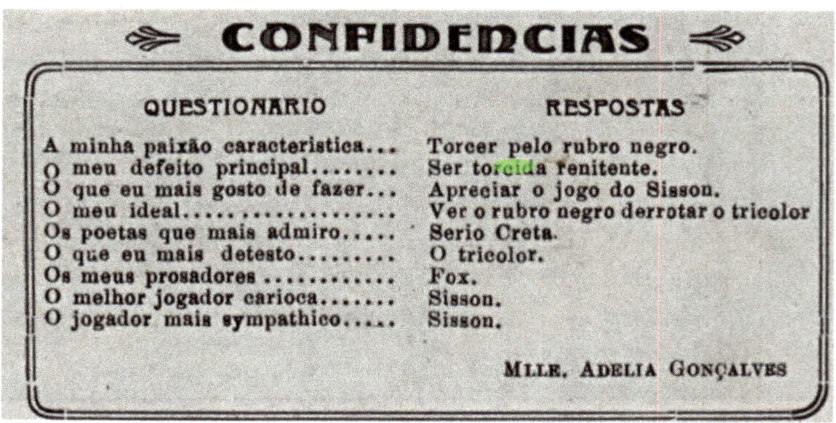

CONFIDENCIAS

QUESTIONARIO	RESPOSTAS
A minha paixão caracteristica...	Torcer pelo rubro negro.
O meu defeito principal........	Ser torcida renitente.
O que eu mais gosto de fazer...	Apreciar o jogo do Sisson.
O meu ideal....................	Ver o rubro negro derrotar o tricolor
Os poetas que mais admiro.....	Serio Creta.
O que eu mais detesto.........	O tricolor.
Os meus prosadores............	Fox.
O melhor jogador carioca.......	Sisson.
O jogador mais sympathico.....	Sisson.

MLLE. ADELIA GONÇALVES

In fact, the act of cheering denotes the development of female participation in society. Women in the stands did not just serve male interests, but actively cheered on their teams. The myth of the origin of the term torcer (to cheer), as soccer assistance, is credited to the chronicler Coelho Netto who, on observing the nervous movements of the girls cheering their toilettes in the stands, called

2. The French expression means angry, irritated, furious, enthusiastic or passionate.

them torcidas (fans). The words torcer, torcida, and torcedor began to gain notoriety during the 1910s and replaced the Anglicisms sportmen and sportwomen (Malaia, 2012).

It is important to note, as observed in the clippings analyzed, that women's presence in soccer stadiums should not be characterized as a passive act or as merely subservient to male desire. Women showed their passion and loyalty to their team. Moreover, they were often portrayed as expressing their emotions during matches or after the result achieved by their beloved club.

During the early years of the twentieth century, illustrated magazines played an important role in creating a new perspective on society in Brazil. Through their easy narratives and use of photography and caricature, they expanded their audience and became a mass press. Thus, illustrated magazines, like *Vida Sportiva*, portrayed the accelerated transformations of the century, while also contributing to the construction of these changes. Since magazines act during their publication to consolidate the social transformations of their time and, from a historical perspective, to preserve a memory in constant development.

In the development of narrative journalism, the illustrated magazine *Vida Sportiva* shows us the beginnings of the sports sector and its correlation with the daily life of Brazilian society. Despite not being the first publication to focus on sports in the capital, *Vida Sportiva* is a weekly that deserves attention precisely because of the association between social life and sporting life. As the editorial of the first issue itself reveals, for the magazine, these two areas of Brazilian social life, especially in Rio de Janeiro, are inseparable.

In fact, the popularization of soccer also served the purpose of disseminating the ideas of modernity that the elite of Brazilian society sought for the country's new political regime. Therefore, the narratives surrounding the sport and its fans are part of the institutionalization of new habits in light of the Belle Epoch reforms in Rio de Janeiro. The narratives about the women in the stands, above all, express the development of female participation in society at a time when colonial traditions were being broken down and they were almost exclusively confined to private spaces. As Victor Melo (2007) states, the narrative about women in sports and in the stands also reflects "women's struggles and demands for recognition of their broad possibility of participation" (p. 128).

Cheering on the Pinnacles of Fame: Female Presence and Sports Language as an Instrument for Popularizing Soccer

Despite the increase in interest in the sport, the language of representation in the newspaper pages reflected soccer's elitism and the supposed distinction of modern sports (Lopes, 1994). Generally, during this period, newspapers only devoted space to football after the matches had finished, after the public had already heard about what had happened on the pitch. "In general, soccer only occupied one or two columns of pages" (Lopes, 1994, p. 68), as we can see in the *Jornal do Brasil* newspaper. Previously, other sports had already been featured in newspapers, but without much prominence. Sports journalism had not yet achieved notoriety in the newsrooms and was treated as a minor issue.

During the period of consolidation of soccer, or football as it was portrayed, on the Rio de Janeiro scene, its concepts and terms returned to their English origins and the elitist distinction of modern novelty. Soccer was a social event constantly associated with the parties of high-society ladies, as Pereira (1998) states. Therefore, as an event of worldly life, described by the weekly *Vida Sportiva*, sport also gained a place in the publications of illustrated magazines aimed at women.

> At the beginning of the 20th century, soccer was football. The player was a player, or sportsman. The positions on the pitch were goalkeeper, right defender, left defender, center-half, right wing and left wing, as well as striker. The referee was the linesman. Everyone performed on the field, in the stadium, in games full of goals, hands, off-sides and fouls. These terms lasted throughout most of the First Republic in Brazil and generated heated debates about the use of these Anglicisms among intellectuals, chroniclers and the general public. (Malaia, 2012, p. 53)

However, from 1910 onward, a Brazilian term began to gain importance and take on a new meaning in the journalistic narrative about the sport. Cheering began to enter the vocabulary of periodicals as a characteristic of soccer fans. João Malaia (2012) states that terms such as "being a fan or a supporter and being part of a crowd" (p. 54) began to appear on a large scale in the sports narratives of Rio de Janeiro's newspapers. It is worth noting that audiences, whether in sports arenas or cultural shows, were already part of the narratives of sporting, in the everyday and mundane life in the periodicals. Thus, the term audience, supporters, and sportsman referred to the sports public, while audience and spectator referred to theatrical shows or the city's cinemas.

In fact, we can see that during the 1910s, narratives about supporters, referring to an individual or a group of soccer fans, developed and gained space in the sports pages of the periodicals. In *O Paiz*, for example, in the first five years of the decade, it is possible to find less than ten publications referring to soccer spectators. On the other hand, in 1918 alone, "torcidas" had more than twenty articles in the newspaper. During the entire period from 1910 to 1919, the term "torcida," referring to the audience at sporting events, in the periodicals analyzed, exceeded the 130 insertions mark. We analyzed *Jornal do Brasil*, *O Paiz* and *Vida Sportiva: hebdomandário sportivo e mundano*, published between 1910 and 1919, available at the Hemeroteca da Biblioteca Nacional, filtered using the search term "torcida."

For a term recently coined in the journalistic narrative and increasingly used over time, it is possible to see a constant concern in the narrative to characterize the term "torcida" and its expected behavior, for both men and women. It is important to note that the development of the narrative about soccer, its spectators, and the consequent popularization of the sport in Rio de Janeiro, also served the interests of a Brazilian elite in transforming society in light of European modernity. Leonardo Pereira (1998) states that the pride in Brazilian soccer was not wrapped up in national originality; in contrast, it was permeated by the need to faithfully reproduce the models of its matrix in the Old World.

> Having appeared in the country as a foreign sport, it was its supposed modernity, based on European standards, that had sustained its growth–whether among sportsmen or those who took up the game for themselves. Although widespread among all groups, all neighborhoods, all classes, soccer thus maintained its imported profile, appearing until then as a technique from abroad over which Brazilians were beginning to have some mastery. (Pereira, 1998, p. 284)

Thus, the use of a national language term to designate a behavior that is fundamental to the sport is a milestone in the development of soccer. Torcida, which, in its mythical origin, is synonymous with the habits of female spectators at matches, quickly became synonymous with fan, an individual who is passionate about the sport, going beyond the soccer field. Therefore, despite the fact that the term "audience" was still used to designate the public present at sports competitions, from 1910 onward, the journalistic narrative began to use the term "fans" on a large scale. It is also possible to observe attempts to categorize the new meaning of the Brazilian term. It is important to note that torcida, currently used to refer to a group of people who love a particular sport or club, at the beginning of its use could also refer to an individual, whether male or female.

Just as rowing inaugurated the use of the term "sportswoman" to refer to a new panorama of female participation in the sports field, the term "fans and supporters" also points to a change in the status quo of women who frequent the soccer stands and in the most varied social fields. It is important to note that soccer, since its popularization, is a field in which conflicts, developments, and social issues can be observed in a potentiated way. In other words, as Franzini (2005) states, soccer and its fans are a "socio-cultural space" where the nuances of social praxis and paradigms reverberate the issues developing in society as a whole.

According to Pereira (1998), at least since 1917, there has been a movement to nationalize soccer, renouncing the English terms used to designate the sport, its players, their techniques, and positions in the teams. In 1919, there was also an attempt to rename the sport according to the Portuguese language spoken in Brazil. Thus, football would be peból, balidopo, or futiból. This nationalist movement in the language of sport, however, does not take into account the development of the term torcida. Since 1910, we can find evidence of its use to designate an assistant in the stands at the game in journalistic narratives. According to João Malaia (2012):

> [...] it was in the 1910s that the term came into common use among press professionals, sports chroniclers and writers. It was from this period onwards that fans came to be more precisely characterized and became an object of reflection. (p. 60).

The term "torcida," therefore, is configured throughout its insertions in the sports pages. The analysis of its uses points to the construction of a fragmented identification over time, through the narrative of everyday life in sports magazines. More than just watching a match, the fans, later referred to as supporters, play a fundamental role in the sporting spectacle. And their importance is gradually developed in the imagination of the sports spectator. If, for rowing, the board of directors of the stands does not represent a high position in the sports field, we can see throughout the history of soccer that the role of head of the crowd is very expressive in the "microphysics of power" (Hollanda, 2012). João Malaia (2012) observes that in the first decades of the twentieth century, "we can see the supporters as a character projected by a collective of fans of a soccer club" (p. 59).

Thus, the initial insertions of the term "torcida," as well as its characterizations, indicate the conduct expected of those who would lead large crowds of spectators. It is worth noting that many of the fans' behaviors are already described when the meanings of the term are assigned.

> Attempting to classify fans
>
> Torcida is common for two: it both means the pale, scatty, neurasthenic young man, who obeyed the precepts of strict economy long before the presidential councils, as he sacrificed everything to pay the entrance fee to the (game) field, and it can also be applied to the nervous young lady (neurasthenic is too strong and undiplomatic for a girl), who always had ardent and complimentary phrases in mi-mi (it's a musical note and somewhat onomatopoeic, as it lends itself perfectly to interpreting the high-pitched states of a purple torcida).
>
> I'll try, in a few brief lines, to give you a glimpse of the cheerleader and, out of special deference, to the representatives of the so-called weaker sex, but who are really strong, because it is in front of them that we all bow reverently, varying only in the way we do it: preventing the ball from going over the goal we're defending (because we know that our girlfriend is cheering for us), studying to appear brilliantly in the forum, in the teaching profession, in the martial parades on the Avenue, at the bedside of the sick, or…writing chronicles purporting to be about a cheerleader.…writing chronicles with psychological pretensions about balidopo (football).
>
> As I said, out of special deference to the girls, I'll try to say something first about the female "fans": They're generally slim (even if they were fat, the emotions of the game, which when very violent can even kill them, as happened in São Paulo at the Corinthians game, would end up making them thin), cute (the diminutive is a sign of affection), have deep dark circles under their eyes and, in short, are the type of sporting romanticism—They don't allow arguments, let alone criticism of the club they love. It is because it is, it wins because it can't help but win, I want it, and fate couldn't deny it in practice.
>
> That's the gist of his logic (his fans). She gives the supporters "rope" (not to hang themselves…) to all the members of her favorite club, and if, by overcoming party resistance, someone manages to impose themselves on the consideration of the supporters, whether they belong to a club contrary to the predilections of the elected one, they receive an "ultimatum," and within 24 hours they have to turn their backs, change parties, tear up receipts from the other club to the great satisfaction of some and the deepest sadness of others.

> When the fans are watching a game, they are completely distracted, concerned only with the events of the match, so it's not difficult to predict the consequences of their detachment from everything around them. The fans give her familiar gestures and hugs in psychological moments. This perhaps compensates for the distracted pinches offered to mortals who have the fortune or misfortune of meeting them. It's a necessary element in a game for the excitement to be complete!
>
> When the player goes out on the pitch, his first precaution is to look at the stands and see if his devotees are there, if his female followers have already been recruited.
>
> All supporters (except "confirm regulam": the exception confirms the rule, I translated it because that's not balidopo) have a double cult: that of the party they're affiliated to and, in particular, that of Mimi. Mimi is a kind of balidopo soldier's song. It's the hymn of every fan who gets caught up in pronouncing it and falls into a musical monotony, having no "pity" for those who are trampled underfoot by the excesses of their enthusiasms, not coming to "their senses" from their party exaltations and only seeing the "sun" of their predilection shine, completely abandoning themselves to the domination of the sporting prestige of the mi-mi–Robin. (*O Paiz*, issue 12253, April 28, 1918, p. 7)

The lengthy transcript of Robin's chronicle for *O Paiz* is necessary for us to understand the universe in which women soccer fans are inserted. In this narrative, we can also see the development of discussions on the use of football terms in Portuguese, called balípodo, and the characterization of being a fan in the 1910s. It is essential to note that throughout the period under analysis, the "Attempt to Classify Fans" dichotomizes the characteristics of female and male fans. In this case, "the female fan" is commonly exalted, despite her characterization by (a) the negative valence of terms such as "nervous," "hysterical," and "indignant"; (b) the valorization of bodies with adjectives such as puny, cute, physical type of sporting romanticism; (c) the docility of the behavior of gentle and graceful mademoiselles.

Even though women in the 1910s were increasingly gaining a foothold in the public life of Rio de Janeiro society, mainly as a result of structural reforms in the city, female behavior was still shaped by the concepts of docility and subservience present in the private space. The presence of women in sporting environments confers docility, beauty, and domesticity to the space, so more exalted behaviors are characterized negatively in the construction of the meaning of cheering in sports narratives.

As Marina Maluf and Maria Lúcia Mott (1998) state, women must maintain family honor and order, "seen as the most important 'support of the state' and the only social institution capable of damming up the intimidating waves of modernity" (p. 372), even though they enjoy the greatest freedom in social life.

In addition, women's presence is also narrated through the male gaze of newspaper editors and, therefore, exalted through the characteristics of men. In the September 19, 1917 edition of the *Jornal do Brasil*, when portraying the match between Vila Isabel and Botafogo, the narrative states that "the matches that Botafogo takes part in always have an original stamp due to the impenitent and graceful fans of the beautiful sex who with their presence give great enthusiasm to the sporting contest." In other words, the construction of female representation in the soccer stands, and therefore of the ideal type of fans, is permeated by the ideological clash between moderns (who exalted the presence of women in the public space) and conservatives (who limited their experience to the familiar docility of the environment).

As we can see in the analysis by Marina Maluf and Maria Lúcia Mott (1998):

> The duty to be of Brazilian women in the first three decades of the century was thus traced by a precise and vigorous ideological discourse, which brought together conservatives and different shades of reformers, and which ended up dehumanizing them as historical subjects, at the same time as crystallizing certain types of behaviour by converting them into rigid social roles. "The woman who is, in everything, the opposite of the man," was the catchphrase that summed up the thinking of an uneasy and therefore agile era in the construction and dissemination of representations of ideal female behaviour, which limited their horizon to the "confines of the home" and reduced their activities and aspirations as much as possible, until they fit into the role of "queen of the home," supported by the tripod of mother-wife-housewife. (p. 373)

In the context of the sports arena, the female soccer fan can be seen as a variation on this tripod supporting the social role of women. In the stands, the wife–mother–housewife represents the ideal behavior of subservience, docility, and beautification of the environment. In the May 21, 1918 edition of *O Paiz*, a reader sends a letter to the editor expressing his dissatisfaction with the behavior of the female fans of all the teams in the capital, especially Fluminense, and suggests a "campaign by the sports section against the uses and abuses" and "in favor of the morality that should reign among soccer assistants." However, we cannot ignore the fact that the new configuration of soccer attendance also reflects new social dynamics.

In addition to the possibility of enjoying leisure activities outside the home environment, the attendance of women, especially single women, changes the social dynamics of wanting a relationship. The possibility of flirting and dating arises from the choice and interaction of individuals of different sexes. There was an "intolerable corrosion of customs" criticized by intellectuals of the time (Maluf and Mott, 1998, p. 372). In sports periodicals, this contact between men and women in the soccer stands is characterized in a positive and humorous way, when the girl shows inattention to the flirting. Another indication of this characterization is evident in the passage "because we know that our girlfriend is cheering for us," from the aforementioned transcript, when the columnist describes the importance of the female fan in the soccer stands.

Although the chronicle is signed by Robin, it is important to note that the use of pseudonyms and the text's practice of being shared by several people in the newsroom make it imprecise to name the author of the article. However, we can understand it as a positioning of the newspaper. Thus, the construction of a national identity for soccer involves an understanding of fan practices and the categorization of the term in journalistic narratives. As the chronicler Tesoura said in *Jornal do Brasil* on September 22, 1919, from the 1910s onward, "those who don't cheer aren't civilized."

> Cheer, cheer, cheer
>
> It's an adjective verb that has reached the pinnacles of fame.
>
> Anyone who doesn't cheer isn't civilized. However, the fun lies in the varied ways in which both sexes of all ages cheer. Let's see how they cheer and the consequences of their cheering.
>
> The elegant and sympathetic "señorita" J…twists in such a way that she ends up sitting on the lap of the first gentleman on her right or left, depending on the side of the goal.
>
> The sweet and gentle D…was nervous and attentive to the ball that was rolling towards her goal. The crisis was so strong that she pinched a respectable matron on her left. On the right was me, who gave her a formidable ear tug.
>
> Madame B…a very respectable lady, known in high society as a true model type, could not escape the contaminating evil. The situation on the pitch was difficult. She was hoping that her countrymen would score the first goal.

> When Heitor ran with the ball, Madame B…got down on her tiptoes and opened her arms so quickly that she punched the wind out of her husband on the right and another fan on the left.
>
> The gracious and kind N…was having her lunch when the players entered the field. She had a large sandwich in her hands. At the height of the cheering, the gracious N…smacked the sandwich into the cheeks of Dr. F…, an old professor at the F. de…
>
> The wealthy businessman M…went home with his mind so steeped in football that he had a dream so horrible that waking up was alarming.
>
> He dreamt he was playing. He wanted to score a goal and he hit the ball with a shot that was so hard it was a touch of tail. He had kicked his wife in the face. How did he do it? We don't know…
>
> Anyway, if we were to tell you, in writing, about the great and varied way of cheering in foot-ball, I'd be convinced that not all the paper made in North America would do.
>
> What I can guarantee is that I've never seen anything as amusing as watching the spectators as the players drive the ball into the goal. Everything falls apart, and everyone loses track of time, place, and social conveniences. It's crazy, this foot-ball. (Tesoura, *Jornal do Brasil*, issue 263, September 22, 1919, p. 10)

The comicality of the text above comes from the distinction between the profiles of the fans and their reactions during the soccer match. The women, specifically, are characterized as madams, pampered, gracious, and gentle. However, as the emotions of a soccer match rise, their attitudes become distracted, violent, and immoral (when sitting on the lap of an unknown man, for example). The text itself states that social conveniences are shattered in soccer. The concept of cheering, according to *Jornal do Brasil*, reaches the height of its fame and becomes synonymous with the emotional reactions of individuals present in stadiums during and after matches.

The chronicle also shows that the presence of both sexes in the stands is common and socially accepted. The female fans give the atmosphere the social distinction it is intended to encompass in the construction of a modern society in Rio de Janeiro. With this, the behavior of good society girls at soccer matches is portrayed as an ideal type to be observed and replicated in the public spaces of sporting events.

Another important feature of the text is the use of expressions in English, while an "adjective verb" is defined in Portuguese. Torcer, based mainly on female gestures, finds its apex in the journalistic narrative and consolidates itself as a term referring to soccer fans and their behavior. The category of the female fan in the 1910s can therefore be considered the mother of cheering in its myth of origin, just as soccer, as a practice, reveres the founding fathers of the game in various locations, such as Oscar Cox in Rio de Janeiro and Charles Miller in São Paulo.

Thus, we can infer that the presence of female fans is imperative for the popularization of soccer in Rio de Janeiro and, consequently, nationwide. Since its earliest narratives, the public in stadiums has been just as much a part of the spectacle as the players. After all, cheering is "an adjective verb that is on the pinnacles of fame" as early as 1919.

Therefore, according to the analysis in this chapter, soccer was introduced into the Brazilian context at a time of great effervescence of new sporting habits and social customs. It was thus consolidated as an elite sport, originating from a European country and practiced by members of the country's economic elite. It also attracted the attention of young women to watch and practice the sport. As a result, it became a notorious social event for girls and boys from the upper social classes. The halls of the clubs and the grandstands, during the matches, provided the opportunity for individuals of opposite sexes to socialize, just as they did when attending the turf and rowing competitions.

In this way, we can analyze the development of women's participation in Brazilian society, here from the perspective of Rio de Janeiro, the capital of the Republic during this period, based on their involvement in the sporting environment, especially soccer. In addition to the public and its practitioners, the sport of football began to attract the attention of journalists, poets, and intellectuals from the 1910s onward. As a result, both the ways in which it was practiced and the characteristics of cheering began to be narrated more frequently in the periodicals of the time.

Thus, we can infer that during the period when soccer was introduced into Rio de Janeiro society, and by extension Brazilian society, the presence of women was praised. The woman-fan category became the foundation of the ideal fan model of the period. It should be noted that the narrative about women's participation in the stands is through the male gaze. The female voice, despite existing, still lacks social credibility.

REFERENCES

BARBOSA, Marialva. **História da comunicação no Brasil** (History of Communication in Brazil). Petrópolis: Editora Vozes, 2013.

BONFIM, Aira Fernandes. **Football feminino entre festas esportivas, circos e campos suburbanos**: uma história social do futebol praticado por mulheres da introdução à proibição (1915–1941) (Women's Football between sports festivals, circuses, and suburban fields: A social history of football played by women from Its Introduction to its prohibition (1915–1941)). Rio de Janeiro: Dissertação de Mestrado em História/FGV CPDOC, 2019.

DaMATTA, Roberto. "Antropologia do óbvio-notas em torno do significado social do futebol brasileiro" ("Anthropology of the obvious - notes on the social significance of Brazilian football). In: **Revista USP**. São Paulo: n. 22, pp. 10–17, 1994.

FOUCAULT, Michel. **Vigiar e punir**: nascimento da prisão (Discipline and Punish: the birth of the prison). Petrópolis: Editora Vozes, 2014.

FRANZINI, Fábio. Futebol é " coisa para macho"? pequeno esboço para uma história das mulheres no país do futebol (Is Football a Male Thing? A Small Sketch for a History of Women in the Country of Football). In: **Revista Brasileira de História**, v. 25, pp. 315–328, 2005.

GUTERMAN, Marcos. **O futebol explica o Brasil**: uma história da maior expressão popular do país (Football explains Brazil: A history of the country's greatest popular expression). São Paulo: Editora Contexto, 2009.

HOLLANDA, Bernardo Borges Buarque de. **O clube como vontade e representação: o jornalismo esportivo e a formação das torcidas organizadas de futebol do Rio** de Janeiro (1967–1988) (The club as will and representation: Sports journalism and the formation of organized football supporter groups in Rio de Janeiro (1967–1988)). Rio de Janeiro Tese de Doutorado em História /PUC-Rio.

HOLLANDA, Bernardo Borges Buarque de. [et al.]. **A torcida brasileira** (The Brazilian fan base). Rio de Janeiro: Editora 7Letras, 2012.

LOPES, José Sérgio Leite. "A vitória do futebol que incorporou a pelada: a invenção do jornalismo espotivo e a entrada dos negros no futebol brasileiro" ("The victory of football That Embraced 'Pelada': The invention of sports journalism and the entry of black players into Brazilian football"). In: **Revista USP**. São Paulo: n. 22, pp. 64–83, 1994.

MACHADO, Humberto Fernandes. "A voz do morro na passagem do Império para a República" ("The voice of the slum in the transition from the Empire to Republic"). In: BATISTA, M.; CAMPOS G. (Org.). **Cidades Brasileiras II**: políticas urbanas e dimensão cultural (Brazilian cities II: Urban policies and cultural dimension). São Paulo: IEB/USP, 1999.

MALAIA, João. "Torcer, torcedores, torcedoras, torcida (bras.):1910–1950" ("Cheering, fans, and supporters (Brazil): 1910–1950"). In: HOLLANDA, Bernardo Buarque de. [et al.]. **A torcida brasileira** (The Brazilian fan base). Rio de Janeiro: Editora 7Letras, 2012.

MALUF, Marina; MOTT, Maria Lucia. "Recônditos do mundo feminino" ("Hidden Corners of the Feminine World"). In: SEVCENKO, Nicolau (Org.). **História da vida privada no Brasil**. São Paulo: Companhia das Letras, v. 3, 1998.

MASCARENHAS, Gilmar. "Construindo a cidade moderna: a introdução dos esportes na vida urbana do Rio de Janeiro" ("Building the Modern City: The Introduction of Sports into Urban Life in Rio de Janeiro"). In: **Revista Estudos Históricos**. Rio de Janeiro: v. 13, n. 23, pp. 17–40, 1999.

MAUAD, Ana. "Através da imagem: fotografia e história interfaces" ("Through the Image: Photography and History Interfaces"). In: **Revista Tempo**. Rio de Janeiro: v. 1, n. 2, 1996.

MELO, Victor Andrade de. "Mulheres em movimento: a presença feminina nos primórdios do esporte na cidade do Rio de Janeiro (até 1910)" ("Women in Motion: The Female Presence in the Early Days of Sports in Rio de Janeiro (up to 1910)"). In: **Revista Brasileira de História**, v. 27, pp. 127–152, 2007.

MELO, Victor Andrade de. "*Sportmen*: os primeiros momentos da configuração de um público esportivo no Brasil" ("Sportsmen: The First Moments of the Formation of a Sports Audience in Brazil"). In HOLLANDA, Bernardo Buarque de. [et al.]. **A torcida brasileira**. Rio de Janeiro: Editora 7Letras, 2012.

NETO, José Miguel Arias. "Primeira República: economia cafeeira, urbanização e industrialização" ("First Republic: Coffee Economy, Urbanization, and Industrialization"). In: DELGADO, Lucilia de Almeida Neves; FERREIRA, Jorge (org). **O Brasil Republicano**. O tempo do liberalismo excludente—da Proclamação da República a Revolução de 1930. Rio de Janeiro: Editora Civilização Brasileira, 2003.

PEREIRA, Leonardo Affonso de Miranda [et al.]. **Footballmania**: uma história social do futebol no Rio de Janeiro (1902–1938) (Footballmania: A Social History of Football in Rio de Janeiro (1902–1938)). Rio de Janeiro: Nova Fronteira, 1998.

SEVCENKO, Nicolau [et al.]. **História da vida privada no Brasil** (A History of Private Life in Brazil). São Paulo: Companhia das Letras, v. 3, 1998.

SILVA, Marcelino Rodrigues da. **Mil e uma noites de futebol**: o Brasil moderno de Mário Filho. (A Thousand and One Nights of Football: Modern Brazil by Mário Filho). Belo Horizonte: Editora UFMG, 2006.

SODRÉ, Nelson Werneck. **História da imprensa no Brasil** (A History of the Press in Brazil). Rio de Janeiro: Mauad Editora Ltda, 1998.

VOKS, Douglas Josiel. "As representações sociais sobre as mulheres na revista Careta (1910–1920): entre a mulher ideal e a independente" ("Social Representations of Women in *Careta* Magazine (1910–1920): Between the Ideal Woman and the Independent Woman"). In: **Temporalidades**, v. 4, n. 1, 2012, pp. 175–188.

CHAPTER 2

Experiences of the Football Practiced by Women in Brazil: From Its Origin to Its Prohibition (1915–1941)

Aira Bonfim Fernandes

Introduction

The history of Brazilian football mostly gives an account of men's performance. Media narratives still leave their public in the dark on women's practices. Recent research has started to uncover this history. This chapter aims to show incidents, figures, clubs, and places that unveil the public and ongoing practice of women's football in Brazil, from its initial milestones to the year of the prohibition of this sport, in 1941. Stories of female players belong to the complex set of narratives that constitute the History of Football in Brazil. When, despite serious bans, we recognize women as historical subjects in football, we broaden the historiographical discourse in a more generous and extensive way (Rago, 1995).

Notwithstanding that the history of women football has been reckoned to be "non-existent" or "incipient" until the 1980s, when their practice apparently started, the following paragraphs will show a sequence of events that reveal a great many sport experiences that confirm that Brazilian women were introduced into football over one hundred years ago. Evidence shows that there was an expressive number of women's football matches in the late 1930s, i.e. months before the enforcement of Decree law of 1941, a federal bill that prohibited the practice of women's football and hindered its development over the following forty years. Since the primary sources used in this study are little known, they will help demystify the idea that Brazilian women's football supposedly had no tradition and had been of little interest to the female public since its introduction into the country in the late 19th century.

The silence surrounding the history of women (Perrot, 2008) raises questions on where to find and how to access sources on this topic. We therefore chose to use most relevant mainstream media outlets of the period as our main sources for this study: early 20th-century newspapers and magazines. This chapter presents some highlights of the research that gives an overview to which degree Brazilian women of different social groups, who joined the practice, were involved in various historical moments, playing distinct roles.

It is useful at this point to consider where this research is located in relation to studies of the history and development of women's sport, and studies of the significance of sport in Brazilian society. With respect to studies on the significance of sport in Brazil society, this research also stands out from existing studies that have been largely concentrated on "male" sports (Mills, 2005; Pereira, 1998). In relation to the former, this research is original in the sense that it focuses on the development of women's football in Brazil. It is an important contribution to our knowledge of women's history, women's sport history, and in particular, the history of women playing a traditionally male sport, in a Brazilian context.

1910s and 1920s: The Early Years

There is a general consensus in existing research that, in terms of growth in the game, the beginning 20th century was one significant stage in the development of women's football. The first historical signs of the phenomenon "women's football" (newspapers at 1910s and 1920s still used the English word "football" *feminino*) in Brazil trace back to the aristocratic circles that supported the sport centers that were on the rise then, and to clubs that belonged to the very same elite that had introduced football for men.

However, the initial milestones for men's football in Brazil emphasizes that its official status was a criterion for its historical visibility. Pioneering figures, such as Brazilians Charles Miller (born to John Miller, a Scottish railway engineer, and Carlota Fox, a Brazilian woman of English descent) and Oscar Cox (son of an English father and a Brazilian mother from Rio de Janeiro), and Thomas Donohue, a Scottish dye worker in a textile factory in the gritty Bangu district of Rio de Janeiro, are consistently named as "fathers of football" (Mills, 2005, p. 73; Pereira, 1998).

They were not the only ones in Brazil, though, but their biographies are favored, since they were acknowledged in several records of the first clubs they founded and of the first Football Leagues in the 1890s. As public figures they were recognized by the elite in their cities (São Paulo and Rio de Janeiro) and provided game experiences that came closer to the official international play regulations available at that time.

Factors such as social attitudes to women and sport, the influence of the media, the role of the football governing bodies and changes in women's place in society, have combined to mold the development of women's football in the context of Brazilian society. The late organization of women's football was not due to lack of interest and initiatives by Brazilian female players but to the fact that, with the endorsement of renowned sport clubs, the State excluded women from the official sport structure.[1]

The lack of an official status for football matches played by Brazilian women in the early 20th century is yet another point of attention regarding women's sense of belonging and recognition on the sport ground. Women's football did not evolve to be a competitive sport through the official means of that time. One could compare the way women were introduced into football to children's and teenagers' athletic experiences, such as boys playing football on the street, on school and church grounds, in clubs and at sport festivities (Brown and Lanci, 2016; Goulart, 2014). Nevertheless, Bonfim (2019) recently uncovered new evidence that women were introduced into football in Brazil as early as 1915, and new research efforts may reveal even older sources.

For many years, the announcement of a match "between young ladies" of Tremembé and Cantareira—two districts of the city of São Paulo—held in 1921,[2] was reproduced by researchers, institutions, and sport media as the starting point of women's football in Brazil. However, recent research, such as conducted by Bonfim (2019), has revealed earlier and scattered public events of women playing football, for example in clubs of Rio de Janeiro, such as Villa Isabel F.C. (1915),[3] Progresso F.C. (1919),[4] C.R. Flamengo (1919),[5] and River S.C. (1919),[6] which already had mixed teams or girls playing against boys as part of their Sunday sport activities. There is also evidence of Brazilian women

1. About the marginal position of women players in sports, see Knijnik and Vasconcellos (2003); Franzini (2005) and Goellner (2005).

2. (1921, June 26). Um jogo de futebol entre senhoritas. *A Gazeta*, 2.

3. (1915, November 26). Untitled. *A Época*, 4; (1920, December 3) Untitled. *A Rua: Semanario Illustrado*, 5.

4. (1919, April 12). Untitled. *O Dia*, 5.

5. (1919, June 14). Um festival no Flamengo. *Jornal de Theatro & Sport*, 24.

6. (1919, December 10). Untitled. *O Imparcial*, 8.

playing football among themselves in clubs, such as Helios A.C. (1920),[7] C.R. Vasco da Gama (1923),[8] S.C. Celeste (1923),[9] and São Cristóvão A.C. (1929).[10]

It should be noted that the year 1920 witnessed the formation of many women's football teams in Europe, where girls had already been playing football since the end of the nineteenth century. It is estimated that in France alone, nearly 150 groups played football in 1920 (Doble, 2017; William and Hess, 2015). *La Fédération des sociétés féminines sportives de France* had been founded years earlier, and among others established a partnership between French female athletes and the pioneers of women's football, the English female players. The meeting led to the first international women's football match between England and France, which was held in Preston, in 1920, and attracted 25,000 spectators.

This match, which took place on the Chelsea F.C. pitch, received a full-page feature in the Brazilian magazine *Vida Sportiva* of July 1920.[11] The article brought little-known images of women's football to Brazil, gave special mention to captains Macgnemond and Kell, as well as to a save by French goalkeeper Fémina Sport and to a scene of the match. In the 1920s, Brazilian newspapers began to report more and more on women playing football in other countries.

Aside from the pictures of international female players published in the Brazilian press, in 1920, *Vida Sportiva* also invested in several covers featuring sportswomen, two of which dedicated to women's football. The first of these covers showed the caricature of a female football player wearing the jersey of Botafogo Futebol Clube[12] (Rio de Janeiro); the second one featured a picture of the women's team of ABC Sport Clube from Natal, Rio Grande do Norte[13]; this state is located in the Northeast Region of Brazil, distant from Rio de Janeiro, but with a thriving and growing sport scene.

In the 1920s, it was a well-known fact that female fans and members of the Club de Regatas Vasco da Gama,[14] Rio de Janeiro, already had been playing

7. (1920, December 8). Untitled. *O Imparcial*, 8; (1920, December 8). Untitled. *O Paiz*, 7.

8. (1923, September 1). Untitled. *Careta*, 16.

9. (1923, November 16). Untitled. *Correio da Manhã*, 7.

10. (1929, May 14). O S. Christóvão feminino venceu o Vasco feminino por 2X0. *A Manhã*, 9.

11. (1920, July 24). Match de futebol feminino entre a França e a Inglaterra. *Vida Sportiva*, 19.

12. (1920, February 21). *Vida Sportiva*, 1.

13. (1920, March 20). *Vida Sportiva*, 1.

14. (1923, September 1). *Careta*, 16.

football in public since 1923 (Bonfim, 2019). In 1929, during the preliminary match between the men's teams of São Christovão A.C. and Bangu A.C.,[15] the public got to watch a charity football match in the popular Laranjeiras Stadium, Rio de Janeiro, where the girls played against female fans of São Christovão Athletic Club. Recent research confirms that, even if only occasionally, women played football in Brazil, in the 1920s, a time, when regular championships and matches for men sparked an interest in the sport and made it popular even among Brazilian women.

1930s and 1940s: The Girls Are Playing

In the 1930s, men's football started to become an important element in the construction of identity and social bonds by mobilizing new spectators and players in the outskirts of the city of Rio de Janeiro. Throughout the 1930s, women's football events in the amateur sport scene, until then had been considered new or was little known, slowly started to spark the interest of sport associations in the outer areas (Costa, 2017). The recurrence, especially in 1939 and 1940, of sporting events, in which women practiced a male-dominated sport in public, contributed to the expansion of gender boundaries in this sport, and broadened and complexified what was known as the social history of Brazilian football (Bonfim, 2019).

Outside the frame of the official organization of Brazilian football, mobilized by the big leagues and sport clubs run by men and where only men played, women's football—a practice still unknown to the football elite—started to grow and emerge in marginal sport programs. Satellite and low-income districts of Rio de Janeiro, such as Engenho de Dentro,[16] Piedade,[17] Benfica,[18] Cascadura,[19] and Realengo,[20] launched their female players through over fifteen female teams (Bonfim, 2019). It should be stressed that the outskirts of Rio de Janeiro

15. (1929, May 11). *O Paiz*, 8.

16. (1930, June 24). *A Esquerda*, 5.

17. (1931, April 10). *O Jornal*, 10.

18. (1939, December 7). Actividades nos pequenos clubs. *O Jornal*, 12, 7.

19. (1940, April 8). *A Noite*, 30.

20. (1939, May 25). *A Noite*, 8.

encompass a complex, multifaceted society with diverse ways of life, including workers, people of the new middle class employed in retailers, public servants, as well as impoverished migrants from North and Northeast and people of color coming from other regions of Brazil.

In 1940, names, pictures, and districts of these female players started to be featured in the most popular newspapers of Rio de Janeiro.[21] Remaining undefeated—something that still is dear to amateur football today—became a competitive advantage, as well as the technical playing abilities of female players[22] (best player, best goalkeeper, and top scorer). Back then, sport reporters preferred to cover the many amateur men's football championships in the city's outskirts. These events held outside the range of the programming of elite clubs in Rio de Janeiro made for stories and sold newspapers.

Sponsors interested in promoting their brands during women's matches showed their support through awards, tributes, and direct investments in sporting activities with women.[23] Female players, e.g., from Casino do Realengo F.C., S.C. Brasileiro, or A.C. and Primavera, already received gifts or were paid[24] at each new tour or public presentation enabled through football. As per these sources, women received chocolate, parties, a pair of new shoes, or trips. Historical sources indicate that, judging from the consistency with which women's matches were held, female players also had the dream of being financially independent and ascending socially through football, a common and increasing aspiration shared with the population living in the city's outskirts.

With the organization of domestic matches attracting significant numbers of spectators, international invitations (Chile, Uruguay, and Argentina) and the attention received in the press (Rio de Janeiro and São Paulo), women's football had reached a peak of popularity by the year 1940 and saw it evolve into what was undoubtedly its apogee.

---

21. (1940, March 3). *Jornal dos Sports*.

22. (1940, March 14). Mais uma victoria das "meninas" do Casino do Realengo FC. *O Radical*, 7.

23. Example of the football match "Anitta D'Angelo Cup" named after the wife of a Sudanese cigarette factory owner that sponsored the event with female players. (1940, June 9). *Jornal dos Sports*, 4.

24. The survey conducted by newspapers identified that players of the city outskirts were paid from R$ 10,000 to R$ 15,000 (converted to today's currency (2025), approx. R$ 1,230–R$ 1,845 or $0.20–$0.30) per sporting exhibition. (1941, January 11). *A Noite*, 3.

1941: Football Is Inappropriate for Women and Banned in Brazil

The image of Brazilian female players—Black, poor, of mixed ethnic origin, and living in the outskirts—was widespread throughout and not only Rio de Janeiro. On May 17, 1940, the then recently opened Pacaembu stadium, in São Paulo, hosted a match with two teams from Rio de Janeiro.[25] Women's football teams toured cities in the state of São Paulo, e.g. Santos,[26] and in other states, for example Juiz de Fora[27] and Belo Horizonte[28] in Minas Gerais Early 1941, Primavera, a women's football team, was invited to perform on an international level in cities, such as Buenos Aires (Argentina), Montevideo (Uruguay), and Santiago de Chile (Chile). The visibility brought by the many public appearances of women playing football in Rio de Janeiro and outside, as well as the great number of news coverages by different sport reporters were crucial for newspapers from São Paulo and Rio and sport entities to intensify a campaign that publicly demoralized women's football (Bonfim, 2019).

The public confrontational attitudes toward this type of football were indicative of escalating conflicts regarding gender, race, and the social structures that were conceived for Brazilian men and women. Part of the press, such as the newspapers *A Batalha*, *O Radical*, *Jornal dos Sports*, and *Correio Paulistano*, which made an effort to promote women's football, also reinforced gender stereotypes commonly attributed to women such as "charm," "grace," or "sensuality."[29] The other part—based on the opinion of physicians, managers, or other figures of the sport or scientific community—were radically opposed to the practice of football by women, since they considered the sport to be harmful to women's aesthetics and health.[30]

Thus, in the 1940s, women were not denied the right to practice physical activities, as long as they did not involve any kind of intense physical contact or excessive effort. Women—constituted in opposition to male otherness—besides

25. (1940, April 6). Football feminino no "Pacaembú." *O Radical*, 6.

26. (1940, May 18). *Correio Paulistano*, 8.

27. (1940, September 27). *Jornal dos Sports*, 5.

28. (1940, June 6). As filhas da Eva em Bello Horizonte. *O Radical*.

29. (1940, May 16). Untitled. *O Radical*, 7.

30. (1940, May 9). Untitled. *O Radical*, 9.

being wives and mothers, "should" also be responsible for bearing strong and healthy children for their fatherland. Those were two opposing models, as suggested by the press, when it considered the practice of football by women a violent and masculinizing sport, which, according to physicians, would jeopardize the female players' chances of becoming mothers (Goellner, 2005). Franzini (2000) presents several other documents published by the press and written by physicians and physical education teachers, according to which women had to be "protected" from the possible harm of playing football to their bodies and to their morality, which in both cases diverted them from motherhood.

Laqueur (2001) examines the factors that motivated changes in how we perceive different bodies and how this impacted the social construction of gender roles. He thereby demonstrates that however the sexes have been understood throughout history, it is always situational and permeated by political interests that steer scientific research. He further demonstrates that, like other sciences, biology is not disconnected from the society in which it is produced and, therefore, is influenced in all its research phases by social–cultural, political, and ideological factors. Likewise, biological knowledge is built while it is influenced by aspects that are not limited to the scientific field and that seek to validate what is of interest to hegemonic political and social groups at that time. During the 1940s, however, it was this biological knowledge that presented the "scientific evidence" to support the ban of women's football across the country.

In 1941, the National Sport Council (*Conselho Nacional de Desportos*, CND), which was a governmental body under the authority of the Ministry of Health and Education during the *Estado Novo* period (1937–1945), published Decree no. 3.199, issued by President Getúlio Vargas. The purpose of this Decree was to control the national sport and the development of its activities in the country. At the same time, it also strengthened the social role that was expected of women by responding to those railing against women's football in the press.

The regulation also warned that the same would happen to other sports that eventually undermined conservative morality. Paragraph 54 of said Decree stated that "women shall not be allowed to practice sports that are incompatible with their nature; for this purpose, the National Sport Council shall issue necessary instructions to the country's sport entities." This concept of "nature" coincided with the expectation that women should bear and raise strong children for the nation, according to the civic values of the *Estado Novo* dictatorship (Goellner, 2005).

The notion of a "female nature," which was used by the legislation and the media narratives to justify the ban prohibiting women's football matches, is a social and cultural construction—there is no universal biological nature—and can, therefore, be deconstructed and reconstructed. Furthermore, the Brazilian ban prohibiting women from practicing any sport considered not to be adequate to the female nature was not restricted to the tropics. On the contrary, it was connected to a European mentality (Devide, 2005; Knijnik, 2010; Rubio, 2011), according to which this attitude was deemed absolutely fitting and even desirable by the powers that be, such as international organizations, culture, society, medicine, and the Brazilian State.

The unease that the presence of women would cause in public spaces was a quite complex issue. As intersectional studies indicate (Davis, 2016), gender is not the only determining factor for what is considered socially adequate or inadequate, right or wrong for that body. Skin color, family of origin, being married or single were some of the factors that carried weight. Upon reviewing the bibliography on the first decades of this century in Brazil, we notice a clear difference: some of the newspapers in circulation saw the increased presence of women in public spaces as a sign of country's modernization; others—those were the majority—invoked moral codes to justify its unsuitability (Bonfim, 2019; Franzini, 2000).

Evidence shows that there were many instances, in which women had gone on to the field to play football prior to 1941. However, while the press recognized men's football as game, it portrayed women's football as something exceptional, spectacular, strange, different, and inappropriate. Over the four decades, during which women's football was banned in Brazil, the way football was perceived and played changed, as did the hegemony of the social roles of men and women. Changes also affected the forms of resistance and the spaces occupied by women that played football. In the press, their visibility varied according to different factors: media target audience, in which news section the sport was featured, who the female players were, as well as the approach given by journalists, who were mostly men, especially in sport periodicals.

It became more apparent that many in the footballing establishment and throughout Brazilian society regarded the participation of women in football as a curiosity, considering it nothing more than a novelty.

Conclusion–The End of a Starting Fight?

In addition to discussing the damages that the forty years of ban on women's football caused to the sport's growth, this chapter also highlights the challenges to the historicity of football practiced by Brazilian women. It is pressing to reorganize the historiography of Brazilian football. This has contributed to the collapse of the prejudiced arguments against women's football that are still present to this day. The discovery and disclosure of narratives, biographies, and events featuring Brazilian women, dating back to the early 20th century, breaks with the obsolete idea that women would neither be suited nor be interested in football. It also challenges the account that the sport supposedly started only in the 1980s.

Despite the ban, women never stopped playing football. Over time, depending on their social origin—social stratum, skin color, place of residence—their access to the sport changed. Charity matches were also a form of resistance; they were only permitted, because they no longer had sport performance characteristics and because they sought a bigger goal than their final result, namely amateur matches in the outskirts of São Paulo and on the beaches of Rio de Janeiro. Due to the effects of second-wave feminism and a broader concept of what it meant to *be a woman*, they could play football just for fun, even if that meant playing where a large part of society would not see them.

Visibility is, in fact, key to the history of women's football in Brazil. We should not forget that women only played in the outskirts of Rio de Janeiro until they took Pacaembu by storm. The stadium was decisive for the political project of that time and for professional men's football. Although the research has uncovered much about women's football in Brazil, we are still only at the beginning, and have more questions than answers regarding the past of women's football in Brazil. The history of the country's most popular sport is still under construction and is everything but predictable. In contrast, it is filled with ban infringements and collective and individual achievements by Brazilian women.

REFERENCES

Bonfim, A. (2019). *Football feminino entre festas esportivas, circos e campos suburbanos*: uma história social do futebol praticado por mulheres da introdução à proibição (1915–1941) (Women's Football between sports festivals, circuses, and suburban fields: A social history of football played by women from Its Introduction to its prohibition (1915–1941)). [Unpublished master's thesis]. Rio de Janeiro: Centro de Pesquisa e Documentação de História Contemporânea do Brasil (CPDOC).

Brown, M., & Lanci, G. (2016). Football and urban expansion in São Paulo, Brazil, 1880–1920. *Sport in History*, 36(2), 162–189.

Decree No. 3199 (1941, April 14). http://www.planalto.gov.br/ccivil_03/decreto-lei/1937-1946/Del3199.htm.

Conselho Nacional de Desportos. (1983). *Normas Básicas sobre Desportos. Deliberações, 1983 (01 a 15) (*Basic Rules on Sports. Deliberations, 1983 (01 to 15).

Costa, L. M. (2017). O futebol feminino nas décadas de 1940 a 1980 (Women's Football from the 1940s to the 1980s). In: *Revista do Arquivo Geral da Cidade do Rio de Janeiro*. N. *13*, pp. 493–507.

Davis, A. (2016). *Mulheres, raça e classe* (Women, Race, and Class). São Paulo: Boitempo.

Devide, F. P. (2005). *Gênero e mulheres no esporte*: história das mulheres nos jogos olímpicos modernos (Gender and Women in Sports: The History of Women in the Modern Olympic Games). Editora Unijuí.

Doble, A. (2017, July 19). The Secret History of women's football. *Newsbeat*. https://www.bbc.com/news/newsbeat-40654436.

Franzini, F. (2000). *As raízes do país do futebol: estudo sobre a relação entre o futebol e a nacionalidade brasileira (1919–1950)* (The Roots of the Country of Football: A Study on the Relationship Between Football and Brazilian National Identity (1919–1950)). [Published master's thesis, University of São Paulo]. https://ludopedio.org.br/biblioteca/as-raizes-do-pais-do-futebol/

Franzini, F. (2005). Futebol é "coisa para macho"? Pequeno esboço para uma história das mulheres no país do futebol (Is Football "a Man's Thing"? A Brief Outline for a History of Women in the Country of Football). In: *Revista Brasileira de História*, São Paulo, v. 25, n. 50, 315–358.

Goellner, S. V. (2005). Mulheres e futebol no Brasil: entre sombras e visibilidades (Women and Football in Brazil: Between Shadows and Visibility).t. *Revista Brasileira de Educação Física e Esporte*, *19*(2), 143–151.

Goulart, P. C. A. (2014). Pontapé inicial para o futebol no Brasil: o batebolão e os esportes no Colégio São Luís: 1880–2014. (Kick-off for Football in Brazil: The Games and Sports at Colégio São Luís: 1880–2014). Vargem Grande Paulista: A9 Editora.

Laqueur, T. W (2001). *Inventando o sexo: corpo e gênero dos gregos a Freud* (Inventing Sex: Body and Gender from the Greeks to Freud, V. Whately, Trans.) Relume Dumará. (Original work published 1990).

Mills, J. R. (2005). *Charles Miller: o pai do futebol brasileiro(*Charles Miller: The Father of Brazilian Football). São Paulo: Panda Books.

Knijnik, J. D. (Org.). (2010). *Gênero e esporte*: masculinidades e feminilidades (Gender and Sport: Masculinities and Femininities). Rio de Janeiro: Apicuri.

Pereira, L. A. de M. [et al.]. **Footballmania**: uma história social do futebol no Rio de Janeiro (1902–1938) (Footballmania: a social history of football in Rio de Janeiro (1902–1938)). Rio de Janeiro: Nova Fronteira, 1998.

Perrot, M. (2008). *Minha história das mulheres*. ((My Stories of Women, A. M. S. Corrêa, Trans.). São Paulo: Editora Contexto. (Original work published 2006).

Rago, M. (1995). As mulheres na historiografia brasileira (Women in Brazilian Historiography). In Z. L. Silva (Org.), *Cultura histórica em debate*. São Paulo: Editora UNESP, pp. 81–91.

Rubio, K. (Org.). (2011). *As mulheres e o esporte olímpico brasileiro* (Women and Brazilian Olympic Sports). São Paulo: Casa do Psicólogo.

Williams, J., & Hess, R. (2015). Women, Football and History: International Perspectives. *The International Journal of the History of Sport*, *32*(18), 2115–2122.

CHAPTER 3

Forbidden Years: Veto, Resilience, and Gender Resistance among Practitioners of Football Acts (1941–1979)

Caroline Almeida and Carmen Rial

When raised in public debate, the futbolera was shorthand for a woman who went "too far," a red herring, or a strange monstrosity.
Brenda Elsey and J. Nadel, *Futebolera*, p. 2

On April 14, 1941, Decree-Law no. 3.199 was enacted in Brazil to regulate sports practices, which included the creation of the Conselho Nacional de Desportos/ National Sports Council (CND). Article 54[1] of this decree prohibited women from practicing sports that were considered incompatible with their nature.

The CND was established during the Estado Novo period (1937–1945) and was initially linked to the Ministry of Education and Health, which was centered on the presidency of Getúlio Vargas. Although the ban on women's football was in effect from 1941 to 1979, it did not completely prevent Brazilian women from playing the sport (Rigo et al., 2008; Moraes, 2012; Capucim e Silva, 2015; Elsey and Nadel, 2019; Almeida, 2020; Goellner, 2021). Historian Giovana Capucim e Silva (2015, 2020) described the practice of women's football after the prohibition as clandestine and a form of resistance, particularly among young women in the suburbs and "várzeas"[2] in the remote areas of the country. The prejudice against women's football existed before the law and was reinforced by it. Some

[1] "Women will not be allowed to practice sports that are incompatible with the conditions of their nature, and for this purpose, the Conselho Nacional de Desportos must issue the necessary instructions to the country's sports entities" (Brasil, 1941).

[2] Várzea is a term that refers to low-lying, flood-prone areas adjacent to rivers or other bodies of water. In Brazil, the term "várzea" is often used to describe informal football fields that are located in these types of areas. It is a type of grassroots football that is not organized by official leagues or clubs, and is instead played by groups of friends, neighbors, or coworkers who gather to play for fun or as a way to stay active. The games are usually played on unpaved or uneven surfaces.

reports from women who resisted playing the sport revealed that they would justify buying soccer shoes for their brothers. Even in everyday situations, the clandestine status of women's football persisted until the 1970s, highlighting the struggle that women faced to participate in the sport.

In essence, the 1941 decree-law prohibiting women's football not only hindered the professionalization that was already underway but also erased the history of Brazilian women who had dedicated themselves to the sport through practice, organization, and writing. This subversive act challenged the patriarchal society and continued to do so in the years that followed, as noted by Goellner (2021).

The year 1940 was pivotal for women's football in Brazil, beginning with the plan to establish a championship in Rio de Janeiro and ending in newspaper police reports. This unfortunate trajectory influenced the legislation that led to the ban on the sport. In this chapter, we examine the stories of three women who represent this critical moment in the history of women's football in Brazil. These women played three central roles in the football field (Bourdieu, 1977): journalist, club manager, and player. We analyze the resistance of these women to the ban on football and consider their early gender subversive acts (Butler, 1990) within the field. Their life trajectories in football, resilience, and gender resistance predated the prohibitive decree-law and shed light on the years during which the practice of football was forbidden for women.

The Journalist: Cléo de Galsan

One crucial figure in the history of women's football in Brazil is often overlooked: journalist Cléo de Galsan. She played a critical role in promoting women's football in the country during the 1920s, and her efforts were integral to the development of the sport. Cléo was one of the most vocal opponents against negative criticism of women's football during these periods. She argued that women had the right to play the sport they loved and that the ban was an infringement on their basic human rights (Galsan, 1924a). Galsan's activism on behalf of women's football continued even after the ban, as she continued to write articles and organize matches in defiance of the law.

Despite her significant contributions to the development of women's football in Brazil, Galsan is often overlooked in discussions of the sport's history. However, her work as a journalist, organizer, and advocate played a crucial role in laying the foundation for the sport's eventual resurgence in the country.

When writing about the history of women's football in Brazil, it is common to begin with the 1941 ban. However, it is also important to acknowledge the presence and vitality of football played by women in previous years. Taking a global perspective, one can trace the sportivization of football and the presence of women even in its early stages, as noted by Giulianotti and Robertson (2009). The authors argue that football already at this time served as a vehicle for reproducing patriarchal social values.

It is possible to trace the history of women and football in Brazil back to the beginning of football in the country itself, which arrived six years after the Proclamation of the Republic. However, football initially played a secondary role in a hygienist republican project led by the elites, influenced by civilizing ideals (Elias and Dunning, 1992). The muscular and tanned figure of the sportsman emerged as an ideal of modernity to be achieved in Brazil, as opposed to the laziness of the slave-owning nobleman, linked to the retrograde and worn-out image of the monarchy. Nicolau Sevcenko (1998) called this movement the "ethics of activism," "the idea that it is in action and therefore in bodily engagement that the fullest realization of human destiny is concentrated" (Sevcenko, 1998, p. 569).

It is difficult to imagine women being excluded from this process, as they were active not only as spectators in the stands but also as "torcedoras" or supporters, a term coined by journalists in the early 1910s[3] to refer to young women who followed football teams. Brazilian women also played on the field, at least since 1913 (Bonfim, 2019; Almeida, 2020; Rial and Almeida, 2023) and worked in sports sections of newspaper editorial offices in the first decades of the 20th century. However, both of these activities were made invisible by the official history of football in Brazil.

This invisibilization also affected the writings of Cleo de Galsan, a journalist who worked for the newspaper A Gazeta (São Paulo) between 1924 and 1925. It was later discovered that Galsan ardently defended women's access to football in the 1920s, when gender was viewed as directly linked to sex, leading to the belief that women were fragile, delicate, and destined for motherhood. This perspective supported a symbolic power structure of domination, where masculinity was associated with virility (Bourdieu, 2010). According to Bourdieu, the body is constructed as a sexual reality by the social world, and it is infused

[3] It is written in the newspaper *O Pirralho* (October 7, 1911): "was perfectly clear that Mlle. Z was no longer the same 'torcedora' that she had been during the match with Americano." Anonymous. "O Pirralho Sportsman." *O Pirralho* (São Paulo), Outubro 7, 1911, 10.

with principles of sexualization, perception, and division. This social program of embodied perception applies universally, extending to all aspects of the world, and most notably to the body itself in its biological reality. The body is responsible for establishing the distinction between biological sexes, aligning with the principles of a mythical worldview (2002, p. 18).

During the first half of the 20th century, Cleo de Galsan wrote chronicles defending that women should be able to practice any sport, including football (Galsan, 1924a). Her texts were discovered by chance as we were searching for quotes about women's football in the digital archives of periodicals at the National Library's Hemeroteca. Initially, we found the idea of a "possible" woman who translated chronicles from the French magazine *Très Sport* in 1924 for the newspaper *A Gazeta* curious. Gradually, we found several commented translations until we came across the text of her own authorship, which defended the practice of any sport for women. However, doubts remained about who wrote the texts: was Cleo a man or a woman? The confirmation appeared in a few lines in the response to a reader, identified as "curious," in the newspaper's letters section: "No. Cléo de Galsan is not one of our assistants...with a beard. Our appreciated collaborator, in fact, wears a skirt..."

As we could not find any mention of the last name Galsan on the internet, we suspected that Cleo de Galsan was a pseudonym, as she was a woman writing in a newspaper during the 1920s. We searched the separate editions of *A Gazeta* for the words "Cléo" and "Galsan" and found some clues about who could be the author of the chronicles. Among the various mentions of Cléo, there was a rather curious one: Cléo was the name chosen to baptize the daughter of the director of the sports section of the newspaper, Leopoldo Sant'Anna, and his wife, Maria Conceição Rehder Galvão (Sant'Anna), born in June 1925. Based on this fact, we imagined the chronicler as Conceição, as she was known. After all, "Cléo" could be a combination of Conceição and Leopoldo and "Galsan" by Galvão and Sant'Anna. This hypothesis was confirmed by Conceição's own daughter, Cléo, aged 93 at the time, by email to Caroline Almeida in December 2018.

The surprises didn't stop there. We discovered that Cléo de Galsan/Conceição Rehder Galvão had none other than Patrícia Galvão. She was the older sister of Pagu, who was also a journalist and writer and an important name in the feminist struggle in Brazil, having become the first female political prisoner in the country.

Cléo understood early on the important role that football played in understanding the place of women in the gender hierarchy. Her articles also help us better understand the representations of class, race, and sexuality present in Brazil at that time. As a sports journalist, she presented herself as a narrator and critic of the context in which she was inserted. Her texts addressed the urgency of feminist guidelines that thought, from the practice of sports, of equal rights between men and women. In this sense, she believed that only physically strong women would be able to fight the structure of domination, since physical struggle could level the power relations between women and men. (Galsan, 1924b)

The history of Cléo de Galsan makes us think of a contemporary of hers, the German philosopher Walter Benjamin, who drew attention to the fact that history is often constructed by those who have achieved domination, the victors. He asked the question, "Is there not an echo of those who have been silenced in the voices to which we lend our ears today?" (Benjamin, 1987, n.p.). Cléo, it turns out, has become an example of these muted echoes—of the many voices that have been silenced throughout history. For too long, women were excluded from football (and other sports), club management, and sports journalism. She was among the pioneers of this genre, just like her husband, Leopoldo Sant'Ana. But only he and his bearded colleagues achieved recognition, while Cléo's contributions were largely overlooked.

First Manager of Clubs–Carlota Rezende

In the 1940s, football had already become a well-established sport in Brazil. It was no longer a secondary element in the nation-building project, but instead elevated to the status of a national symbol. Football was projected as a symbol of virility, discipline, and victory, in line with the Estado Novo (New State) ideology (Almeida, 2019). During this period, the number of women's football teams increased in the suburbs of Rio de Janeiro (Franzini, 2005; Goelner, 2005; Bonfim, 2019; Almeida and Almeida, 2020).

Primavera A.C.[4] was founded by Carlota Alves Rezende in May 1940, to bring together the best female players in the city of Rio de Janeiro. In an interview with the Rio de Janeiro newspaper *A Noite* (1941), Carlota confirmed that the footballers received payment for each match played. She was affectionately

4. The name of the club is presented in the newspapers as Primavera A.C. (Athletic Club) and Primavera F.C. (Football Club), the latter being highlighted by Carlota in an interview: "I can only attribute the denunciation to respect; the Primavera F.C.—you see, Mr. reporter, F.C.—has only lost one game since it began to exist." See: PINTO, Ricardo. Futebol Feminino. Diário de Notícias: January 22, 1941, p. 7. We have chosen to use "A. C." because of its connection to the group since its foundation.

called "little mother"[5] ("mãezinha") by the players and besides managing the club's agenda and finances, she also advised and took care of "her pupils." In addition to Primavera, Carlota founded eight other clubs in the North Zone of Rio de Janeiro.[6]

Primavera A.C. participated in games in Rio, and, following a tradition at the time among men's football clubs, intended to expand its reach with a tour. Afonso Doce, a well-known Argentine businessman in the football business, expressed his interest in sponsoring the trip of a group of Brazilian women football players for competitions with Argentine and Uruguayan teams.[7] The practice, although condemned by FIFA, was quite common among men, and Doce had been working for at least two decades intermediating football matches between clubs in Brazil, Argentina, and Uruguay (Almeida and Almeida, 2020). At first, the players were enthusiastic about the possibility of touring again, this time abroad, but after the negative repercussions and the campaign against women's football in Rio de Janeiro newspapers, led by *O Imparcial* (Bonfim, 2019), they knew it would be difficult.

This possibility of travel motivated Carlota's arrest the day before the journalist visited the club's headquarters. The accusation of leading the players to dances and cabarets after the games was raised by the chief of police, Dulcídio Gonçalves, and disseminated by different press vehicles. The narratives turned the Primavera founder into a recruiter of women for prostitution (Almeida, 2019; Bonfim, 2019; Almeida and Almeida, 2020), with the football club being a disguise for the scheme that would now gain an international dimension with Doce's participation. The defendant also had a lawsuit filed by Maria de Lourdes,[8] a former left midfielder of *Brasileiro.*[9] In an article, *O Imparcial* stated: "The controllers of the women's team are seen as suspicious *creatures* by the police, who know them as unfortunate patients worthy of admission to the judicial asylum. [...] In a letter addressed to the Juvenile Court, the *aforementioned* authority *explained.*"[10]

---

5. Anonymous. "Soluçava de Chuteiras." A Noite: Saturday, January 11, 1941, p. 3.

6. Among the football teams are S.C. Brazilian, A.C. Independent and Mavilis. Anonymous. "Soluçava de Chuteiras." A Noite (Rio de Janeiro), January 11, 1941, p. 3.

7. This practice was commonplace among male football players at the time, and years later, Pierre Geoffroy (Rial, 2020) in France and Eurico Lyra in Rio de Janeiro used it to promote women's football and build a network of clubs and businessmen overseas.

8. Anonymous. "Está sendo processada a mentora do foot-ball feminino." O Imparcial, January 18, 1941, p. 14.

9. Anonymous. "Presa uma das mentoras do foot-ball feminino" ("One of the Mentors of Women's Football Is Arrested"). *O Imparcial* (Rio de Janeiro), January 11, 1941, p. 8.

10. Anonymous. "Bailarinas ou jogadoras de foot-ball?" Imparcial, January 22, 1941, p. 14.

The newspaper *A Noite* provided firsthand details about the house in Pilares on the afternoon of January 11. The report emphasized the poster at the entrance and the challenge of obtaining interviews with the Primavera members, as they had all been instructed by Carlota not to make any statements. Regarding this matter, the journalist wrote:

> Salette reluctantly agreed to provide information stating that all the players were authorized by their respective parents to participate in football matches, and therefore, they were surprised by Ms. Carlota's arrest.
>
> Before leaving, the reporter noticed a picture on one of the walls and was drawn to a message that read "Bring your lipstick, rouge, and powder."[11]

After her release two days later, the case was once again highlighted by the same newspaper. "D. Carlota, introducer, director, and promoter of women's football is accused of diverting her pupils from the pitches to the "dancings," after playing football during the day, they spend their nights dancing tangos and congas in infamous ballrooms."[12] Despite claiming innocence and highlighting the qualities of Primavera's Football Club (F.C.), he attributed the accusations to moral issues: "I can only attribute the complaint to respect; the Primavera F.C.—you see, your reporter, F.C.—has only lost one game since it was founded" (Pinto, 1941, p. 7). However, a week later, the tour to the Prata region countries was forbidden by the Rio de Janeiro justice system, and the Theater and Cinema Division, linked to the Department of Press and Propaganda (DIP) of the Vargas government, announced the censorship of sports programs featuring Women's Football contests. The police closed down the Primavera headquarters. There is no further news regarding Carlota. Journalist Ricardo Pinto (1941) wrote about the situation that led to the arrest and closure of Women's Football clubs:

> Women's football is widely practiced in several countries, including the United States, where it thrills crowds. In Brazil, however, it is just beginning, and it started on the wrong foot, as we are seeing, because it began with an open fight with the police. The result of the investigations, led by the chief of police Cota,

11. Anonymous. "Soluçava de Chuteiras." A Noite: Saturday, January 11, 1941, p. 3.

12. Anonymous. "Da noite para o dia." A Noite, January 13, 1941, p. 2.

> has not been revealed yet. The newspapers have been silent lately. In any case, it is assumed that the existence of "Primavera" was not considered entirely regular, as it is certain that the champion team from Rio de Janeiro did not participate. Nor will they ever again, as some say. The chief of police Cota does not like to make his investigations public, especially related to sports. Therefore, it is possible that the result of the inquiry about the "spring games" will not be known. (Pinto, 1941, p. 7)

The arrest of Carlota Rezende on pimping charges marked the initial move toward criminalizing Women's football. The effort to professionalize Women's football at the time was likened to Tzvi Migdal, a mafia group that ran a prostitution network of Jewish women in major American cities, including Rio de Janeiro, Montevideo, and Buenos Aires (Almeida and Almeida, 2020). This moral appeal was followed by Decree Law No. 3199 in April 1941, which established the National Sports Council and regulated sports in the country. The decree prohibited women from participating in physical activities deemed incompatible with their "nature" as mothers. This biological argument prevented the development of the sport for the next forty years (Franzini, 2005; Goellner, 2005; Pisani, 2018; Almeida, 2019).

In May 1941, the *Primavera A.C.* headquarters in Pilares, located on Rua Gaspar, was put up for rent in a newspaper ad.[13]

Carlota Rezende was arrested and charged with procuring prostitution for the players of the team when she attempted to organize their trip to matches in Argentina and Uruguay. In addition to her work with CAF and Primavera F.C. However, unlike the men managers, Carlota's story was erased, and the contributions of many other women who played crucial roles in the development of football were made invisible.

The Footballers

In Brazil, unlike in other countries where football was started by workers, women's football was first played by the wealthy. From the 1920s, there was an increase in the organization of women around football, and clubs such as *Vasco da Gama*, *River F.C.*, and *ABC* (Natal/RN) began creating teams. The spread of women's football was as broad and encompassing as men's football, and newspapers and

[13] *Jornal do Brasil*, May 11, 1941, p. 14.

magazines began to feature chronicles and editorials warning of supposed dangers to the health of women who played football. Despite some journalists considering it scandalous and inappropriate for women to play football, some football players stood out in the news, particularly from 1940 onward. The sisters Nicéa, Sally, Aida, Wisleína, and many others played during the years of prohibition, and their stories offer valuable insights into the history of football in Brazil.

The success of women's football in the suburbs of Rio de Janeiro was documented in articles and interviews with footballers in important newspapers such as *Jornal dos Sports*, *Diário Carioca*, *O Radical*, and *A Noite*, which was owned by Irineu Marinho, who would later found the *Grupo Globo*. Even Leônidas da Silva, the most famous football player in Brazil at that time, expressed interest in following women's matches. Reports show that he had seen a women's football match in Pacaembu—a preliminary match between the men's teams *São Paulo F.C.* and *C.R. Flamengo*, a few days after the inauguration of the stadium in April 1940.

> Women's Football is arousing enthusiasm throughout Brazil. Rio had the primacy of awakening the attention of women and even of the leaders of the States, as can be seen from the invitation that comes from receiving the teams from the Cassino do Realengo F.C. and S.C. Brasileiro, from the Mayor of São Paulo, for the 27th of this month to inaugurate sports activities in that majestic stadium.[14]

It was at that moment that the professionalization of women's football began to be discussed, based on payment for games and even the creation of a municipal league in Rio de Janeiro—an issue defended by Salathiel Campos (1940a, 1940b) in his column in *Correio Paulistano* called *Ao correr da penna*. The journalist became known for his political position in relation to professionalization in football and for black militancy, being also the founder of the Frente Negra Brasileira in the early 1930s (Jeuken, 2017). Regarding the moralistic tone regarding the payment negotiations for the women's football preliminary match at Pacaembu, Salathiel asks: "if women's football manages to attract a large number of spectators, isn't it fair that it demands for itself a little of the much it produces?" (Campos, 1940a).

During that time, Nicéa, Sally, and Aida were members of S.C. Brasileiro, a team established by their aunt Carlota Rezende. The three sisters, who had been orphans since childhood, had been living with Carlota. Following their journey

14. Anonymous. "Football Feminino no 'Pacaembu'." *O Radical*, May 6, 1940, p. 8.

to São Paulo, Carlota founded Primavera FC, and her nieces joined the same team. The team had a remarkable record since its inception, losing only twice in seventeen games. Nicéa, Sally, and Aida were often mentioned in sports news articles for their impressive performances on the field.

> True "virtuous women" in the leather sphere, the blonde girls from Cascadura already have countless fans, thanks to the intense spontaneous publicity with which women's football has been focused, since there was even a moralist who deigned to write an open letter to Mr. President of the Republic, combating the practice of violent Breton sport by our country girls. It was the definitive consecration of women's football in our land.[15]

Nicéa and Sally were the most visible players on the team, with Nicéa receiving praise for her technical skills and being called "ace no. 1" or "Leonidas in a skirt."[16] She had been playing with her sisters since she was nine years old in games organized by children on their street. Sally, on the other hand, was referred to as the "super production girl"[17] and even visited the editorial office of *Diário Carioca* with Aida to talk about Primavera's debut on the women's football circuit.[18] Her photos were often featured in newspapers, with journalists not only highlighting her performance in football but also her beauty.

The social space assigned to these suburban women who played football in Rio de Janeiro in the 1940s is well exemplified in the chronicle "O feijão queimado" by Puck (1941). As a fascinating illustration of the gender and race ideology prevalent at the time, we present the following extended excerpt:

> [...] The police have just put a stop to the women's football game, sending the players back to their kitchens and pantries, restoring peace to Rio homes. If Miquelina is upset while washing the dishes and humming the latest samba for Carnaval, don't worry, dear reader: revenge is coming. The maid who couldn't go to Buenos Aires with "Esperança F. C." has already signed up with "Inocentes do Encantado." From goalkeeper, she will become the standard-bearer [...].

15. Anonymous. "Vamos ter mais um match de football feminino." *Diário Carioca*, May 25, 1940.

16. Anonymous. "Não quer mais nada com o football..." *A Noite*. Rio de Janeiro, January 12, 1941, p. 1.

17. Anonymous. "Vamos ter mais um match de football feminino." Diário Carioca, May 25, 1940.

18. Anonymous. "Estréa hoje a equipe feminina do Primavera A.C." Diário Carioca, June 9, 1940.

> The demise of women's "football" had the merit of bringing peace back to the homes of Rio de Janeiro residents, who were faced with a serious dilemma: either football or roast beef. Those who boasted having the "leading scorer" in their kitchen could expect burnt beans three times a week—days dedicated to team training. Those who wanted a good maid had to search for them in nursing homes where invalids, who were no longer able to chase after a ball, were kept. This was because the "association" was exciting the world of pots, pans, and desserts.
>
> The Rio de Janeiro police did the population a great favor. Now, the "extremes" that made the "supporters" delirious are doing laundry, while the great "back" stirs the frying pan that makes the French fries. What remains for them are memories, the only right of the ostracized "aces."
>
> "Imagine our success in Buenos Aires, huh?"
>
> "That's true. Just for that, I'll let the 'bishop' invade the penalty area of the Mrs.!" (Puck, 1941, p. 2)

After Carlota's arrest and the passing of Decree-Law 3199, newspapers ceased reporting on women's football games in Brazil. The Rio de Janeiro police, with the support of the DIP's censorship, prohibited matches of this sport. However, movements to promote women's football persisted, particularly toward the end of the 1950s, as seen in Pelotas (Rigo et al., 2008), Bahia (Moraes, 2012; Capucim and Silva, 2015), and Minas Gerais (Capucim and Silva, 2015). It is worth noting that during the same decade, Rio de Janeiro and São Paulo businessmen organized football games between "superstars" as a form of entertainment, which resulted in legal disputes with the CND (Capucim and Silva, 2015). Additionally, women's football teams played during this period in games organized by charitable actions in the suburbs of Rio de Janeiro and nearby cities, such as São João do Meriti and Nova Iguaçu. Notably, these events received support from parish priests of the Catholic Church.

Wisleína was an exemplary footballer of the 1950s. As a player for *Clube Atlético Mineiro*, she was compared to Didi,[19] a black midfielder of the same era. During the short championship held among Minas Gerais teams in Belo

[19] Referring to midfielder Waldir Pereira, star of the Brazilian national team, world champion in 1958. About Wisleína, see: Anonymous. "Elas jogam mais do que muito barbado." Revista dos esportes, n. 15, 1959, pp. 4–7.

Horizonte, she received the best reviews from journalists who covered the event for sports media.

> The game was tied, but among the *Atleticanas* was Didi, who was determined to win. With one run, the jambo-colored mulatto girl dribbled past the entire defense of *América* and, facing the goalkeeper, kicked the ball into the net. Didi, also known as Wisleina, was inconsolable for having made such a serious mistake earlier in the game. She stamped her feet, put her hands on her head, and cried. She was a girl of pride, running for the colors she defended, not just for a contract renewal. Despite the attention of 50,000 spectators, she filled herself with courage and, pardon my language, put her body on the line in pursuit of victory, which had been eluding them. After five minutes, Wisleína (Didi) saw her efforts crowned with success, scoring the most beautiful goal of the afternoon and securing the win for her team thanks to her class, determination, and, above all, her feminine intuition.[20]

It is important to remember that the Brazilian football chronicle of the 1950s had very distinctive characteristics, including some well-known names like Nelson Rodrigues, João Saldanha, and Thomaz Mazzoni. These individuals represented that generation of football in Brazil. However, the author of this chronicle points out something that is not often addressed in texts about women's football during this period. He highlights a characteristic attributed to women that goes beyond beauty and motherhood: intuition as a differentiating factor in the game.

On the contrary, many of Nelson Rodrigues' chronicles were sexist, including those that dealt with football. In his 1955 chronicle "Flamengo at Sixty" [O Flamengo Sessentão], published in the newspaper *Manchete Esportiva*, Nelson Rodrigues discussed the differences between C.R. Flamengo in 1911, the year in which football was introduced at the club, and the present day. One of the changes he observed was the absence of what he called "female hysteria" in the stadium stands. According to Rodrigues, in the past, supporters demonstrated a grandiose and operatic enthusiasm, and when a goal was scored, the women would go into frenzied ecstasy. Rodrigues (1993, p. 12) lamented the fact that modern football lacked this kind of passionate expression, stating that "the

20. Anonymous. "Elas jogam mais do que muito barbado." Revista dos esportes, n 15, 1959, p. 7.

absence of female hysteria lyrically impoverishes football today" [Eis o que empobrece liricamente o futebol atual: a inexistência do histerismo feminino].

In his 1970 article "The Most Beautiful Football on Earth is from Brazil" [O mais belo futebol da terra é do Brasil], published in the newspaper, Nelson Rodrigues wrote about a football match between Brazil and the Soviet Union. Instead of focusing on the game itself, however, he argued that the Brazilian team played better when they were discredited and humiliated by their fans. To illustrate this point, he used an analogy involving a supposedly beautiful woman he knew. She was almost as beautiful as Ava Gardner, if not more so, tell us Nelson Rodrigues. Whenever her husband entered the room, instead of throwing herself into his arms, she would throw herself at his feet and proceed to kiss each of his shoes. She could afford to do this because of her beauty and charm, which sparked passions and even suicides wherever she went. Rodrigues noted that her humility was her way of expressing her vanity as a beautiful woman (Rodrigues, 2013, p. 146).

Moving from this example to the topic of football, Rodrigues believed that a team was made by the people, and that in the case of the Brazilian team, the people motivated them through booing. He claimed that there had never been a team so humiliated and offended, yet still managed to perform well. These examples reveal how deeply sexist Rodrigues' chronicles were and how he often reduced women to mere sexual objects or belittled them for their football skills. Unfortunately, he was not the only writer of his time who held such views.

João Saldanha was renowned for his strong political convictions, his opposition to the military dictatorship in Brazil (1964–1979), and his uncompromising approach to football. However, his chronicles were also marred by instances of sexism. In his paper titled "Is football a thing for 'macho'?" [Futebol é coisa pra macho?], football historian Fábio Franzini (2005) describes a speech by Saldanha that became famous and was recounted by his fellow journalist and colleague, Sérgio Cabral, at an event in the 1990s. The exchange, narrated in an anecdotal style, is said to have transpired as follows: When asked for his opinion on women's football, sports commentator and former coach João Saldanha expressed his disapproval, justifying it with a sharp tongue: "Imagine this scenario: A guy has a son, and the son introduces his girlfriend to his father-in-law, who then asks her, 'What do you do, my daughter?' And she replies, 'I'm a defender for Bangu.' It just doesn't sound right, does it?" (Franzini, 2005, p. 316).

Thomaz Mazzoni, like many of his contemporaries, also made sexist comments about football. In his book *History of Football in Brazil* [*História do Futebol no*

Brasil], Mazzoni wrote about the game between São Paulo and Rio de Janeiro in Pacaembu in 1940, stating that "in this game, as a preliminary, women's football was launched, whose interest was limited to this single game. Girls' football soon died" (Mazzoni, 1950, p. 289). According to Fábio Franzini (2005), this reference by Mazzoni is written in a manner that portrays women as outsiders to the history of Brazilian football.

Final Considerations

In order to establish football as a sport for women in a country where it was a male-dominated field, women had to navigate various social arenas (fields, in Bourdieu's words): the journalistic world, the business world (which, unfortunately, proved less successful), and the practice of the sport itself.

Cléo de Galsan and Carlota Rezende were staunch defenders of women's football and fought against the prejudice and discrimination faced by women who played football at the time. Carlota also advocated for the professionalization of women's football and worked to have female players recognized as professional athletes. Their work was fundamental to the development of women's football in Brazil and paved the way for women who play football today.

The sexism present among the detractors of women's football, who opposed Cléo de Galsan in the 1920s, remained alive in the chronicles of the 1950s and 1960s with important voices for football, such as those of Rodrigues, Saldanha, and Mazzoni. Female sports journalists were rare until the mid-1980s, and unfortunately, prejudices against women club leaders have been long-lasting, with few large (or even small) clubs having women as presidents. As for players, thanks to pioneers like Nicéa, Sally, Aida, and Wisleína, they overcame the barriers of prejudice, but they also had to wait until the 21st century to have their practice recognized and valued.

REFERENCES

Almeida, Caroline S. Nas praias e nas várzeas: o movimento de retorno do Futebol Feminino entre fins da década de 1970 e início de 1980 (On the Beaches and in the Open Fields: The Revival Movement of Women's Football Between the Late 1970s and Early 1980s). In: Kessler, Claudia; Costa, Leda; Pisani,

Mariane (org.). *As mulheres no universo do futebol brasileiro*. Santa Maria, RS: EDUFSM, 2020.

Almeida, Caroline S. *Mulheres futebolistas*: debates sobre violência e moral durante o Estado Novo brasileiro (Women Footballers: Debates on Violence and Morality During Brazil's Estado Novo). *Lusotopie*. 18 (2019): 95–118.

Almeida, Caroline S. and Thaís R. Almeida. Deve ou não deve o football invadir os domínios das saias? histórias do futebol de mulheres no Brasil (Should Football Invade the Realm of Women? Histories of Women's Football in Brazil). *ICSOnline—Revista Eletrônica de Ciências Sociais*. 31 (2020): 168–191.

Benjamin, Walter. Teses sobre o conceito da história (Theses on the Philosophy of History). In: Benjamin, Walter. *Ensaios sobre literatura e história da cultura*. São Paulo: Brasiliense, 1987, vol. 1, pp. 222–232.

Bonfim, Aira F. *Football feminino entre festas esportivas, circos e campos suburbanos*: uma história social do futebol praticado por mulheres da introdução à proibição (1915–1941) (Women's Football between sports festivals, circuses, and suburban fields: A social history of football played by women from Its Introduction to its prohibition (1915–1941)). Master's thesis. Rio de Janeiro: Fundação Getúlio Vargas, 2019.

Bourdieu, Pierre. *Outline of a theory of practice*. Cambridge: Cambridge University Press, 1977.

Bourdieu, Pierre. *A dominação masculina* (Male Domination). Rio de Janeiro: Bertrand Brasil, 2010.

Brasil. Decreto-Lei n. 3.199, de 14 de abril de 1941. Estabelece as bases de organização dos desportos em todo o país (Decree-Law No. 3,199, of April 14, 1941. Establishes the Foundations for the Organization of Sports Nationwide). Portal da Câmara dos Deputados. https://www2.camara.leg.br/legin/fed/declei/1940-1949/decreto-lei-3199-14-abril-1941-413238-publicacaooriginal-1-pe.html (accessed March 07, 2022).

Butler, Judith. *Gender troubles*. New York: Routledge, 1990.

Campos, Salathiel. Ao correr da penna...(As the Pen Flows...) Correio Paulistano (São Paulo). May 5, 1940a, 16.

Campos, Salathiel. Ao correr da penna...(As the Pen Flows...) Correio Paulistano (São Paulo). May 21, 1940b, 10.

Capucim e Silva, Giovana. *Narrativas sobre o futebol feminino na imprensa paulista*: entre a proibição e a regulamentação (1941–1983) (Narratives About Women's Football in São Paulo Press: Between Prohibition and Regulation (1941–1983)). Master's thesis. São Paulo: Universidade de São Paulo, 2015.

Elias, Norbet; Eric Dunning, E. 1992. *A busca da excitação* (The Quest for Excitement: Sport and Leisure in the Civilizing Process). Lisboa: DIFEL.

Elsey, Brenda; Nadel, Joshua H. *Futbolera: a history of women and sports in Latin America.* Austin: Texas University Press, 2019.

Franzini, Fábio. Futebol é coisa para macho? Pequeno esboço para uma história das mulheres no país do futebol (Is Football "a Man's Thing"? A Brief Outline for a History of Women in the Country of Football). In: *Revista Brasileira de História*. São Paulo: n. 50 (2005): 315–328.

Galsan, Cléo. "A mulher e o esporte—O futebol feminino é o jogo recommendado à mocidade feminina," ("Women and Sport—Women's Football is the Game Recommended for Young Women"). A Gazeta (SP), n. 5481b, p. 3, 1924a.

Galsan, Cleo. "As melindrosas e o...esporte" ("The Flappers and...Sport"). A Gazeta (SP), n. 5488, p. 3, 1924b.

Goellner, Silvana. Mulheres e futebol no Brasil: entre sombras e visibilidades. In: *Revista Brasileira de Educação Física* (Women and Football in Brazil: Between Shadows and Visibility). São Paulo: n. 19 (2005): 143–151.

Goellner, Silvana. V. Mulheres e futebol no Brasil: descontinuidades, resistências e resiliências (Women and Football in Brazil: Discontinuities, Resistance, and Resilience). *Movimento, 27*, (2021), e27001.

Jeuken, Bruno. *Salathiel de Campos: esporte e política (1926–1938)* (Salathiel de Campos: Sport and Politics (1926–1938)). Master's thesis, Universidade de São Paulo, 2017.

Mazzoni, Thomaz. *História do futebol no Brasil: 1894–1950* (A History of Football in Brazil: 1894–1950). São Paulo: Edições Leia, 1950.

Moraes, Enny Vieira. *As mulheres também são boas de bola*: histórias de vida de jogadoras baianas (1970–1990) (Women Are Also Skilled with the Ball: Life Stories of Women Football Players from Bahia (1970–1990)). 2012. 288 f. PhD diss, Pontifícia Universidade Católica de São Paulo, 2012.

Pinto, Ricardo. Futebol Feminino (Women's Football). *Diário de Notícias*: January 22, 1941, p. 7.

Pisani, Mariane. *Sou feita de chuva, sol e barro*: o futebol de mulheres praticado na cidade de São Paulo (I Am Made of Rain, Sun, and Mud: Women's Football Played in the City of São Paulo). PhD diss, Universidade de São Paulo, 2018.

Puck. "O feijão queimado," ("The Burnt Beans"). A Noite (Rio de Janeiro), January 18, 1941, 2.

Rial, Carmen. A memória do futebol praticado por mulheres—semelhantes trajetórias no Brasil e na França? In: Grossi, Miriam and Leandro Oltramani, Vinicius Ferreira (eds). *Família, gênero e memória*: diálogos interdisciplinares entre França e Brasil. Brasília: ABA; Florianópolis: Tribo da Ilha, 2020: 295–321.

Rial, C., & de Almeida, C. S. (2023). Football, lesbianism and feminism in Brazil: subversive acts. *Soccer & Society*, *25*(2), 174–186.

Rigo, Luiz and others. Notas acerca do futebol feminino pelotense em 1950: um estudo genealógico (9 Notes on Women's Football in Pelotas in 1950: A Genealogical Study). In: *Revista Brasileira de Ciências do Esporte*. São Paulo: n. 29 (2008): 173–188.

Rodrigues, Nelson. Flamengo Sessentão (Flamengo at Sixty). In: Castro, Ruy (org.). *À sombra das chuteiras imortais*. São Paulo: Companhia das Letras, 1993.

Rodrigues, Nelson. *A pátria de chuteiras* (The Nation in Boots). Rio de Janeiro: Nova Fronteira, 2013.

Sevcenko, Nicolau. A capital irradiante: técnica, ritmos e ritos do Rio. In: Novais, Fernando and N. Sevcenko (eds.). *História da vida privada no Brasil*. São Paulo, Companhia das Letras: 3(1998): 513–619.

No Author

Anonymous. "A censura não approvará programas com partidas femininas." O Imparcial (Rio de Janeiro), January 23, 1941, 15.

Anonymous. "Bailarinas ou jogadoras de foot-ball?" O Imparcial (Rio de Janeiro), January 22, 1941, 14.

Anonymous. "Campo do Volante Interditado." Última Hora (Rio de Janeiro), November 12, 1959, 2.

Anonymous. "Da noite para o dia." A Noite (Rio de Janeiro), January 13, 1941, 2.

Anonymous. "Elas jogam mais do que muito barbado." Revista dos esportes, n 15, 1959, pp. 4–7.

Anonymous. "Está sendo processada a mentora do foot-ball feminino." O Imparcial (Rio de Janeiro), January 18, 1941, 14.

Anonymous. "Jogos internacionaes entre quadros femininos." A Gazeta (São Paulo), December 16, 1920, 2.

Anonymous. "Meninas do Meriti também jogam bola." Última Hora (Rio de Janeiro), September 21, 1959, 7.

Anonymous. "Não quer mais nada com o football." A Noite (Rio de Janeiro), January 12, 1941, 1.

Anonymous. "O Pirralho Sportsman." O Pirralho (São Paulo), Outubro, 7, 1911, 10.

Anonymous. "Presa uma das mentoras do foot-ball feminino." O Imparcial (Rio de Janeiro), January 11, 1941, 8.

Anonymous. "S. Paulo assiste, pela primeira vez, a uma partida de futebol feminine." Correio Paulistano (São Paulo), May 19, 1940, 16–18.

Anonymous. "Soluçava de Chuteiras." A Noite (Rio de Janeiro), January 11, 1941, 3.

Anonymous. "Vamos ter mais um match de football feminino." Diário Carioca (Rio de Janeiro), May 25, 1940.

CHAPTER 4

Soccer as Work in Brazil: An Analysis of *the Making* of a Women's Soccer Player from Childhood to Professionalism (1983–2023)

Fernanda Haag

Introduction

In 2020, when we recorded, I played for fun. I still do, but now I have that direct focus on my career, right?

The sentence in epigraph was said by Juju Dinis, a youth athlete from the *Associação Desportiva Centro Olímpico* (an important grassroots soccer team), in the second season of the São Paulo Football Federation-produced series *Absolutes.*[1] The young woman projects her future as a player and highlights the focus on the development of her career. The construction of a career as a professional soccer athlete is intertwined with the logic of the sports field, as well as the structure of class society. Moreover, the players have agency in the development of their project (constantly called a dream) and undertake diversified strategies to achieve it, also reaching different results.

Borrowing Thompson's perspective on the making of the working class, we can understand that *making oneself* a player as an "is a study of an active process, which owes as much to agency as to conditioning" (Thompson, 2011). Thus, the objective of this text is unveiled: to understand the process of building a soccer player's career or, in other words, the process of *becoming a* professional player. Due to the limits of this article, a historical cutout was established; therefore, this analysis will focus on the moment of transition, i.e., when soccer becomes a job, and they start to recognize themselves as professional players.

[1] FEDERAÇÃO PAULISTA DE FUTEBOL. Absolutas—Ep. 1 Foguete não tem ré. 20 sep 2022. 1 video (7min34sec). Available on: https://www.facebook.com/watch/?v=635630088280491&_rdc=1&_rdr. Accessed: 11 April 2023.

Thus, this chapter follows the trajectory and narrative of eight Brazilian women's soccer players, who played from 1983 to 2023. The last year is 2023 (when this text was written) since two of them are currently playing, and the initial milestone is 1983 due to the regulation of women's soccer in Brazil, published in the Deliberation 01/1983, by the National Sports Council,[2] during the political distension of the country's civil-military dictatorship. In other words, the eight players played professionally after the regulation, and one of the reasons is precisely that before that it was not a career or a possible job for them.

All of them had soccer as a job at some point in their careers and sought to build a career in the sports field. They played for national clubs—from the so-called smaller ones to the most important in the sport—and six of them played outside Brazil, more specifically, in Europe. They played in the main women's soccer leagues, either in their country of origin or in the countries that received them as immigrant players. All eight had stints with the Brazilian National Team and played in the most important tournaments: World Cup, Olympics, South American, Pan American, São Paulo International Women's Football Tournament. But there is some variation, because not all of them played every tournament. In any case, they experienced the national team, and in the words of one of them, "It is the accomplishment of a job of a lifetime" (Aggio, 2022).

The chapter does not seek to generalize the experience of all women's soccer players and recognizes that the experiences of other athletes may be different, so it is limited to the study of specific cases. It emphasizes that the analysis of the soccer players' trajectories is not limited to an individual perspective and considers the social relationships that influenced their careers.

Oral History: Between Memories and Narratives

The present chapter starts from oral history as a method. Therefore, we have conducted interviews, which constitute as a source intentionally constructed in a collaborative and dialogical way, because it involves the researched subject (the players) and the researcher (Hollanda and Ribeiro, 2019). Thus, according to Alberti (2013), the interviewees' narratives are themselves our object of analysis—when conducting oral history research, it is fundamental to consider

2. Deliberação n. 01/1983, Conselho Nacional de Desportos.

the relevance of the question, "How did the interviewees used to perceive, and still do, the subject matter?"

Portelli complements this notion by stating that oral history is not only about the event but also about the place and meaning of the event within the narrators' lives. Regarding oral sources, the historian highlights their active character, since the interviewees do not passively recall the facts, instead elaborating from them and *creating meaning* through memory's work (Portelli, 2016). Another important element linked to oral sources is that they are "a necessary (not sufficient) condition for the history of non-hegemonic classes" (Portelli, 1997). We can extend such reasoning beyond the notion of class, thinking about other minority groups from a race and gender perspective.

In this sense, analyzing the trajectory of *women players* is pertinent to the understanding of the soccer's development in Brazil and to the understanding of the way in which gender inequality engenders labor relations in the sports field. Talking about the experiences of female players is also justified because, as previously mentioned, women in soccer have long been invisible and their stories neglected (Goellner, 2005; Kessler, 2015; Silva, 2015; Goellner and Cabral, 2022) and it is necessary to shed light on such historical subjects. It is not, however, to adopt an arrogant or naive posture of "giving voice" to the silenced, as if they did not already have it; on the contrary, it is to offer them a listening to their memories (Tonini, 2016).

Furthermore, the use of oral history is especially useful for us to look beyond the circuit of male spectacle soccer, a constant focus of media and memorialist coverage (Hollanda and Ribeiro, 2019). For this chapter, unique and targeted interviews were conducted. They were directed, due to our choice of conducting a thematic oral history. A script was prepared with the purpose of establishing a minimum logical chain of recollection. It does not, however, mean to imprison the interviewees' narratives, instead allowing them to follow their memory flow.

A Brief Periodization of Women's Soccer in Brazil

To have a career as a professional player started to become feasible for women in Brazil after the regulation of women's soccer with the publication of Deliberation CND 01/1983. However, it is important to point out that in its Article 3 the deliberation vetoed professionalism for women: the practice should be amateur—hence the idea of it *starting* to become viable, and many female soccer players starting to consider such a project. However, it is not an automatic process. In any case, the regulation was the result of intense mobilizations against the prohibitions in place until then,[3] and in defense of an organized and recognized sport.

Due to the present chapter's limitations, it is not possible to further delve into the historicity of women's soccer during the period from 1983 to 2023, but a brief periodization is necessary in order to historically situate the players' narratives. This period can be divided in three phases: (1) from 1983 to 1995, starting with Deliberation 01/1983 and ending with the 1985 FIFA World Cup in Sweden; (2) from 1996 to 2019, beginning with the Atlanta Olympics and continuing until the start of the 2019 FIFA Women's World Cup in France; (3) from 2019 onward, precisely considering the World Cup in France as a rupture and inaugural cornerstone of our phase.

The first phase is characterized by the struggle for regulation and recognition of the modality. It is directly connected to the democratic transition process[4] and to the social struggles waged in the 1980s and 1990s in the Brazilian context. There was a concern to mark the existence of women's soccer, therefore, the "pioneer generation's" performance stands out (Goellner and Cabral, 2022)—those who experienced and dedicated themselves to soccer soon after the regulation.[5] The initiatives to structure soccer practice by women were less articulate in this phase: teams existed, albeit with management woes, and tournaments were established mostly at regional and national levels, diffusely supported (or not) by sports institutions such as the CBF and the state federations. Other elements that stand out from this period are the call-up of the first Brazilian National Team, first World Cup challenge, and the South American Championship.

The Atlanta Olympic Games, in 1996, are a milestone for women's soccer in Brazil, inaugurating the second phase. There is a degree of recognition of the sport's existence—professionalism, however, was still as absent as it was needed. Such absence permeates the whole structure of this soccer: teams, federations, calendar, competitions, media, (lack of) investment. Similarly, there were demands

3. Women's soccer in Brazil was officially banned for almost forty decades. The prohibitions were established by Decree 3.199, 1941, of the Estado Novo and by Deliberation 7, 1965, of the National Sports Council (CND) in the civil-military dictatorship. In 1979, Deliberation 10/79 revoked the previous one from 1965, which, despite removing the prohibition, kept the sport clandestine, since there were no regulations.

4. The process of transition from a civil-military dictatorship to a regime of liberal democracy in Brazil.

5. The pioneering here refers to the first women who played soccer after the regulation. Still, it is important to point out that women have always been on the field, even before 1983, including during prohibition.

and calls for improvements. One must remember the iconic banner "Brazil, we need support" raised by the female players of the Brazilian National Team in the final of the 2007 FIFA Women's World Cup in China. Moreover, this phase is also characterized by a significant growth in the emigration of Brazilian players, the consolidation of international tournaments, an increase in media coverage (often filled with gender stereotypes, however), and by active state participation and incentives for maintaining the sport.

The third phase started with the 2019 FIFA Women's World Cup in France. It continues to the present day and has no end in sight. The tournament was a milestone for women's soccer and the culmination of previous constructions, both inside the sports field, with the charges and disputes for improvements, and outside of it, related to the "Feminist Explosion" (Hollanda, 2018). This phase opened countless possibilities with respect to greater professionalization of the sport, not only in Brazil. It seems to be a consensus among the agents involved with women's soccer that the growth that occurred from 2019 onward is quite significant and covers all spheres (athletes, clubs, federations, investors, states, other professionals, managers and directors, media).

Sticking to the Brazilian case, it is important to highlight examples of said professionalization: occupation of management positions in CBF by women, such as Aline Pellegrino and Eduarda Luizelli; women coaches in charge of the Brazilian National Teams, Simone Jatobá (Under-17) and Pia Sundhage (main); equalization of per diems and awards for men and women in the National Team; creation of more divisions in the national championships (A1, A2, and A3 series), organization of youth championships (Under-18, Under-16, and Under-14); effective growth of the viewership and of the spectating public in stadiums, more sports coverage, increase in investments and sponsors.

One caveat about periodization: not understanding it in a hermetic way—any one phase is not entirely independent from another, with continuities and ruptures—nor as a progressive line: advances and setbacks occur throughout all these periods. In the wake of this movement, there is a specificity of women's soccer in Brazil: the cyclical effect. This is not new, and researchers Mourão and Morel (2005) already highlighted it at the beginning of the 21st century: "There is in female football an cyclical movement, when the context seems to represent a condition of stability one dynamically observes a retraction of this practice." Kessler (2015), ten years later, agrees: "The ineffectiveness in terms of perennial actions generates a framework of instabilities, of 'cyclical effect', of frequent expansion and retraction of women's soccer."

The Women's Soccer Player Profession

The link between the worlds of labor and soccer has been built by researchers in Human Sciences and constitutes one of the central axes of the social history of sports in Brazil. By highlighting the relationship of the sports' genesis with nationalism, industrialization, and urbanization, it too addresses the identity formation of the working class, as well as its connection with modern sports (Hollanda and Fontes, 2021). There is also an important bibliographic production on the historical process of professionalization of men's soccer (Pereira, 2000; Santos, 2010) as well as fundamental anthropological analyses on the formation and profession of players (Araújo, 1980; Damo, 2005). However, it is a field of study with plenty of room for growth and with gaps to be filled. Thinking about gender and class, dialectically imbricated, is one of such possible paths.

For this, it is necessary to approach the discussions about the soccer profession and its specificities. Roderick (2006) lists some of them.

(1) It is a job that demands a highly specialized manual skill and is different from industrial workers because the player's involvement with their profession is more intense, and sometimes they can find a sense of self-fulfillment in it, especially at the beginning of their career. Moreover, the idea that the player can build a career as a professional becomes an integral part of their own sense of identity.

(2) It is a short career: for athletes, the standard is to start their careers at a young age or as children, but few continue after the age of 35. During these years, they are exposed to relatively high risks, which can result in early termination of their career, and they undergo intense and prolonged periods of physical exercise. In their narratives, it is common to talk about the need for great dedication and discipline to succeed.

(3) Allied to that, the soccer player profession has a specific temporal dimension: their career is very vulnerable to aging, so getting older and retiring are strong presences, and these elements relate to identity and reputation. Thus, the older the player, the more sensitive he becomes to job insecurity, as important characteristics of the physical activity involved vary with age.

(4) Regarding job insecurity, soccer is a highly competitive labor market characterized by short-term contracts. The hiring institutions (i.e., the clubs) are composed of highly specialized and highly mobile workers, that is, ones who move continuously between one employer and another. As such, the vast majority of players sign fixed and short-term contracts (usually lasting from one

to five years), in which there is a gigantic concentration of profit in the hands of a small number of employers.

(5) Career progression is also quite peculiar. Unlike other jobs, in which there is the notion (or at least the perspective) of progressing to better positions as time goes by, career advancement is never guaranteed for athletes and, since their physical peak occurs years before retirement, the tendency at the end is an increase in insecurity to find other employers, probably without the same prominence or the same working conditions. Furthermore, career progression is marked by insecurity thanks to the possibility of injury. Excessive concern with the body is a constant, making cases in which players are led to have a behavior marked by abstinence and sacrifice in order to preserve their physique common.

Roderick's propositions are fundamental for us to better understand what soccer as work involves. However, his approach covers only men's soccer. It is necessary to think about the place women occupy in this context and how soccer as work is configured for them. Culvin (2019) seeks to understand why and how women try to develop a career as a professional player, given that soccer encompasses a precarious and insecure employment situation. She also recalls that in the world of work there are more women in precarious and/or part-time positions, and in subordinate spots.

Precariousness can be felt in the insecurity of labor contracts. Women players around the globe operate on short-term contracts, usually one to three years (lower than men's), and many do not even have contracts (FIFPro, 2017). Culvin (2019) explains that the consequence of this insecurity is similar to those of *freelance* workers: there is no denying a job, leading them into a continuous cycle of competitions and matches—and thus intense periods of training, high performance, and of course, work. In such a way, women's soccer operates in very unstable market conditions.

Moreover, women's soccer players perform all these activities in an environment of male hegemony. Men predominantly occupy the positions of power in the sport and thus control its development. In this decision-making environment, women's teams are often seen as charity, as a benefit offered by the club itself. Even if men and women play the same game, within the same club, the power relations that dominate the teams and organizations reinforce a supposed distinction between "real soccer" and women's soccer. Therefore, male and female players are unlikely to have similar experiences when it comes to the sports management, training, and structure they receive.

Female soccer players are also under greater pressure to meet an athletic ideal within soccer—with all its demands for dedication, sacrifice, and discipline—and an ideal of femininity in society in general. In addition, among the reasons that make female players give up their careers earlier, are motherhood and family obligations. These family obligations, in turn, involve women disproportionately more than they do men. There is a difficulty for them to negotiate these specific obligations with their gender. Culvin adds as reasons: the lack of financial incentive to stay in the sport and the desire to seek professional opportunities outside of soccer.

With all these difficulties and mishaps, it is worth asking the following question: what leads women to become professional players? How does *making oneself a* soccer player happen? McGillivray et al. (2005), despite analyzing the reality of Scottish soccer, brings us a way to think about answers. For the researchers, soccer players are "caught up in and by the game." Based on this premise, they use Wacquant's research on boxing athletes to explain that the soccer field is relatively autonomous, has its own logic, and the soccer player is "inhabited by the game he inhabits," finding it difficult to gaze outside the logic of this field.

For many players, soccer is the only thing they have ever done, and the only thing they know how to do. Another of the author's points is that the identity of professional players is rooted in their body: soccer is, going back to Wacquant, an *embodied practice*. Thus, the body is the site that embodies a story. A third element pointed out about the players is that even if they had opportunities in other professions, they would persist in soccer, because it enables them to escape the insecurity they would face in other spaces. This is related, above all, to the popular classes and to the view of soccer as a vector for social ascension.

Culvin brings the perspective of female players and complements all that reasoning. For her, women's love for playing soccer is underestimated, considering there is immense financial insecurity involved. Many of the female players interviewed by Culvin portrayed an authentic "labor of love," as soccer was part of their identities and from a young age, they based many of their important life decisions on their love for the game. Therefore, soccer can be considered a relatively autonomous field, which simultaneously forms players and is formed by them, where players build their own identities linked to the sport, directly influencing their decision-making and professional choice. Let's see how this appears in the interviewees' narratives:

> Soccer, literally everything I have lived. My life, it is my life. It was like I said, I don't know if I got lucky, but soccer was what I conquered. It was learning other languages, getting to know other cultures. I think soccer is my life. Literally,

> it is my life. I based myself...everything I've been living has been on this. **So, soccer is what I am, soccer is me** (Moreno, 2022).
>
> It is my profession; it is what I want to do. It's just that some things you discover and identify yourself while you experience them, **when I walk into the field, I am myself there. I feel like myself** (Wahlbrink, 2022).

These are just two registers; but soccer as a central element of identity is present in the speech of all the interviewees, always a defining axis of their lives. The passages above are quite symbolic of this process. Thus, we must now analyze how the women's soccer players' trajectory happened until the moment the sport became a job for them—in other words, how their *making* as players occurred.

The Making of a Player: From Childhood to Soccer as Work

Araújo (1980) carried out a case study in his master's dissertation with eight professional soccer players, with the objective of understanding why they chose soccer as a profession and their conceptions on their careers. For the anthropologist, a career as a player is a choice made with much "reflection and calculation," considering the risks involved with the choice, but especially the possibility of social ascension and financial independence. Therefore, the decision to play soccer professionally is made based on a *project*, an "eminently conscious activity."

Astruc (2021), when analyzing the individual trajectories of players who represented Brazil in the World Cups from 1954 to 1978, and also concerned with thinking about soccer as a profession, disagrees with such proposition.[6] For him, the choice of soccer as an occupation is not the result of strategic reflection or a long-term project aiming at social ascension. There are two arguments to support such positioning: (1) being a professional player was the fulfillment of a childhood dream, to transform a personal passion into an occupation; (2) the emphasis on luck and occasional circumstances to become a player. Thus, they *became* players, rather than they *chose to*.

[6] Even though both concern soccer as a profession, Astruc himself points out that since the testimonies collected from the two surveys occurred under distinct conditions, the interviewees' profiles and the questions also differ, which contributes to the different results.

As we have seen, the playing profession, besides the difficulties inherent to a soccer career, suffers from the aggravating effects of gender inequality. The question arises: do women consciously and strategically choose to be players, or do they become players because of occasional situations in their lives? The interviewed women's soccer players, in their majority, declared that playing soccer professionally was a goal since childhood or adolescence, despite all the existing challenges: "Always, always. I had always said I was going to be a soccer player" (Oliveira, 2022). They report an obstacle experienced at that point of their lives: perceiving the material conditions to make this project come true, mainly due to the absence or small number of women's teams. Jatobá mentions a change when she saw women playing professionally:

> There was a preliminary game where the girls played. And that enticed me, so I said "wow, now I can be an athlete, a professional soccer player, in the future." [...] That happened when I was, I think, 6 or 7 years old, that is it. I think the final was in 87, 88. So we all went to São Paulo to watch it, the whole family, and it really caught my attention. So, I said "oh, this is what I want." (Jatobá, 2022)

Only three athletes were categorical in stating that being a soccer player was not in their plans. Two of them are from the pioneer generation:

> No, it never crossed my mind, and things were happening like that...As they were happening, I was giving it some thought, and then things were happening. (Luizelli, 2022)

> And I wrote a history in soccer. I had not foreseen this for myself. I did not dream; at that time we didn't dream of becoming a soccer player. At least, I did not dream of being a soccer player, but I managed to get there. [...] Nothing planned, nothing dreamed of, as a player. [...] but it was child's play that became serious, and I am very grateful for that. (Abreu, 2022)

Perhaps the explanation for their not envisioning a soccer career in the beginning lies precisely in the period when they started playing. The existing prohibition and that initial phase right after regulation, in which there is a significant growth of the sport—far, however, from a professional structure, or professionalizing conditions for athletes. Being from a pioneer generation, they needed to pave this road which, when they started practicing the sport, was still non-existent.

They were part of the generation that Jatobá saw in the stadium and that made her see soccer as a possible profession for women.

Moreno also stated that she did not imagine a career as a soccer player—ironically, she is one of the interviewees who still plays professionally. The reason for this, according to Moreno, is the same as Leda's: "at the time we didn't have that much visibility, so I just wanted to have fun." There are continuities in Brazilian women's soccer thanks to the deficient structuring of the sport, or as we saw above, the cyclical effect. Moreno also relates the lack of visibility for women in the sport considering she grew up in a city in the countryside of the Paraná state with a population of 5,000 people.

Regarding their initial contact with the practice of sports, all of them said that they started playing during childhood, at around 5 or 6 years old. They developed different strategies, such as turning their dolls' heads into balls, or incessantly kicking a ball against the wall. All of them also played with boys during their childhood, either at school, on the farm, in city squares, or on the streets. Some reported that this helped their physical and even technical development, because they felt the difference when they played against girls. It was during adolescence that the game became more institutionalized. Some said they started playing in soccer schools, others received scholarships thanks to the sport, and some had, by then, joined professional and/or youth teams.

The making of a player is not an individual and entirely autonomous process—both because of the issue between agency and structure, as previously mentioned, and because of the possibility of understanding careers as a collective construction, in the sense that the players, throughout their trajectory, receive fundamental support for the consolidation of their professional activity. Characters from inside or outside the sports field directly intervene.

Families make decisive interventions. Unlike many common reports on women's soccer, in which family members were against girls playing ball, the interviewees' families were not only favorable but fundamental in encouraging the practice. Some of them reported that soccer was an important part of family life, that a family member played (at the time) or had played soccer before, or that they were fans and followed the sport, passing these practices and feelings forward. Besides the sharing of a common passion and the introduction to the environment of soccer, many family members were responsible for concrete actions in the player's trajectories: enrollment in soccer schools, helping face prejudice from people close to them, providing advice and guidance during decisive moments in their careers, giving emotional and financial support, or helping in the search for women's teams.

Fathers and mothers were the most often cited in this case—fathers, mainly, in the introduction to soccer: they already had greater contact with the sport, either as fans or as players, which is not by chance, as soccer is a sport of male hegemony. Fathers would also be proud to see their daughters playing ball and being successful. Mothers were portrayed as important throughout the career, assisting with decision-making demands, helping with day-to-day activities, and encouraging (or even demanding) regular school learning. It is the perspective of women as a person linked to care. In Jatobá's narrative, the one who assumes this role is her grandmother: "She used to take the bus with me; she used to walk, so we would go to the square with the boys, and she would sit there. So yeah, she was someone who was always very present."

Mothers also stand out because, at first, they tended not to be enthusiastic about the possibility of their daughters being soccer players. Not because they considered that girls should not practice soccer, but because there was concern both with money and discrimination:

> My mother supported me too, but she was very afraid because she had no support. She dreamed of a career for me, I come from a humble family. My mother, my parents, they studied a little. My mother is a day laborer, she was a maid, and my father is also a domestic worker, so there is this concern with studies, with intellectual development, with a profession. So, if today it is already a little difficult, imagine back then? Myself, at the age of 10, saying that I wanted to be a soccer player, it was 1995. Imagine my mother's concern about what I would go through, both in terms of prejudice and money. (Oliveira, 2022)

Oliveira's speech is quite elucidative of this perspective of concern and care, especially for the material reality that involved the soccer career for women. This contrasts with the notion proposed by Araújo of players seeing soccer as a means of social ascension; for women, the sport could imply more a possibility of financial woes than one of social mobility. This also evidences their socio-economic background. Our interviewees belong to what Antunes (2009) named *class-who-lives-from-work*, aimed at giving contemporary validity to the Marxian concept of working class while considering the diversity of the jobs performed. They come from the middle or working classes.

Only one of the players' families did not play such a decisive role, even though in her childhood she played the sport with family members, but that was because Maravilha left home early and cut ties with her father—he was against her continuing her studies. Beyond family, however, players often establish or become part of a support network that boosts and assists their careers. For Maravilha it was a friend from the Landless Workers' Movement settlement who started to look for women's teams and gave her the opportunity to try out for a team in Porto Alegre, or other church pastor friends who took up a collection at a service and gave her part of the money. Oliveira mentions her mother's employer, responsible for helping her stay in college, where she continued playing futsal and improving her skills.

Agents in the sports field are also part of support networks. Oliveira remembers Dona Inês, manager of Campo Grande, one of the first teams where she played, who gave her food, rides, and accommodation. They developed a close relationship: "So, until today, for example, on Mother's Day I send her a message, on Christmas I send her a message. This is someone who has been with me since I was fifteen. Today I am thirty-seven. So, Dona Inês was indispensable. Along the same lines, other players mention male and female coaches who were fundamental in their trajectories. Aggio exemplifies this with the coaches of her first school: "My coaches gave me the opportunity to play in Zico's school, among the boys. Because if they had said 'no, we don't have women's soccer and Marina won't be able to play', I would not have pushed forward. These are the opportunities people give us."

The path taken by women to have soccer as their profession is far from being linear or progressive. The intention now is to understand, from the interviewees' narratives, the transition from soccer as leisure to soccer as work. All of them started to practice the sport when they were children, and when they became teenagers the first opportunities started to appear. It happened in different ways: Entrance in women's teams, either in the youth categories or in the main squads, scholarships, call-ups to the Brazilian National Team (Rocha was called up when she was 16 years old), competing in high level championships (Luizelli played her first Brazilian Cup when she was only 13 years old; Aggio played in the Paraná State Championship when she was 15; Moreno played in the Brazilian Futsal Championship when he was 15), took part in tryouts, changed positions to ensure a spot on a team (Maravilha tried to play as a forward, but when she realized she would be cut off she decided to play as a goalkeeper). It was at this moment of transition that the first financial gains happened. Initially, it was more like an allowance, without a safe and recurrent income:

> My first money was 50 Reais, as an athlete. We always played on weekends in the countryside of São Paulo, when I was 15, 16 years old. We would play there for a team called "Make Plans," and then they would pay the athletes. So, my first money as an athlete was to play on weekends. Every weekend, we earned 50 Reais. (Jatobá, 2022)
>
> I remember at the time that Cianorte [a soccer team from the Paraná state countryside] said: "come over, I will pay you 80 Reais for you to play for us." I said: "Mom, there is a team that wants me to play for them, they will give me 80 Reais." Back then, remember, 80 Reais was kind of all right. So, my mom said: "then go." I was 14 years old, and I got 80 Reais, I think. I said: "Mom, there are people wanting to pay to play, see?"
>
> My first Real was with the Brazilian National Team, and it was that Real, sweaty, limited. I know that people will say "it was years ago." Even still, it was not much. Yes, that is the truth. Even still, it was not much. (Oliveira, 2022)

Another element of this transitional phase is the realization that sport ceases to be a game and becomes a responsibility, which involves sacrifices and great responsibility with the body:

> I always had sports as something very important in my life. When I left my small town and went to Zico's school, I already had the responsibility of being an athlete. I already knew what my responsibilities were. I knew I had to sleep early, I knew I had to sleep well, I knew I had to be well rested. I knew I had to drink lots of water. I knew that to be an athlete, I had to give up some things and live others, and that is what I did. (Aggio, 2022)

> I think [it happened during] my first tryout, because I always imagined myself playing soccer. From the moment I decided that I wanted it, I took it very seriously, so I trained for myself. It was very serious about taking care of my body. I always studied far away, so if I had to leave home at 6:00 in the morning, I had to wake up at 5:30. In fact, I would wake up at 5:15, do a series of abdominal crunches, a series of squat thrusts, that sort of thing, and then take a shower and go to school. For me it was not a sacrifice, in fact, it was a single goal. (Oliveira, 2022)

The next phase of the making of a player is precisely the start as a professional: the arrival at a club that creates a labor bond with the athlete—not necessarily formalized with a work contract, a continuous salary and not only the occasional income, and the participation in official and institutionalized tournaments:

> When I went to play for Vasco, I realized that I was becoming a real player. That was in 1992. Look, it took me from '81 to '92, 11 years to kind of realize that I was starting a soccer career. Not that it was a conscious thing, though. It was not conscious for me because I worked, I was forced to work. Until then, when I was eighteen, I studied and played, and then I worked and played. And then, when I arrived at Vasco, there yes: you will get paid X, but it was not enough to survive. I had to work and play, but that was when I started to compete in the most important competitions of my life. They were the Brazilian futsal championships and the Brazilian field championships, called Taça Brasil. So, this turning point was when I started to play for Vasco. It was playing for Vasco that I started to actually earn a salary. "Man, I am doing my effort, doing my work, and I am getting paid." (Abreu, 2022)

> I played my first Paranaense [state championship] in 1999, for Londrina Futebol Clube. The [Zico's] academy coaches themselves started to look for places for me, so I was there from when I was 13, 14 years old, and at 15 I was already playing the Paranaense for Londrina Futebol Clube, which was a team that already had an organization in Paraná and competed in several places. At that time, we had a strong Paranaense and competed in Londrina, Maringá, Curitiba, Cascavel, Toledo, Foz do Iguaçu, and it was there that I started to enter my first professional competitions. Moving on, from there I went to São Paulo, because that is the focal point of women's soccer. Even today, it is São Paulo. I thought I had to leave Paraná to get something better. (Aggio, 2022)

Abreu's speech is significant because it shows that reaching the level of being a professional player could take many years—after all, she started playing in 1981, and only became a professional in 1992, when she arrived at Vasco da Gama. Again, it is necessary to consider the context of this pioneering generation, which built these new paths. And even when soccer became a job, it was not the only one, for in 1992 she still had to work in other places to make ends meet. Soon after, that changed, and Abreu began to live off soccer alone for a few years. She played for two clubs at the same time: Vasco, in Rio de Janeiro, and Sabesp, in São Paulo, as a futsal athlete. Aggio's trajectory shows that this start as a professional can happen early: for her, it was already at the age of 15. Another interesting element is the migration to another state, the search for better opportunities. As she herself pointed out, São Paulo was and is an especially important center for women's soccer in Brazil.

The migration of the athletes did not happen only within Brazil. As mentioned, six of the eight interviewees played in Europe. Emigration was a defining moment for them as players, because thanks to the better working conditions they found in European clubs when compared to Brazilian clubs, they felt professional and considered soccer as work. This is a consensus among all those who emigrated:

> I think when I signed my first contract abroad. I think when I arrived there and at Lyon, in France, and saw all that structure. I said "wow, I am really going to make a living out of soccer." […] In my point of view, the professional thing I had was outside Brazil. (Rocha, 2022)

> Ah, no doubt: when I went to Italy. I think that when I went to Italy I experienced very cool moments, because, like, a tournament structure that did not exist here in Brazil. Periodization of training, which was very amateurish back then. I would say that when I went to Italy at that time, we are talking about 30 years ago, soccer was "dilettante" in Italy. A dilettante would be somewhere between an amateur and a professional, because the girls, in this case in Italy, also worked or studied and we trained at evening, late hours. But in that case, I was already living off soccer, because I was a foreigner. (Luizelli, 2022)

> That is when I went to Sweden. Without a doubt. There is a very big transition from leaving Brazilian soccer and going to Sweden, because here I considered myself a professional, I did it as such, but the clubs did not have the structure to offer you that. […] So I left Brazil for Sweden, and it made me change gears. I had a house, I had a car, I had a professional life, the same thing that men have today. When you go to Europe you go there because there is a club that hired you, when you get there, your salary is already in your account, without you having to ask "for the love of God" for someone to pay you. (Aggio, 2022)

Rocha immigrated to play for Lyon, but then ended up playing in Italy, where she plays to this day:

> The milestone for me was when I made the leap from soccer to futsal. In people's minds, I was an unknown quantity. But in my mind, I always had a sure thing here. So, in my mind, I never had any doubts [...] So, I think that it was then I had greater recognition as an athlete in sports, because there I started to be valued. There I started to see teams coming after me all the time, there I started to see teams that changed the way they played because I was on the court. I began to see that in Italy I was creating roots as a player, you know? (Rocha, 2022)

The player points at two milestones in her trajectory to identify her professionalization. The first is precisely her departure to Europe. The second is another migration: this time to the courts. Rocha followed a tradition of Brazilian athletes moving between indoor and outdoor soccer. What is interesting about this second milestone is that it is linked to recognition, because she had already achieved structure and good working conditions at Lyon. The differential in Italy was to be individually recognized. In other words, the making of a player obviously considers material factors (salary, contract, working conditions, physical structure, specialized professionals, etc.), but it also considers subjective gains, such as recognition, that are present in different ways, even tactically, when the team is adapted to play according to the characteristics of a certain athlete.

Final Remarks

The regulation of women's soccer in Brazil in 1983 was an important achievement and paved the way for a long (and unfinished) process of structuring the sport, as well as for professional avenues for women in the sport. The construction of a soccer career is characterized by the athletes' actions in the development of their dreams/projects, and by the conditioning of both the social structure and the sports field.

It is fundamental to understand that *the making* of a player includes these two elements. When we looked at the trajectories and narratives of eight Brazilian players, we noticed that this process is not entirely individual or homogeneous, because they develop different strategies and achieve different results. Soccer as work also occurs in diverse ways depending on the context: the place, the club, and the other agents of the sports field involved. Similarities and continuities also permeate the careers of the interviewees, such as the precariousness of the work or its cyclical nature, the accordion effect.

Finally, it is necessary to consider the characteristics of the players' careers (short, unstable, short contracts, sacrifices, high concern and connection with the body, *embodied career*, and soccer as an element of identity), and to highlight the challenges arising from gender inequalities (acting in an environment of male hegemony in which women are systematically marginalized and subordinated) to effectively promote gender equity in the sports field.

REFERENCES

Oral Sources

AGGIO, Marina. **Marina Aggio**: interview [Sep 27, 2022]. Interviewer: Fernanda Haag. Digital document (1h37). Personal archive.

DE ABREU, Leda Maria. **Leda Maria de Abreu**: interview [October 23, 2022]. Interviewer: Fernanda Haag. Digital document (1h30). Personal archive.

JATOBÁ, Simone. **Simone Gomes Jatobá**: interview [October 31, 2022]. Interviewer: Fernanda Haag. Digital document (1h12). Personal archive.

LUIZELLI, Eduarda. **Eduarda Luizelli (Duda Luizelli)**: interview [October 24, 2022]. Interviewer: Fernanda Haag. Digital document (54 min). Personal archive.

MORENO, Thaisa R. M. **Thaisa R. M. Moreno**: interview [Nov. 3, 2022]. Interviewer: Fernanda Haag. Digital document (1h07). Personal archive.

OLIVEIRA, Carla S. **Carla Santos de Oliveira**: interview [Oct. 18, 2022]. Interviewer: Fernanda Haag. Digital document (1h38). Personal archive.

ROCHA, Dayane F. **Dayane Fátima da Rocha**: interview [Oct. 14, 2022]. Interviewer: Fernanda Haag. Digital document (1h19). Personal archive.

WAHLBRINK, Marlisa. **Marlisa Wahlbrink (Wonder)**: interview [Dec 5, 2022]. Interviewer: Fernanda Haag. Digital document (1h35). Personal archive.

Bilbliography

ALBERTI, V. **Manual de História Oral** (Manual of Oral History). 3. ed. Rio de Janeiro: Editora FGV, 2013.

ANTUNES, R. **Os Sentidos do Trabalho** (The Meanings of Work)**.** Ensaio sobre a afirmação e a negação do trabalho. 2. ed. São Paulo: Boitempo, 2009.

ARAÚJO, Ricardo Benzaquen De. **Os gênios da pelota**: um estudo do futebol como profissão (The Geniuses of the Ball: A Study of Football as a Profession). 1980. 100 f. UFRJ, Rio de Janeiro, 1980.

ASTRUC, C. O futebol como profissão: origem, ascensão social e o mundo do trabalho dos futebolistas brasileiros (1950–1980) (Football as a Profession: Origin, Social Mobility, and the World of Work for Brazilian Football Players (1950–1980)). In: HOLLANDA, B. B.; FONTES, P. (Orgs.). **Futebol & mundos do trabalho no Brasil**. Rio de Janeiro: EdUERJ, 2021.

CULVIN, A. **Football as work**: the lived realities of professional women footballers in England. 420 f. 2019. Thesis (PhD in Philosophy)—School of Sport and Wellbeing, University of Central Lancashire, 2019.

DAMO, Arlei Sander. **Do dom à profissão**: uma etnografia do futebol espetáculo a partir da formação de jogadores do Brasil e na França (From Gift to Profession: An Ethnography of Spectacle Football Based on Player Development in Brazil and France). Tese (Doutorado)–Universidade Federal do Rio Grande do Sul, 2005.

FIFPro World Players' Union. **Global Employment Report**: Working Conditions in Professional Women's Football: Hoofdddorp, Netherlands, 2017.

GOELLNER, Silvana Vilodre. Mulheres e futebol no Brasil: entre sombras e visibilidades (Women and Football in Brazil: Between Shadows and Visibility). **Revista Brasileira de Educação Física e Esporte**, v. 19, n. 2, pp. 143–151, 2005.

GOELLNER, S. V.; CABRAL, J. R. **As pioneiras do futebol pedem passagem**: conhecer para reconhecer (The Pioneers of Women's Football Demand a Place: Knowing to Recognize). São Paulo: Editora Ludopédio, 2022.

HOLLANDA, B. B.; FONTES, P. Introdução (Introduction). In: HOLLANDA, B. B.; FONTES, P. (Org.). **Futebol & mundos do trabalho no Brasil**. Rio de Janeiro: EdUERJ, 2021.

HOLLANDA, B. B. B.; RIBEIRO, R. R. História Oral, prática futebolística e cidades no Brasil: conflitos e apropriações nas narrativas de ocupação dos campos de "futebol de várzea" de Belo Horizonte (Oral History, Football Practices, and Cities in Brazil: Conflicts and Appropriations in Narratives About the Use of "Várzea Football" Fields in Belo Horizonte). **História Oral**, v. 22, n. 2, pp. 33–57, 2019.

HOLLANDA, H. B. **Explosão Feminista**: arte, cultura, política e universidade (Feminist Explosion: Art, Culture, Politics, and University). São Paulo: Companhia das Letras, 2018.

KESSLER, Cláudia Samuel. **Mais que Barbies e Ogras**: uma Etnografia do Futebol de Mulheres no Brasil e nos Estados Unidos (More Than Barbies and Ogres: An Ethnography of Women's Football in Brazil and the United States). Tese (Doutorado)—Universidade Federal do Rio Grande do Sul, 2015.

MCGILLIVRAY, David; FEARN, Richard; MCINTOSH, Aaron. Caught up in and by the beautiful game: A case study of Scottish professional footballers. **Journal of Sport and Social Issues**, v. 29, n. 1, pp. 102–123, 2005.

MOURÃO, Ludmila; MOREL, Marcia. As Narrativas Sobre O Futebol Feminino (What Makes Oral History Different). **Revista Brasileira de Ciências do Esporte**, v. 26, n. 2, 2005.

PEREIRA, L. A. M. **Footballmania**: Uma História Social do Futebol no Rio de Janeiro (Footballmania: A Social History of Football in Rio de Janeiro (1902–1938)). Rio de Janeiro: Nova Fronteira, 2000.

PORTELLI, Alessandro. O que faz a história oral diferente (What Makes Oral History Different). **Projeto História**, v. 14, n. fev., pp. 25–39, 1997.

PORTELLI, A. **História Oral como a Arte da Escuta** (Oral History as the Art of Listening). São Paulo: Letra e Voz, 2016.

RODERICK, Martin. **The Work of Professional Football. A labor of love?** London: Routledge, 2006.

SANTOS, J. M.C. M. **Revolução Vascaína**: a profissionalização do futebol e a inserção sócio-econômica de negros e portugueses na cidade do Rio de Janeiro (1915–1934) (Vasco Revolution: The Professionalization of Football and the Socioeconomic Integration of Black People and Portuguese in the City of Rio de Janeiro (1915–1934)). Tese (Doutorado)—Universidade de São Paulo, 2010.

SILVA, Giovana Capucim. **Narrativas sobre o futebol feminino na imprensa paulista**: entre a proibição e a regulamentação (1965–1983) (Narratives About Women's Football in São Paulo Press: Between Prohibition and Regulation (1941–1983)). Dissertação (Mestrado)—Universidade de São Paulo, 2015.

THOMPSON, E. P. **A formação da classe operária inglesa**. A árvore da liberdade (The Making of the English Working Class). 6. ed. São Paulo: Paz e Terra, 2011.

TONINI, Marcel Diego. **Dentro e fora de outros gramados**: histórias orais de vida de futebolistas brasileiros negros no continente europeu (On and Off Other Fields: Oral Life Histories of Black Brazilian Footballers in Europe). Tese (Doutorado)—Universidade de São Paulo, 2016.

CHAPTER 5

Press Narratives on the Participation of Women's National Teams in the FIFA World Cups[1]

Leda Costa, Ronaldo Helal, and Gustavo Fernandes

2007 Women's World Cup and the 2008 Olympic Games: Denunciation, Fear, and Talent

In terms of the history of the relationship between the media and women's football, the 2023 World Cup occupies a unique place in Brazil. The event received robust media coverage, especially from Grupo Globo, the country's largest media conglomerate, which broadcasted on public-access channels matches not only from the Brazilian team but also from the knockout stages of the competition.[2] As well as being exhaustive, there is not enough space here to undertake an in-depth study of the sports journalism coverage of the Brazilian women's team's participation in World Cups and Olympic Games, the two main competitions in which the national team takes part.[3]

Brazil has taken part in all nine editions of the FIFA Women's World Cup and all editions of the Olympic Games since the sport was included in this event. In both competitions, Brazil has never won the title, but some of its defeats have been notable and have gained media coverage, and the meanings attributed to these defeats have undergone a significant change in the 2023 World Cup. Until

1. This study was funded by CNPQ—National Council for Scientific and Technological Development. Process number 421784/2021-0

2. Rede Globo carried out multiplatform coverage of the 2023 World Cup, involving public-access TV, cable TV, and digital channels. During the event, the broadcaster put together a team of around 200 professionals including reporters, narrators, commentators, producers and cameramen working outside and inside its studios. In the 2019 World Cup, Rede Globo broadcast only the Brazilian team's matches on public-access TV.

3. The team also takes part in the Copa America, a competition in which they have won eight times out of the nine editions, and the Pan American Games, in which they have won eight gold medals.

then, there had been a peaceful coexistence in the face of significant defeats by the women's national team, so a change in the way this type of result is narrated points to alterations in the meanings of the national team and of women's football itself in Brazil.

This article aims to briefly analyze the narratives of the Brazilian women's football team's defeats at the 2008 Olympic Games and the 2007 and 2023 World Cups. To this end, the coverage of the newspapers *O Globo* and *Folha de São Paulo* will be focused on. These newspapers were chosen because they are traditional vehicles with national circulation and because access to their collections available is available through the internet.[4] The criterion for choosing these competitions is guided by reasons related to the aforementioned uniqueness of the 2023 World Cup and the fact that the national team reached the finals of the respective competitions in 2007 and 2008,[5] a relevant issue if we consider some of the specificities of sports culture in Brazil.

The possibility of winning titles is a relevant factor for sports media in Brazil to pay attention to sports other than just men's football (Guedes, 2023). In 2007 and 2008, the women's national football team consecutively reached the final of a World Cup and competed for a gold medal, which was newsworthy enough to lead the team to occupy more space than usual at the time on the sports pages of newspapers such as *O Globo* and *Folha de São Paulo*. In 2007, the expectation of an unprecedented triumph was sustained, above all, after Brazil beat the US in the semifinal of the World Cup. Defeating one of the biggest powers in women's football by an elastic 4–0 score led the *Folha de São Paulo* outlet to use superlative tones to create the headline "*Seleção* shines and humiliates the Americans" (September 28, 2007). *O Globo* attributed to Marta the role of conductor of a victory considered spectacular by the newspaper (September 28, 2007). However, the team lost the World Cup final to Germany.

Despite this negative result, the women's team managed to escape the harsh treatment given by the sports media to teams that are defeated in the finals of football competitions, which is often the case when it comes to the men's team

[4] Access to these archives is available through subscriptions to both newspapers. It is worth emphasizing the importance of studies that focus on media narratives produced by outlets exclusively dedicated to women's football or that are not linked to the main media corporations in Brazil (Januário, 2020; Fon, 2022; Souza et al., 2023).

[5] It is worth mentioning a historically important defeat for the national team, which occurred in the semifinal of the 2016 Olympic Games at the Maracanã stadium. However, we chose to focus on defeats in championship finals and the 2023 tournament due to the unprecedented context of the competition.

(Costa, 2020).[6] The analyses made of the defeat to the German team postulated that the result on the pitch was a reflection of the unfavorable conditions facing women's football in Brazil. Both newspapers adopted a denunciatory perspective, warning of the lack of care with which the women's team—and the sport as a whole—was treated by the Brazilian Football Confederation. The day after the match against Germany, *Folha de São Paulo* declared: "Germany makes Brazilian women wake up."

This headline pointed to the need to look at the reality of women's football in Brazil, which is marked by a lack of support and structure for the sport (*Folha de São Paulo*, October 1, 2007). While, according to the newspaper, Germany was investing in women's football, what we saw in Brazil was neglect and abandonment from the sporting authorities. The newspaper *O Globo* strengthened its denunciatory approach by reporting the defeat as follows: "Girls ask for help," a phrase that refers to a banner produced by the players themselves and which was shown to the public when they stood on the podium to receive their runners-up medal. The banner read: "Brazil, we need support" (*O Globo*, October 1, 2007).[7]

In addition to the aim of alerting the public and the authorities, the emphasis on the precariousness of women's football can also be understood as an integral part of a type of approach that made it possible to trigger emotions in the construction of journalistic discourse, which is common practice in much of the sports press in Brazil (Oselame, 2013). Some communication theorists have drawn attention to the fact that narrative structures interfere in the process of converting an event into news (Schudson, 2010; Traquina, 1999). As Gaye Tuchman (1999) said, "being a reporter who deals with facts and being a storyteller who produces stories are not antithetical activities."

This is not to equate journalistic reports with fiction, but only to emphasize the possibility of thinking of journalistic practice as an activity that makes frequent use of narrative formulas, since reporting something implies selecting facts that need to be ordered in a sequence that gives them meaning. In Brazil,

6. The men's national football team's defeats at the World Cup often provoke controversy and lengthy analyses that seek the answer to the question "Why did Brazil lose." This question is usually answered by choosing a villain, i.e., a player or coach whom we consider to be to blame for the defeat.

7. This episode was recalled in the article "The World Cup in which Brazil charmed the world, but begged for support," written by journalists Laís Malek and Tatiana Furtado and published on the GE.com portal. This article reports that the banner raised by the players caused unease within the CBF, with direct consequences for the career of defender Daiane Bagé, who would only be called up to the national team again four years later (available at: https://oglobo.globo.com/esportes/noticia/2023/06/relembre-a-copa-em-que-o-brasil-encantou-o-mundo-mas-implorou-por-apoio.ghtml).

this process of selection and ordering follows the tendency to produce effects of dramatization of the narrated facts obtained from narrative strategies that use emotion to provoke it in readers and consumers of sports news (Costa, 2020).

In the case of women's football, fear and despair were basic emotions in the narratives of the two remarkable defeats in question, and they dovetailed very well with the scenario of misfortunes presented in the form of denunciations by the newspapers, as shown earlier. These feelings were represented by images of crying, especially that of Marta, the team's main player. In 2008, the lack of financial support featured prominently in analyses of Brazil's defeat to the US in the gold medal match at the Olympic Games in China. At the time, the shot of Marta with her hands on her face and a body expression of despair very similar to that of the figure in Edvard Munch's painting *The Scream* was printed on the front page of the newspaper *O Globo* (August 22, 2008) and reproduced in the sports section of *Folha de São Paulo* (August 22, 2008). According to these newspapers, the gesture indicated not only sadness at the defeat itself but also the fact that Marta had stated on several occasions that winning such a title would be fundamental for the women's team to gain legitimacy and greater support from the Brazilian Football Confederation.

Still on the subject of the 2008 defeat, in the sports section of *O Globo,* an article by Gilberto Scofield Jr., the newspaper's correspondent in Beijing, describes the moment when Marta, just after the final whistle of the match against the US, raised her head toward heaven and asked God what she had done wrong to justify losing the gold medal (*O Globo*, August 21, 2008). For the reporter, it was a clear demonstration of the player's despondency in the face of yet another defeat in a championship final. A photo of Marta lying on the pitch and crying accompanies the report (*O Globo*, August 21, 2008). Goalkeeper Bárbara, who at the time played for the national team without any club ties, vented her frustration by saying that football in Brazil did not offer players the conditions to survive (*Folha de São Paulo*, August 22, 2008, D3).

More than sadness at the defeat, the players' tears represented fear of an uncertain future, as we can see on the front page of *Folha de São Paulo,* which announced the team's silver medal by showing a photograph of players Maycon and Pretinha crying with their heads down on the podium (*Folha de São Paulo*, August 22, 2008). This fear would be in relation to the future of women's football in Brazil, an absolutely justifiable feeling if we consider that the sporting culture in Brazil—with the exception of men's football—is very dependent on winning significant titles (Guedes, 2023). Sports that do not have a winning tradition tend to fall by the wayside or even into the indifference of the public and the sports media. This issue will be revisited in the following.

As well as fear, the issue of the players' talent was emphasized. According to the newspapers selected here, the players' talent for playing the ball is what made it possible for the national team to reach important stages of competitions. In 2007, this aspect was highlighted in the newspaper *O Globo,* which attributed the players' ability to be the only reason they won second place in a World Cup, considering that in Brazil there were not even properly organized championships capable of occupying an entire year's sports calendar (October 1, 2007). In this competition, the team included Marta, who had been voted the best player in the world by FIFA the previous year, and Cristiane, who had come third in the same award.[8]

As an explanation for the defeat, *Folha de São Paulo* emphasized that Germany's focus on collective play had surpassed the individual skill of the Brazilian team (*Folha de São Paulo*, 2007). In 2008, *Folha de São Paulo* followed the same logic of thought and published an article in which it emphasized that the team's defeat to the US in the final of the competition was due to the US team's ability to play collectively and defensively, which would have prevented the individual talent of the Brazilian players from leading the team to victory (*Folha de São Paulo*, August, 22, 2008).

The talent attributed to the players is a relevant factor in the press' representation of the women's national team and, in this sense, Marta is the one who manages to capitalize on much of the praise (Moreira, 2013). Exalting the ability of the players points to the possibility of constructing narratives of athletes overcoming obstacles to reach important competitions even without the necessary support. In 2006, when Marta was honored by FIFA for the first time as the best female player in the world, *O Globo* described her achievement as "Victory over a country's sexism. The best in the world left home at 14 to play football" (Rodrigues, 2006). The following day, the same narrative followed, "Number 1 in overcoming barriers [...] Behind the fragile figure of 1.61m is the strength of the poor, underprivileged Brazilian woman who only relies on her own talent and sweat" (Gueiros, 2006).

8. Marta was voted FIFA's best player in 2007 and Cristiane Rozeira de Souza Silva, or simply Cristiane, came third. The following year they both won the same award.

However, even if this is not necessarily the aim of the sports media, the exaltation of talent allows the possibility of deconstructing the assumption that football in Brazil is only for men. Although they have not yet won a title of international importance, such as the world championship or an Olympic gold, a large part of the sports media supports the view that the Brazilian women's team is capable of embodying "football-art," a category so dear to the identity of Brazilian football.[9] In this area of the ability to play "football-art," it must be reiterated that the spotlight is on Marta, especially after her consecutive wins of the World Player of the Year award.[10] In 2018, when Marta won this award for the sixth time, journalist Juca Kfouri said in a chronicle that there is "Nobody who plays football and was born in Brazil with the mastery of all the fundamentals of the game like Marta. Nobody!" (Kfouri, 2018, p. B7).

Even without being a starter, Marta was the protagonist of the coverage of the 2023 World Cup, a competition for which the national team could count on a strong incentive from the Brazilian Football Confederation. It was Marta's last World Cup and, once again, the women's team failed to win the title, leaving the competition prematurely. However, unlike in previous years, a significant defeat was received in a less patient manner. This kind of reception could point to important changes in the meanings attributed to the national team and to women's football in general.

2023 World Cup, Expectation and Disappointment

In recent decades, there have been many questions and protests about sexism in the national football environment, which reverberated on social media networks and are often supported by marketing actions by various Brazilian clubs (Bertoncello, 2022). At an organizational level, former player Aline Peregrino stands out. She became the director of the sport at the São Paulo Football Federation and, during her tenure, managed to reinvigorate the championships and teams. We can highlight the actions of groups of female fans who, on social media and in the stands, demanded respect and safety from harassment (Bandeira, 2019; Pinto, 2022).

9. On the football-art category, see Hollanda, 2004; Helal and Soares, 2003.

10. Marta won the World Player of the Year award in 2006, 2007, 2008, 2009, 2010, and 2018.

The same kind of gesture can be seen in sports newsrooms in initiatives such as the video manifesto "Let Her Work," that in 2018 united fifty-two journalists who work in sport, including presenters, reporters, producers, and advisors (Meirelles, 2022). It is worth highlighting the emergence of communication channels focused exclusively on news about women's football, such as the ESPNW portal in 2016 and the Brazilian portal *Dibradoras*, created in 2015 (Fon, 2022; Gonçalves, 2021).

In traditional television media, there is a greater presence of women narrating, commentating and acting as reporters in various football championships. Many of these changes are the result of demands that have arisen in Brazilian society. It would not be an exaggeration to say that a kind of "football feminism" has emerged in Brazil over the last ten years, which means that football has been an important arena for debate, visibility and the promotion of actions linked to issues of gender equality and its intersectional aspects, not restricted to the sport, but which resonates in society as a whole.[11]

The 2019 World Cup was the first to be broadcast by Rede Globo, the country's main television channel, which for some years held a monopoly on football broadcasting rights in Brazil (Santos, 2013). However, this same broadcaster gave little space to women's football in its programming schedule, which is an aspect that has changed. The possible reasons for this transformation are part of a broad context of significant changes in the scenario of sports broadcasting rights in Brazil, in which Rede Globo is facing the threat of losing its hegemony (Santos, 2021).[12]

In addition, platforms such as YouTube and Twitter have been reconfiguring the map of sports broadcasting in Brazil. The 2023 World Cup, for example, was broadcast by Cazé TV, a *streaming* channel that is considered a popular phenomenon in Brazil and has won the right to broadcast important championships (Balacó, 2023).[13] In this context, Rede Globo is trying to adapt to the demands of

[11] The term feminism is used in its broadest sense to encompass demands related to struggles for gender equality in various spheres of society. Many women's football movements do not call themselves feminists, not least because it is a word that has become the target of negativity, especially after the rise of the far right in Brazil with the government of Jair Bolsonaro (2018–2022).

[12] This phenomenon has been developing since the beginning of the COVID-19 pandemic, driven, among other reasons, by the explosion of streaming consumption in Brazil and the change in the legislation on sports broadcasting rights, with the approval of Law 14.205 (BRASIL, 2021), known as the Principal's Law, which boosted the pulverization of sports broadcasting rights.

[13] Cazé TV is the result of a partnership between LiveMode (a media and sports marketing company that manages various sports rights in Brazil) and the streamer Casimiro Miguel, known as Cazé. Cazé TV currently has more than eight million subscribers on YouTube.

an audience, especially young people, who want to consume a variety of sports and are no longer restricted to the "malestream" football (Moreira, 2014) that we were used to. On the other hand, this broadcaster has also shown itself to be attentive to the demands of Brazilian society in general and of female footballers.

Another aspect is the gradual demonstration of the potential of women's football as a sporting spectacle that attracts fans and consumers, a fact that was evident at the 2007 Pan American Games when the women's team won the championship by beating the US in the Maracanã stadium with an estimated crowd of 67,788 people.[14] In 2016, in the same stadium, around 72,000 people watched the semifinal of women's football at the Olympic Games between the Brazilian and Swedish teams.[15] In 2022, the final of the Brazilian women's championship brought a crowd of 41,070 to the Corinthians stadium, a record surpassed in 2023 in the same stadium, which welcomed 42,566 people.[16] In 2019, the Brazil–France match had a record audience of thirty-five million viewers, and was symbolically relevant as it was narrated by Galvão Bueno, one of Brazil's most popular sports narrators in the country (Januário et al., 2020).

The broadcaster's participation in this process was—and is—very relevant as it is the most watched public-access TV channel in the country and is part of the largest media and communications conglomerate not only in Brazil but in Latin America. As a result, women's football gained visibility both in advertising and in Grupo Globo's news programs, including the exclusive sports channels on cable TV. The 2019 World Cup represented a valuable moment in the insertion of Brazilian women's football into a sports–media–commercial complex already consolidated in men's football (Maguire, 2011).

These facts certainly do not mean that Rede Globo has built a journalism that favors the equal participation of men and women in sports coverage (Bueno and Marques, 2020). In addition, sexism and misogyny are far from leaving the football scene in Brazil, as shown by data from the Observatory of Racial

14. According to an article by Debora Gares in the newspaper *O Globo*: "Goals and emotion at the Maracanã on a historic day. Champions are disarmed by a crowd of 67,000, the third largest in women's football" (*O Globo*, Rio2007, June 27, 2007, p. 9).

15. Source: http://rededoesporte.gov.br/pt-br/noticias/brasil-para-na-marcacao-da-suecia-perde-nos-penaltis-e-adia-o-sonho-do-ouro

16. In 2002, the final was between Corinthians (from São Paulo) and Internacional (Rio Grande do Sul) (Source: Fabbri, Beatriz. Corinthians women's Brazilian champions 2022: what it was like (September 24, 2022; available at: https://www.dci.com.br/esporte/brasileirao/corinthians-feminino-campeao-brasileiro-2022-como-foi-a-conquista/272942/). In 2023, the final was Corinthians (from São Paulo) vs. Ferroviária (from São Paulo) and the attendance was 42,566 (Source: https://noticias.uol.com.br/ultimas-noticias/agencia-brasil/2023/09/10/corinthians-vence-ferroviaria-e-leva-o-brasileiro-feminino-pela-5-vez.htm).

Discrimination and the *Canarinhos* LGBTQIA+ collective.[17] It is worth remembering that according to data from the Brazilian Public Safety Yearbook, in 2022, for example, one woman was murdered every six hours.[18] It is in this context, and in spite of it, that women's football is moving forward, still surrounded by difficulties and prejudices, but we must recognize that there are important and promising changes to look out for. This aspect is evident in the coverage in the newspapers *O Globo* and *Folha de São Paulo of* the national team's participation in the 2023 World Cup.

It was necessary to wait until 2023 for the women's team to have a roof over their heads, to refer to the famous phrase by Virginia Woolf (2014). As well as having a robust media structure, the 2023 World Cup did not have to compete for attention with another major tournament in which the men's team also took part, as is usually the case with the Olympic Games and the 2019 World Cup.[19] In addition to this, since 2020, the CBF has equalized the amount of per diem and prize money received by the men's and women's national teams while they are at the service of the Brazilian national team. In 2023, the women's team competed in football's most important competition with the partnership of nineteen brands in three sponsorship categories.[20] Marta was the protagonist of several marketing campaigns and for the sixth time was called up to play in what would probably be her last World Cup.

Until then, the real vulnerability of the sport, which had been banned for forty years, allowed for a narrative characterized by the tears of defeat and the fear caused by doubts about the future not only of the national team but of women's football itself. To this kind of perspective, the exaltation of the ability to play the ball, praise that allowed the focus to be on the overcoming of so many obstacles faced by the players, was added. However, in 2023, it would be narratively unrealistic to persist with this type of interpretation because, although women's football is still in the process of being built, the national team has had time to train and prepare for the World Cup, with Pia Sundhage, who has a winning

17. Report on racial discrimination in football 2021. 8th report on racial discrimination in football (available at: RELATORIO_DISCRIMINACAO_RACIAL_2021.pdf (observatorioracialfutebol.com.br). *10 clubs went on trial for homophobia at the STJD in 2022* (available at: https://canarinhoslgbtq.com.br/10-clubes-foram-a-julgamento-por-homofobia-no-stjd-em-2022/).

18. *Brazilian Public Safety Yearbook* 2022 (available at: https://forumseguranca.org.br/wp-content/uploads/2023/07/anuario-2023.pdf)

19. In 2019, almost at the same time as the Women's Cup, the Men's Copa América was held in Brazil.

20. Master sponsors: Nike, Guaraná Antarctica, Vivo, Itaú, and Neoenergia; Official sponsors: Cimed, Free Fire, Gol, Kavak, Kwai, Mastercard, Pague Menos, Rappi, TCL Semp, and Zé Delivery. Supporters: Três Corações, Technogym, STATSports, and Globus Italian Excellence.

record to her name, at the head of the coaching staff. Women's football has been gradually strengthened in Brazil, with organized competitions and with the support of important clubs in the country, such as Corinthians. There is certainly a lot of room for improvement, but we no longer have the scorched earth scenario of 2007 and 2008.

With greater financial support, accompanied by an unprecedented media apparatus (Januário et al., 2020), expectations were high for a good performance in the competition. However, elimination came sooner than expected and this time the defeat was received differently. Instead of a sympathetic tone, the narratives of the 2023 World Cup defeat were based on questioning and criticizing the performance on the pitch. As has been said, sports journalism narratives in Brazil tend to be guided by the expression of emotions, and if, until now, fear had been the keynote of the reception of notable defeats, such as those in 2007 and 2008, in the case of the team's elimination from the 2023 World Cup, the emotion that guided the media reception was disappointment. Furthermore, for the first time, a villainous figure was depicted, embodied in coach Pia Sundhage, who was blamed for the team's elimination from that World Cup.

Brazil's elimination took up about a quarter of the front page of *O Globo,* which featured an image of Marta waving her hand as if she were saying goodbye, followed by the headline *No adeus de Marta, anatomia de uma decepção* (At Marta's farewell, anatomy of a disappointment) (August 3, 2023). In the sports section, almost an entire page is dedicated to telling the story of Marta's career through an infographic illustrated with iconic scenes of her playing for the national team. Starting with her first participation in a World Cup, the infographic highlights the awards she won for best player in the world, the records she achieved, such as in 2019, when she became the highest scorer in World Cups, and in 2023, the moment of her "melancholic farewell," called as such by the newspaper because it occurred after the national team was eliminated in the first phase of the competition. A defeat which, however, according to the newspaper, would not have been enough to erase the player's history in the national team (August 3, 2023).

On the last page of the section in question, a photo of the players Adriana and Debinha appeared at the top, with their faces showing a sense of disbelief at being eliminated against Jamaica. In the caption for this image, the word chosen to describe the situation was "Disappointment" (August 3, 2023). The premature exit from the World Cup was highlighted and the poor quality of the Brazilian women's football was criticized as a determining factor in their downfall (August 3, 2023). According to the article, despite the obstacles that could still weigh them down, it had been a defeat on the pitch, of a technical nature, in which the team had played poorly, without any demonstration of individual talent.[21] In the same article, in the words of *O Globo*, coach Pia Sundhage was responsible for a large part of the team's problems, because since she was hired in 2019, the Swede had been unable to get the team to play in a safe and convincing manner (*O Globo*, p. 31).

The newspaper reiterates this opinion, using a statement by Rafaelle, who said: "If there is someone with more condition, with more quality, women's football deserves it" (August 3, 2023). At the end of the page, there are some brief comments from Carlos Eduardo Mansur, Marcelo Barreto and Martin Fernandez, regular columnists for the newspaper and renowned sports journalists in Brazil. The former alarmingly mentions the fact that Brazil had been eliminated by a team, Jamaica, which had to resort to *crowdfunding to* go to the World Cup (August 3, 2023).[22] Marcelo Barreto was surprised by the elimination, especially in the face of a team that was inferior in several respects, which was reflected in the fact that Jamaica was forty-third in the FIFA rankings (August 3, 2023). Finally, Martín Fernandez said that the team's campaign in the World Cup was disappointing, and compared it to the performance of other South American and African teams, whose structures in their countries are inferior to Brazil's, but who managed to qualify in their respective groups (August 3, 2023).

In *Folha de São Paulo,* Brazil's elimination was reported on the front page of the newspaper with the headline, "Brazil falls and loses Marta" as a reference to the fact that the player had played for the last time in a World Cup (August 3, 2023). In the "2023 World Cup" section, a photograph of Marta waving goodbye is placed above the headline "Marta says goodbye to the national team as Brazil is eliminated from the World Cup" (August 3, 2023). The sub-headline highlights what it considers to have been the most disappointing World Cup campaign for Brazil since 1995.[23] Just as in O *Globo*'s accounts of the defeat, Marta is the predominant figure in *Folha de São Paulo*'s images and texts throughout the coverage of the competition, and especially in the team's last match. In the "2023 World Cup" section, Marta is the protagonist of the analysis of the match against Jamaica.

21. It is important to remember that Marta was a reserve for most of the matches.

22. Available at: https://theathletic.com/4652279/2023/06/29/jamaica-womens-world-cup/

23. In 1995, the Brazilian team came ninth in the World Cup in Sweden.

It emphasizes the player's dedication: even though she only played from the second half onward, in the minutes she was on the pitch, Marta had tried everything, playing in several different positions and being sought out excessively by her teammates. The newspaper offers a list of the player's achievements in the national team, such as the number of goals for Brazil, the number of goals in World Cups, and Olympic and Pan American medals (August 3, 2023). In the same issue, it is worth noting the two columns written by two of the country's most renowned sports journalists, Paulo Vinícius Coelho and Juca Kfouri.

According to Paulo Vinícius Coelho, the elimination of the women's team was due to technical and, above all, emotional reasons. For the journalist, the team played poorly, but the psychological component would have been predominant in the game against Jamaica, since all the players knew they were being watched by the whole of Brazil, unlike in previous World Cups (*Folha de São Paulo*, August 3, 2023). This interpretation points to the possible consequences of high media visibility on the psychological state of the athletes, a concern that has drawn attention to some research carried out in Brazil (Rubio, 2000; Morão, 2020; Verzani, 2017). It is worth noting here that the 2023 World Cup was the first time that the Brazilian women's national team received professional psychological support, although this type of specialized support is not common throughout athletic training. Recent studies show a high incidence of *burnout* in the main ranks of Brazilian women's football, and part of this phenomenon is related to the increased amount of training and competitions to which players have been exposed, without the proper monitoring by a team of psychologists (Rinaldi, 2020).

Juca Kfouri, for his part, opted for a more blunt criticism, emphasizing the feeling of disappointment caused by the team's elimination. According to the journalist, the women's national team had frustrated the expectations of the fans, who had expected much more than what was achieved (August 3, 2023). For Juca Kfouri, coach Pia Sundhage had made a mistake in setting up the team's tactical scheme, above all by not favoring the presence of Marta who, according to him, in her last World Cup deserved a more honorable farewell. At the end of the article, the journalist says that a draw against Jamaica was "unthinkable" and that the elimination was just as painful as that of the men's team in 2022 (*Folha de São Paulo*, August 3, 2023).

A few observations are in order here. Although Juca Kfouri showed his anger at the national team's elimination, it is worth noting that this journalist, who is very well known in Brazil, barely touched on the 2023 World Cup, at least in the chronicles published between July 19 and August 3, precisely the period that encompasses the national team's participation in the competition.

On the eve of the Brazilian national team's debut, his column was dedicated to the match between the clubs São Paulo and Corinthians, valid for the semifinal of the *Copa do Brasil* (Brazil Cup), a men's competition.[24] On July 24, the Brazilian national team's opening match, Juca Kfouri wrote about the performance of Botafogo, a club from Rio de Janeiro that, at the time, was leading the country's main men's football championship.[25] To comment on Brazil's defeat to France, Juca Kfouri turned to memories of the men's team's defeats to the French throughout World Cup history. The journalist focused exclusively on the 2023 World Cup and the women's team on just two occasions, on July 20 when the tournament started and on August 3, after the team's elimination. In the case of the latter, as has been said, there was strong criticism of the team's performance in the draw against Jamaica and an assessment that the result had been disappointing. However, the question remains as to how it is possible to make a judgement about the participation of the women's national team in a World Cup if the team and the competition in which it participates are rarely analyzed.

In this respect, Juca Kfouri is no exception, at least when it comes to *Folha de São Paulo*'s coverage of the 2023 World Cup. This newspaper, one of the largest in Brazil, ran a small "World Cup 2023" section that did not take up a whole page, even on days when the national team was playing. *Folha*'s approach was less economical than its coverage of the 2019 World Cup, for which it did not even create a special section to report on the event and the national team's participation. However, it would be incorrect to say that the newspaper tends to neglect the women's national football team; after all, at the 2016 Olympic Games, *Folha* gave more space to women's football than men's football, which is noteworthy given that the competition was held in Brazil and featured celebrity player Neymar, in which the men's team won the gold medal (Costa, 2019). However, when it comes to the World Cup, at least since 2019, *Folha de São Paulo has* paid little attention to this competition. And this statement is modelled on another national newspaper, *O Globo*.

There is one factor that most likely influenced this phenomenon. As of 2019, the Women's World Cup had its broadcasting rights bought by Rede Globo. Holding the broadcasting rights is a factor that, to a large extent, explains the abundant attention given by the newspaper *O Globo*—which is part of the same

24. Kfouri, Majestáticos Majestosos. There's a lack of superlatives for the games that will qualify Corinthians or São Paulo for the final of the Copa do Brasil (*Folha de São Paulo*, July 23, 2023).

25. Kfouri, Botafogo, Botafogo, champion since...(*Folha de São Paulo*, July 24, 2023).

television conglomerate—to the 2019 and 2023 World Cups, the latter of which is the subject of this analysis. On the eve of Brazil's opening match in 2023, the newspaper published a special section exclusively dedicated to the World Cup. It announced: "The biggest World Cup in history. A project in the making. Brazil is heading for a promising future at the Women's World Cup!" (July 23, 2023) and throughout its eight pages, data and expectations surrounding the competition, the main teams and the players are shown.

Obviously, the Brazilian national team is the one that arouses the most interest, and it is worth highlighting the publication of advertising for the national team starring female players, including an entire page dedicated to advertising for Itaú bank, one of the main sponsors of the Brazilian Football Confederation. The national team's opening match takes up a considerable amount of space on the front page of the newspaper, featuring a sequence of four images showing one of Ary Borges' goals, which the newspaper calls a "masterpiece" (July 24, 2023).[26]

The coverage generally provides information on other national teams, as well as raising important issues such as allegations of sexual abuse involving some players from Zambia and Haiti who suffered harassment in their national teams.[27] Journalists Tatiana Furtado and Lais Melek were in charge of producing a variety of articles, as well as opinion pieces, which means that the narratives were not just the responsibility of men who say very little about women's football throughout the year. The main story about the team's elimination against Jamaica was written by Tatiana Furtado, who put forward the opinion that the team had played badly on the pitch, with no tactical variation and an inability to beat Jamaica's defense.

According to the journalist, the responsibility fell on Pia Sundhage, who had failed to give the team a tactical standard (*O Globo*, August 3, 2023). Laís Malek, on the other hand, evaluates the players' performances at the World Cup in order to make a judgement on which players might or might not remain in the squad. Unlike the defeats of 2007 and 2008, the future no longer provokes fear and anguish at the possibility of the sport's demise, but rather fuels speculation of renewal. The presence of women acting as the ones who build stories and analyses is a strong differentiator in the *O Globo* newspaper's coverage.

26. The photo is of Brazil's third goal in their 4–0 win over Panama. The goal came from a beautiful move in which the ball passed from foot to foot—Debinha, Adriana, Debinha again, Ary Borges, and Bia Zaneratto.

27. The British newspaper *The Guardian* brings new elements to the accusation of sexual abuse against coach Bruce Mwape, brought before FIFA in September last year. In April 2020, the British newspaper *The Guardian* reported this: Dadou, the nickname of Yves Jean-Bart, president of Haiti's football federation since 2000, allegedly sexually abused several female players.

Provisional Considerations

In Brazil, the only sport that manages to survive defeats is football. There are defeats for the men's national team, such as those in the 1950 and 1982 World Cups, which have become mythical moments in Brazilian football and are revisited in a continuous process of maintaining and re-elaborating their memories. Sports other than football, especially men's sports, depend on a victorious event to remain the focus of interest for the sports media and the general public. When Gustavo Kuerten won the Roland Garros title three times, tennis became incredibly popular in Brazil, but as soon as the winning results became scarce, the sport fell into near oblivion (Guedes, 2001).

The imperative to win was something that could actually provoke fear in players like Marta, who saw the team's defeats as an obstacle to legitimizing and supporting women's football. This feeling was the basis of the narratives of the women's team's defeat in 2007 and 2008, when they reached the final of the World Cup and the Olympic Games. However, the loss of the championship trophy and the Olympic gold medal were received with understanding by the sports media, which chose to take a denunciatory tone by emphasizing the various problems surrounding women's football in Brazil. In 2023, the reception of the Brazilian team's elimination against Jamaica, still in the group stage of the World Cup, proved to be very different from those important previous defeats.

Obviously, the distance in time between the defeats may seem like an obvious explanation for the different treatment given by sports journalism. However, a quick visit to the reception of the national team's defeat in 2019 shows that there is a certain welcoming movement toward the Brazilian national team that is taking shape in the narrative of the newspapers selected here. The elimination against the French team was reported by the newspaper *O Globo* on its front page "In defeat, Marta's victorious message" (June 24, 2019). In the sports section, the newspaper reiterates Marta's request regarding the need for support for women's football, but this time Marta's request is directed at the players who should commit themselves more effectively to the future of women's football:

> The national team's star player [Marta] has appealed for yet another generation not to be wasted at the moment of the category's greatest visibility. In 2007, when the national team finished as the runners-up against Germany in the World Cup, the No. 10 helped raise a banner calling for more investment in women's football. Now that they are actually starting to arrive, more than a decade late,

> she is demanding more commitment from everyone. Without naming anyone specifically, she demanded more professionalism in a message to the new generation of girls. (*O Globo*, July 24, 2023)

In 2023, Marta once again starred in the coverage of the national team's participation in the World Cup, even though she did not start in most of the games. This would be the last World Cup of the career of a player whose career was intertwined with that of the national team itself. It was a unique competition in terms of media visibility and investment in women's football, which created an atmosphere of expectation about the team's performance. Added to this was the investment in Marta's farewell and the result was narratives in which disappointment was the main theme of the comments made about the team's defeat to Jamaica. Coach Pia Sundhage was blamed for failing to give Brazil an effective tactical standard capable of taking the team to the final stages of the World Cup. For the first time, a villainous figure was depicted in the accounts of the women's team's defeat, the antithesis of the heroine Marta.

The reception of the defeat in the 2023 World Cup points to the fact that women's football in Brazil is no longer the same, and that it has shown itself to be more organized in terms of its sporting structure. Hence the impatience with the defeat and an even greater expectation of winning a title with repercussions. The notable demands in the journalistic narratives, especially in the newspaper *O Globo,* are partly due to the investment that the sports media has made in this product called women's football, which in turn has been inserted into the globalized market of sport. To a large extent, what is evident is the growing importance of this sport as a spectacle and the commitment to the national team as a fundamental element of a new scenario of possibilities for women's football. There remains the challenge of not having Marta, the player who played a key role in maintaining media interest in the women's national team, even without winning a major title. However, this is an opportunity to broaden and diversify the reach of the media and public spotlight toward other players.

Despite the fear, the truth is that the team has survived the defeats, which shows that, above all, the strength of the country's most popular sport is at stake, and that it has historically become one of the basic elements in the construction of the very idea of Brazil. Defeat has become a nuisance, which means that there is a demonstration that the women's national team matters. The construction and maintenance of this importance is due to the performance on the pitch of players who, throughout the history of women's football in Brazil, have in fact fought against prejudice and precariousness (Goellner, 2022). It is also due to a broad agenda that is not restricted to football but is part of women's daily struggles for rights. Part of this struggle is the need for women to make their presence felt in the concrete and imaginary shaping of the "country of football." This is a long process and requires constant care to cultivate a football that no longer allows itself to be a vehicle for exalting sexism.

REFERENCES

BALACÓ, Bruno. On the Heels of Cazé TV, YouTube Consolidates Itself as a Sports Broadcasting Platform (*No embalo da Cazé TV, Youtube se consolida como plataforma de transmissão esportiva*). In: **Ludopédio**, São Paulo, v. 169, n. 16, 2023.

BANDEIRA, Gustavo. **A History of Cheering in the Present**: Elitisation, Racism and Heterosexism in the Masculinity Curriculum of Football Fans (*Uma história do torcer no presente: elitização, racismo e heterossexismo no currículo de masculinidade dos torcedores de futebol*). Curitiba: Appris, 2019.

BERTONCELLO, Soraya Damasio. **Football as a Media Instance of Social Advertising**: An Analysis of the Discourse of the Bahia Sports Club Campaigns (*O futebol enquanto instância midiática da publicidade social: Uma análise do discurso das campanhas do esporte clube Bahia*). Master's dissertation. School of Communication, Arts and Design—Famecos—Postgraduate Programme in Social Communication Master's Degree in Social Communication, 2022.

BUENO, Noemi Correa; MARQUES, José Carlos. Sports journalism and gender relations: the space for female participation (*Jornalismo Esportivo e Relações de Gênero: O Espaço para a Participação Feminina*). In: **Comunicação & Inovação**, v. 21, n. 45, pp. 110–128, Jan–Apr 2020.

COSTA, Leda Maria da. Marta versus Neymar. The "War of the Sexes" at the 2016 Olympic Games *(A "Guerra dos Sexos" nos Jogos Olímpicos 2016).* In: **Intercom**—Brazilian Society for Interdisciplinary Communication Studies 42nd Brazilian Congress of Communication Sciences, Belém (PA), September 2 to 7, 2019. (available at: https://portalintercom.org.br/anais/nacional2019/resumos/R14-1423-1.pdf)

COSTA, Leda Maria da. **The Villains of Football**: Sports Journalism and the Melodramatic Imagination (*Os vilões do futebol. Jornalismo esportivo e imaginação melodramática).* Curitiba: Appris, 2020.

FON, Pei Shung Bezerra Alves. **Dibradoras**: An Analysis of the Importance of Social Networks in Strengthening Women's Soccer in Brazil (*Caiu na rede é Dibradoras: análise sobre a importância das redes sociais para o fortalecimento do futebol feminino no Brasil*). Dissertation (Final Coursework in Public Relations)—Federal University of Alagoas. Institute of Sciences, History, Communication and Arts. Maceió, 2022.

GOELLNER, Silvana Vilodre; CABRAL, Juliana. ***Pioneers* Ask for Passage**: Knowing in Order to Recognise (*As* pioneiras *pedem passagem: Conhecer para reconhecer*). São Paulo: Editora *Ludopédio*, 2022.

GONÇALVES, Eduarda dos Passos. **Women's Football in the Media**: Journalistic Coverage of the FIFA Women's World Cup 2019 on the Globoesporte.com and Dibradoras portals *(O futebol de mulheres na mídia: a cobertura jornalística da Copa do Mundo de Futebol Feminino FIFA2019 nos portais Globoesporte.com e Dibradoras)*. Dissertation (master's)—Federal University of Santa Catarina, Centre for Educational Sciences, Postgraduate Programme in Education, Florianópolis, 2021.

GUEDES, Simoni. Authorised Discourses and Rebel Discourses in Brazilian football. (*Discursos autorizados e discursos rebeldes no futebol brasileiro*). In: **Esporte e Sociedade**, Ano 6, n. 16, Nov. 2010/Feb, 2001.

GUEDES, Simoni. **Brazilian football**: Zero Institution (*O Futebol brasileiro. Instituição zero*) SP: Editora Ludopedio, 2023.

GUEIROS, P. M. Number 1 in Overcoming Barriers (*Número 1 em superar barreiras*). In: **O Globo**, *Sports*, December 20, 2006, p. 42.

HELAL, Ronaldo and SOARES, Antônio Jorge. The Decline of the Shoe Country: Football and National Identity at the 2002 World Cup (*O Declínio da Pátria de Chuteiras: futebol e identidade nacional na Copa do Mundo de 2002)*. In: Associação Nacional Dos Programas De Pós-Graduação Em Comunicação, XII, 2003, Recife. **Compós**. Congress: National Association of Postgraduate Programmes in Communication, 2003.

HOLLANDA, Bernardo Borges Buarque de. **The discovery of football**: modernism, regionalism and sporting passion in José Lins do Rego (*O descobrimento do futebol: Modernismo, regionalismo e paixão esportiva em José Lins do Rego*). Rio de Janeiro: National Library, 2004.

JANUÁRIO, Soraya Barreto, LIMA, Rodrigues Cecília Almeida, LEAL, Daniel **Women's Football on the Media Agenda**: A Thematic Analysis of the 2019 World Cup Coverage on Brazilian News Websites. (*Futebol de mulheres na* *agenda da mídia: uma análise temática da cobertura da Copa do Mundo de 2019 em sites jornalísticos brasileiros)* Observatory (OBS*) Journal, v. 14, n. 4, 2020.

KFOURI, J. Marta Phenomenon (*Marta Fenômeno*). In: **Folha de São Paulo**, *Sports*, September 27, 2018, p. B7.

MAGUIRE, J. A. The Global Media Sports Complex: Key Issues and Concerns. In: **Sport in Society**: Cultures, Commerce. Media, Politics, 2011.

MEIRELLES, Rebeka Vaz da Costa. **Sexism in Sports Journalism**: How Women Journalists Experience and Deal with the Patriarchal Organisational Culture of Sport (*Sexismo no jornalismo esportivo: como as mulheres jornalistas vivenciam e lidam com a cultura patriarcal organizacional do esporte*, Niterói, 2022. 158 f). Dissertation (master's degree)—Fluminense Federal University, Niterói, 2022.

MORÃO, Kauan Galvão; BAGNI, Guilherme; VERZANI, Renato Henrique et al. The Dangers of Digital Media: Psychological Changes in Brazilian Footballers (*Os perigos das mídias digitais: alterações psicológicas em futebolistas brasileiros*). In: **Revista Brasileira de Futsal e Futebol**. São Paulo. v. 12, n. 47. pp. 67–74. Jan./Feb./Mar./April. 2020.

MOREIRA, R. P. Marta past Messi: (re)definitions of Gender and Masculinity, Patriarchal Structures and Female Agency in International Soccer. In: **Soccer & Society**, 15(4), 2014, 503–516.

OSELAME, Mariana Corsetti. **The End of News**: The "Funny". In the Field of Television Sports Journalism (Fim da notícia: o "engraçadismo". No campo do jornalismo esportivo de televisão). Master's dissertation. Faculty of Social Communication, Postgraduate Programme in Social Communication. PUCRS, 2013.

RINALDI, Igor Malinosqui. **Stress, Mood and Burnout in female football players. (*Estresse, humor e Burnout em atletas de futebol feminino.*)** 2020. 60 f. Dissertation (Master's in Psychology)—Faculty of Sciences, Universidade Estadual Paulista, Bauru, 2020.

RODRIGUES, J. L. Victory Over a Country's Sexism. The Best Woman in the World Left Home at 14 to Play Football (*Vitória sobre o machismo de um país. A melhor do mundo saiu de casa aos 14 anos para poder jogar bola*). **O Globo**, *Sports*, December 19, 2006, p. 36.

RUBIO, Katia. (org.). **Encounters and Mismatches**: Discovering Sports Psychology *(Encontros e desencontros: descobrindo a Psicologia do Esporte).* São Paulo: Casa do Psicólogo, 2000.

PINTO, Maurício Rodrigues. All-Powerful Corinthian Women: The Trajectory of the All-Powerful Corinthian Movement. (*Corinthianas todo-poderosas: a trajectória do Movimento Toda Poderosa Corinthiana.*) In: Kessler, Claudia Samuel; Costa, Leda Maria da; Pisani, Mariana da Silva (Orgs.). **Women in the Universe of Brazilian Football. (As mulheres no universo do futebol brasileiro**) 1st ed. Santa Maria: Editora UFSM, 2022. pp. 123–138.

SANTOS, Anderson David Gomes dos. **The Consolidation of a Monopoly of Decisions**: Rede Globo and the Broadcasting of the Brazilian Football Championship (*A Consolidação de um Monopólio de Decisões: A Rede Globo e a Transmissão do Campeonato Brasileiro de Futebol*), f. 271. 2013. Dissertation (Master's in Communication Sciences)—Universidade do Vale do Rio dos Sinos, São Leopoldo, 2013.

SANTOS, Anderson David Gomes dos. **A Model for Regulating Football Broadcasting Rights** (*Um modelo para regulação dos direitos de transmissão de futebol*). Thesis (Doctorate in Communication)—University of Brasília, Brasília, 2021.

SCHUDSON, Michael. ***Discovering the News***: A Social History of Newspapers in the United States (*Descobrindo a notícia*: Uma história social dos jornais nos Estados Unidos). SP: Vozes, 2010.

SOUZA, R. C. de; EUGÊNIO, F. R.; VIMIEIRO, A. C. She for She: The News Coverage of Women's Football in Brazilian Podcasts from 2018 to 2022 (*Elas por elas: a cobertura noticiosa do futebol de mulheres em podcasts brasileiros de 2018 a 2022*). In: **FuLiA/UFMG** [Journal on Football, Language, Arts and other Sports], [S. l.], v. 8, n. 2, pp. 101–129, 2023. DOI: 10.35699/2526-4494.2023.45281. Available at: https://periodicos.ufmg.br/index.php/fulia/article/view/45281. Accessed on: November 26, 2023.

TRAQUINA, Nelson. **Journalism**: Issues, Theories and "Stories" (*Jornalismo: questões, teorias e "estórias"*). Lisbon: Vega, 1999.

TUCHMAN, Gaye. Telling Stories. In: TRAQUINA, Nelson (org.). **Journalism**: Issues, Theories and "Stories" (*Jornalismo: questões, teorias e "estórias"*). Lisbon: Vega, 1999.

VERZANI, Renato Henrique. **New Social Media, Athletes and Coping**: Impertinent Relationships (*Novas mídias sociais, atletas e o coping: relações impertinentes*). Dissertation (master)—Universidade Estadual Paulista, Instituto de Biociências de Rio Claro, 2017.

WOOLF, Virginia. **A Roof All Your Own** (*Um teto todo seu*). Rio de Janeiro: Nova Fronteira, 2022.

CHAPTER 6

To Cheer, Transitive Verb: Women in the Stadiums (Brazil, 1940–2023)[1]

Nathália Fernandes Pessanha

This chapter aims to present an overview of the forms and representations of being a woman and a fan in the Brazilian stands, with a special focus on the analysis of stadiums in Rio de Janeiro. In order to do this, a small retrospective analysis will be carried out on the presence and actions of women supporters throughout the 20th century, seeking to demonstrate the changes and permanence of these actions by supporters throughout the period. Then, the different ways of cheering in the stadiums will be discussed, as well as the role of women in them. This chapter is anchored in the perspectives of social history and gender, understood as a power relationship established between different spheres of society.

Being a woman and a fan is not an easy combination. Football and the stands, as representatives of the society to which they belong, reproduce and, at many times, create barriers and gender stereotypes that female fans need to confront and adopt attitudes that are never demanded from men.

Since the beginning of the practice of the sport in Brazil, men and women have frequented stadiums and nurtured attendance at matches. Although both football itself, with its regulations and arenas, and the practice of cheering have varied over the years, having crowds of fans following their clubs and teams in Brazil has been a constant.

This chapter will analyze the presence of female fans in the Brazilian stands, with an emphasis on Rio de Janeiro. To this end, a short retrospective of the fans throughout the 20th century will be carried out. Subsequently, the distancing, resistance, and return of the female presence in large numbers in the stadiums

1. This study was funded by CNPQ—National Council for Scientific and Technological Development. Process number 421784/2021-0.

will be observed and, finally, the ways of being a supporter in Brazil will be discussed, as well as the belonging and disputes that this awakens.

This chapter has as its theoretical foundation gender studies, and understanding the concept, as Scott points out, as power relations established in society.[2] This power is expressed in various ways in the social environment, and, in the stands, it is represented as barriers imposed on women participating in some acts carried out by fans. And, most of the times, with the argument, reiterated countless times, by sports entities and communication vehicles, that the football arena is not a feminine space.

A Brief Retrospective: Women And Football in Brazil in the First Half of the 20th Century.

The football matches of the early 20th century, initially played by amateurs, began to draw an increasingly large audience. It is interesting to note that during the first two decades of the 20th century, female fans were such a prominent presence in the stadiums that they were seen as "professional fans." Associated to the excitement of the game or to the consolation and encouragement of a certain player, female fans were seen as key characters of the match. As João Malaia states,

> Two notes from the Gazeta de Notícias, a Rio de Janeiro newspaper, in 1914 show that, in *Botafogo's* game against the *Associação Atlethica Palmeiras* in the *Alvinegro* stadium on General Severiano street, a noble area of the Federal Capital, the attendance was not large. Even so, "the feminine presence there was to be noticed, being represented by gentle elegant ladies who lent the sportive party the charm of their beauty." However, more particularly in the stadiums of Rio de Janeiro, the so-called "feminine element" was not only destined to a secondary role. "With their nervous and enthusiastic applause shouts," as the same newspaper stated a few days later, the female fans gained importance and prominence in the spectacle.[3]

2. SCOTT, Joan. Gender: Uma categoria útil de análise histórica [A useful category of historical analysis, translated title]. *Revista educação e realidade* [Education and Reality Journal, translated title]. July/December 1995.

3. MALAIA, João. Torcer, torcedores, torcedoras, torcida (Bras.): 1910–1950 [Cheering, fans, female fans: 1910–1950, translated title]. In: HOLLANDA, Bernardo Buarque de.; MALAIA, João M.C.; TOLEDO, Luiz Henrique de.; MELO, Victor Andrade de. (orgs.). **A torcida Brasileira [The Brazilian fans, translated title]**. Rio de Janeiro: 7letras, 2012, p. 64.

Being a guaranteed presence in the football spectacle of the early 20th century, they were not necessarily recognized for being fans and for being in the stands supporting their team. They were seen, above all, as a piece of embellishment to the spectacle, thus contributing much more to the visual composition of the game rather than being demonstrators of some fan passion.

Some decades later, Decree-Law 3.199 of April 14, 1941, created the National Sports Council (CND) and had the purpose of regulating the bases of organization of sports throughout the country. In its Article 54 it established that "Women shall not be allowed to practice sports incompatible with the conditions of their nature, and for this purpose the National Sports Council shall issue the necessary instructions to the sports entities of the country."[4] The sports prohibited by the subsequent CND regulations were, among others, boxing, polo, and football.[5] For authors such as Brenda Elsey and Joshua Nadel "Women's exclusion from the national sport, particularly as it became a cornerstone of Brazilian identity writ large, was part and parcel of marginalizing them as active agents of the nation."[6] Thus, the banning of women from football has deep roots in gender discrimination and the association that women's social role is that of procreation. That said, Silvana Goellner reminds us that:

> In the beginning of the 20th century, the strengthening of the feminine body through physical exercise was seen as a way to better prepare women to lead a good maternity, thus complying with the maxim that strong mothers are those who make strong people (Thardiére, 1940, p. 60). However, not all activities were recommended to them and football, designated as too violent for the female body conformation, was not one of them.[7]

4. BRAZIL, Federal Senate. Decree Law No. 3199 of April 14, 1941. Available at: https://www2.camara.leg.br/legin/fed/declei/1940-1949/decreto-lei-3199-14-abril-1941-413238-publicacaooriginal-1-pe.html. Accessed on March 15, 2023.

5. The CND's determination that specifically mentioned football as a forbidden practice was published in the official gazette in September 1941, as reported in the newspaper *Diário da manhã,* on September 14, 1941, p. 14. Although it is possible to argue that the restriction of women's football had been established in society long before the publication of the decree.

6. ELSEY, Brenda; NADEL, Joshua. **Futbolera. A History of Women and Sports in Latin America**. US: University of Texas Press, 2019, p. 66.

7. GOELLNER, Silvana Vilodre. Mulheres e futebol no Brasil: entre sombras e visibilidades [Women and football in Brazil: between shadows and visibilities, translated title]. *Revista Brasileira de Educação Física e Esporte,* São Paulo, v. 19, n. 2, pp. 143–151, abr./jun. 2005, p. 144.

During this period of prohibition of football practice, the female presence in the stands remained perennial. The *historically organized fan clubs* are a phenomenon that arose around the 1940s in Rio de Janeiro.[8] Their main exponents are the *Charanga Rubro-Negra,* from the *Clube de Regatas do Flamengo* (1942); and the *Torcida Organizada do Vasco,* the TOV, from the *Clube de Regatas Vasco da Gama* (1944), whose leadership stands out for being a woman in times when women were prohibited from playing football. According to Leda Costa, Dulce Rosalina took over the leadership of TOV in 1956, replacing its founder João de Lucas, and became then, the first woman to lead an organized fan club, remaining in the leadership of the fan club for two decades before leaving, in 1976, for one of its dissidences, *Renovascão,* of which she was a founder and member until her death in 2004.[9] To Costa,

> The fact that they are women contributed a lot to the popularity of both Dulce Rosalina and Elisa do Corinthians, giving them uniqueness, after all, in the decades in which they appear in the football scene the fans, in their vast majority, were formed by men. The feminine condition may grant some privileges and this aspect is quite clear, especially in the case of the symbolic female fans.[10]

Already in the period of emergence of the so-called *youth fan clubs* (1960–1970), the feminine presence in the stands was also seen as a restraining and surveillance look, or even as an offence and creation of stereotypes, as is the case of the nickname *Maria-Chuteira (Mary with the football boots),* of which Costa deals with, conferred to the women who followed football, as if all of them were there in search of a good marriage.[11] The reduction in the number of female fans in the stands in Rio de Janeiro, if compared to later moments and even to the moment of "birth" of the female fans at the beginning of the 20th century, was

8. The nomenclature of the *historically organised fans* was used in my master's thesis to serve as a differentiation between the first organised fan clubs for those that appear after the youth ones, and that carry many of their traits. Cf. PESSANHA, Nathália Fernandes. **Arquibancada feminina. Relações de gênero e formas de ser torcedora no Rio de Janeiro [Women's bleachers. Gender relations and ways of being a fan in Rio de Janeiro, translated title]**. Dissertation (Master's degree). Postgraduate Programme in History. Fluminense Federal University. Niterói, 2020.

9. COSTA, Leda Maria. O que é uma torcedora? Notas sobre a representação e autorrepresentação do público feminino de futebol [What Is a female fan? Notes on the representation and self-representation of the female football audience, translated title]. *Esporte e Sociedade (Sport and Society, translated title)*, n. 4. Rio de Janeiro. 2006.

10. Idem, p. 9.

11. *Marias-chuteiras* was the name given to the women who followed football as a function of the players, seeking a love affair with them.

reduced during the period of emergence of these new fan clubs, the youth fans. A reduction that is due to a series of reasons that may range from the banning of the leaderships of these new fans, changes in the football practice and, of course, the political moment Rio de Janeiro and Brazil were going through.[12]

Departure and Return: The Female Presence in the Stands Between 1960 and 1990

Created from groups of friends, in their majority, and marked by youthful effervescence, the *youth fan clubs* appeared on the Rio de Janeiro scene at the end of the 1960s. According to Bernardo Borges Buarque de Hollanda:

> The epithet youth came to be conveyed as a kind of motto associated with everything that was considered new and modern, with its impregnation in the most diverse areas of society. It denoted less the biological condition of a particular age group, arbitrarily defined as between fifteen and twenty-five, and more the manifestation of a free spirit, of a new way of being and being in the world.[13]

Still according to Hollanda, the first group of *youth fan clubs* in Rio de Janeiro was from the *Clube de Regatas Flamengo's* fan club, created in 1967 by dissident members of the historical *Charanga Rubro-Negra,* which was headed by the symbolic supporter Jaime de Carvalho, and was initially named *Poder Jovem do Flamengo* (Flamengo's Youth Power), claiming for itself all the mystique around the name and later adopted the title of *torcida* ("fan club"), finally becoming the *Torcida Jovem do Flamengo* (Flamengo's Youth Fan Club). In the following year, it was *Botafogo's* turn to create its own fan club, the *Torcida Jovem do Botafogo* (Botafogo Youth Power), formed by a group of friends from Miguel Lemos Street, in Copacabana, who used to go to the games at the stadium together and, following the same path of the red-black (Flamengo) fan club, it was renamed, after a few games, *Torcida Jovem do Botafogo* (Botafogo's Youth Fan Club).

12. Since 1964, Brazil had been living under a civil military dictatorship, installed after a coup d'état, which lasted 21 years, only ending in 1985.

13. HOLLANDA, Bernardo Buarque de. **O clube como vontade e representação: o jornalismo esportivo e a formação das torcidas organizadas de futebol do Rio de Janeiro [The club as will and representation: sports journalism and the formation of organised football fans in Rio de Janeiro, translated title].** Rio de Janeiro: 7letras, 2010, p. 175.

In the same year, *Jovem Flu* (Flu Youth Fan Club) was born, created by a group of artists, supporters of Fluminense, among them the actor Hugo Carvana, the composer Chico Buarque de Hollanda and the journalist Nelson Motta. It is important to mention that the *Jovem Flu* referred to here is not the current and well-known Fluminense fan group, *Young Flu,* which was created later, in 1970, although it also used the weight of the title *Young Flu*. Again according to Hollanda, Vasco da Gama will create their own fan club, *Força Jovem do Vasco* (Vasco Youth Force), in the following year, in 1969. [14]

In this sense, it is important to mention the importance of the football stadium as a space of sociability of these supporters and of meeting between sister and opposing identities. For Rosana Teixeira, the stadium is also a place of social and temporal framing which allows selecting certain memories, besides providing a sense of continuity, of connection between past and present, which organizes the supporters' collective memory.[15] In a context in which youth movements erupted all over the world, the *youth fans* embraced a protest movement within their clubs, against the traditional managers and their conservative choices, and against the behavior of the old and consecrated *historically organized fan clubs*, who had friendly relations with the managers, the owners (known as top-hats, or *cartolas*) and the clubs, who, in memory or respect for their leaders, kept a position that forbade swearing or more offensive phrases. For Hollanda, the reasons that defended the creation of new fan clubs, arising from within the *historically organized fan clubs* were several, where some of them stood out:

> There were explicit justifications that were on the surface of the discourse of disgruntled supporters. The reasons alleged comprised apparently simple reasons, caused by the illness of older leaders and the observance of the need to replace them. Other explanations had a harsher, accusatory tone. They were motivated by the restriction of the leaders of the fan clubs, who hindered the free manifestation of the fans. The manifest allegations revolved, finally, around the right to boo and to criticize the team more forcefully, whether against its managers, its coaches or its players, in situations of crisis in team performance.[16]

14. Cf. HOLLANDA, 2010. *Op.Cit.*

15. TEIXEIRA, Rosana da Câmara. **Os perigos da Paixão. Visitando jovens torcidas cariocas [The dangers of Passion. Visiting young carioca fans, translated title]** São Paulo: Annablume, 2003.

16. HOLLANDA, Bernardo Borges Buarque de. A festa competitiva: formação e crise das torcidas organizadas entre 1950 e 1980 [The competitive party: formation and crisis of the organized fans between 1950 and 1980, translated title]. In: HOLLANDA, Bernardo Buarque de.; MALAIA, João M.C.; TOLEDO, Luiz Henrique de.; MELO, Victor Andrade de. (orgs.). **A torcida Brasileira [The Brazilian fans, translated title]**. Rio de Janeiro: 7letras, 2012, p. 109.

These fan clubs, with their ideals and motivations that sought to differentiate themselves from the previous formats, shall serve as inspiration, as time goes on, for new fan clubs. Whether through internal subdivisions or through the birth of new niches, with no relation with the original *youth fan clubs*, these supporters end up exporting their ideals and ways of expressing their passion to the groups to come. Even the new forms of associations, such as the *barras* and *torcidas de alento,* which are born with the purpose of opposing the current way of cheering, have as a parameter most of the ideals and ways of cheering of the *youth fan clubs.*

In the late 1970s, feminist movements began to gain greater importance in Brazil, particularly through many women who, during their period of exile, came into contact with feminist groups in other countries and, on their return, began to give new meaning to this experience.[17] The UN defined 1975 as the International Women's Year and the first of the Women's Decade, giving women and feminist issues more space. Although, in the case of Brazil, women's football continued to be prohibited by law for practically the whole decade, the prohibition decree being revoked only in 1979.

With regard to supporters and fan clubs, contrary to what had happened in the fields, no legislation prohibited women's participation. However, the prohibition of the practice of women's football had effects off-field. Football was and is considered a male sport, to be played, and also watched and followed, by men. The Brazilian grammar itself corroborates this silencing, since it is the rule to use the masculine plural term—*torcedores* (fans)—to refer to the crowd of supporters in the stands.[18] It is important to highlight that, in fact, the male presence in the stands was higher than the female and it is reasonable to argue that this was reflected in the newspapers, where most of the articles published dealt with male supporters. However, the exclusion or silencing of female fans due to grammatical usage or, sometimes, the position adopted by the newspaper should not be underestimated.

17. For more information on the experience of women in exile and in contact with feminist groups abroad, see: PEDRO, Joana Maria. *Narrativas do feminismo em países do Cone Sul (1960–1989) [Feminist narratives in Southern Cone countries (1960–1989), translated title].* In: PEDRO, Joana Maria. WOLFF, Cristina Sheibe (orgs.). **Gênero, feminismos e ditaduras no Cone Sul [Gender, feminisms and dictatorships in the Southern Cone, translated title]**. Santa Catarina: Editora Mulheres, 2010.

18. For more information see: BUTLER, Judith. **Problemas de gênero. Feminismo e subversão da identidade [Gender Trouble. Feminism and the Subversion of Identity, translated title].** Rio de Janeiro: Civilização Brasileira, 2017.

At times, the female participation was highlighted and received the attention of sports journalism, especially the *Jornal dos Sports* (Sports Newspaper), owned by journalist Mario Filho and his family. Thus, the female presence in the stands at the time of birth of the *youth fan clubs* in Rio de Janeiro, more specifically in 1968, was reported in specific cases, such as those analyzed here, whether through the remembrance of a sport worker, whether due to some event in the stands. What the selected reports aim to highlight is that, even if in a smaller number and related to specific events that for the journalistic gaze of the time deserved attention, women were present in the stands when the *youth fan clubs* were being formed and affirmed. Additionally, as already seen, they were present even before that, a fact that goes against the argument often used in "common sense understanding," which says that women's interest in football and their presence in the stands is something recent.

The first reporting of the sports journal that will be highlighted was entitled "*Vasco tem mil bossas.*"[19] The text narrated the day of a *Vasco* versus *Botafogo* match, in which the leader of the *Botafogo* fan clubs, Tarzan, announced the fan clubs' strategies for the spectacle. On the other hand, Mrs. Dulce Rosalina, leader of TOV—Vasco's organized fans—stated that the club would not "hand it over," and that a 15-year-old Vasco fan, Katia Sale, had even composed a march song for the match. The lyrics were as follows:

> *Com a minha bandeira vou para o Estádio ver*
> *Vou tranquila porque sei que o Vasco vai vencer*
> *Danilo, Buglê e Nei Me fizeram esquecer*
> *Os dias tristes que passei*
> *Agora tudo é alegria, agora tudo é motivação*
> *O expressinho voltou é o Vasco campeão.* [20]
>
> "With my flag I'm going to the stadium to see
> I'll go quietly because I know Vasco will win
> Danilo, Buglê and Nei made me forget
> The sad days I've spent
> Now everything is joy, now everything is motivation
> The little expresso is back and Vasco is champion" (Translated text)

19. "Vasco tem mil bossas" [Vasco has a Thousand Bossas, translated title]. *Jornal dos Sports*. April 28, 1968. P. 8.

20. "Vasco tem mil bossas" [Vasco has a thousand bossas, translated title]. *Jornal dos Sports*. April 28, 1968. p. 8.

This report shows not only the leadership of dona Dulce Rosalina in Vasco's fan club but also the female participation in important roles within them, composing songs for the match. Songs have always been an artifice used by fans, and still are today. Starting with the parody of carnival songs and going through several musical rhythms, the songs cheer the audience and highlight the teams' achievements during the game. Moreover, it is also important to mention the rivalry between the fans of the two Rio de Janeiro clubs, Vasco and Botafogo, made explicit by the efforts of the supporters to provide beautiful spectacles during the event.

In the news article "*Fla cantou como nunca*" (Fla sang like never before), the title, which can be interpreted in a double sense, refers to an event that took place in the stands of a *Flamengo* game against *Vasco*.[21] The report, reproduced here, fundamentally demonstrates the female presence in the stands and their interest in observing the match. Besides serving as a backdrop for broader debates regarding the sexism suffered by female fans, many of which remain until today:

> the rubro-negro (Flamengo) side became agitated when a woman passed with a (Vasco) flag. She was booed and saved from further trouble by a kinder rubro-negro man who stood behind her. Another, more fanatical, fan assaulted his own teammate for helping the enemy. In the midst of the commotion, two (Flamengo) beauties asked permission to get a more comfortable seat in the stands. And the red-black crowd forgets the war to toast their appetizing female fans with the indispensable fiu-fius (whistles).[22]

As stated earlier, these reports serve to illustrate a regular female presence in the stands in Rio de Janeiro, although it is not possible, nor is it the purpose of this work, to state that it was a majority or that it numerically equaled the male presence, also because, as already argued, the space of football was considered eminently male, and women were considered mere embellishments of the spectacle, allowing the press to make comments like the one in the last report. Besides, it is possible to infer that the prohibition of women's football has also influenced the lower female presence compared to the male one in the stands. The symbolic force, in Bourdieu's words, that was inserted in society through the banning of women's football and the definition of this sport as a male field had its reflections on the fans. For him:

---

21. "Fla cantou como nunca" [Fla sang like never before, translated title]. *Jornal dos Sports*. May 02, 1968. p. 10.

22. "Fla cantou como nunca." (Fla sang like never before, translated title). *Jornal dos Sports*. May 02, 1968, p. 10.

> "Symbolic force is a form of power that exerts itself over bodies, directly and as if by magic, without any physical coercion; but this magic only acts with the support of predispositions placed, like propulsive springs, in the deepest zone of the bodies."[23]

In 1973, the *Clube de Regatas Vasco da Gama* created the *Camisa 12* women's fan club. It was formed by club members who decided to attend the *carioca* championship matches of that year together. They sat in a specific area of the stands and brought musical instruments, which caught the attention of the press and even appeared in several articles in the *Jornal dos Sports* (Sports Newspaper). In May 1973, the journal reported the presence of the stadium supporters for the next round of matches, determining the location of the new movement. In an article entitled "*Elas são 30 e a Camisa é 12*" (They are 30 and the Shirt is 12), *Jornal dos Sports* described how the supporters, called "luluzinhas vascaínas" (Lucy's of Vasco), would act, with a big flag and percussion instruments.[24]

Another report from this journal, also from 1973, talked about the *Mario Filho trophy*, a prize of a contest promoted by the newspaper and that used to be given to the one elected as the best fan club. In the dispute, different criteria were evaluated, such as animation, singing, presence of members, among others. In the editorial, entitled "In the Fla party, Vasco also had a cup," the newspaper reported the delivery of the award to Jaime de Oliveira, leader of *Charanga Rubro-Negra,* who won the cup next to the representative of the Torcida *Camisa 12*.[25]

Throughout the decade, the leader of the *Camisa 12* fan club, Iara de Barros, even promoted several contests with female fans from Vasco associations, aiming to elect the Queen and Princess of the supporters groups. The 1978 party, as reported by *Jornal Vasco,* had Dulce Rosalina as the leader of the organization, and had Odaléia from *Camisa 12* and Aída from *TOV* as secretaries. Also according to the report Isabel Cristina of the *Vasteles fan club* was chosen Queen of the Fan Clubs, in a contest with nine competitors. In 1979, a new edition of the contest

23. BOURDIEU, Pierre. **A dominação masculina. A condição feminina e a violência de gênero [Male domination. The Female Condition and Gender Violence, translated title].** Rio de Janeiro: Bertrand Brasil, 2019, p. 69.

24. "Elas são 30 e a Camisa é 12" [They are 30 and the Shirt is 12, translated title]. *Jornal dos Sports*, April 05, 1973, p. 3.

25. "Na festa do Fla, Vasco teve taça também" [In Fla's party, Vasco had cup too, translated title]. *Newspaper Jornal dos Sports*, May 10, 1973, p. 05.

had nineteen competitors, when the young Sandra Sena, from *TOV*, became the new queen, according to a new report by *Vasco Newspaper*.[26]

In addition to the emergence of new forms of supporter sociability, as already mentioned, the 1970s also represent a new moment in the formation and definition of supporters. Particularly as of the presidency of Emilio Garrastazu Médici—who liked to have his image associated with that of a football supporter, always following the matches through a small battery operated radio and who even turned this image into a government advertisement, through the AERP—Assessoria Especial de Relações Públicas (Special advisory office for public relations, translated title), and from the commotion that the victory in Mexico caused among the Brazilian population in general, the military government started to actually put into practice a political project using football. According to Magalhães, the effective action of the State in sporting life took place, above all, through massive funding for the construction of stadiums and gyms.[27]

With the implementation of the Nacional, supporters started traveling to follow their teams in several states of the country, making caravans and acquiring the habit of traveling, which, according to Hollanda's argument, on the one hand, increased the supporters' identity cohesion, but on the other, reduced their contesting power.[28] Moreover, thanks to the spread of media such as radio and television in Brazilian homes, football began to be a sport watched at home and with the family, and not only in fan clubs and stadiums.

While men's football was consolidating its new league, women's football managed, in 1979, to have the decree banning its practice revoked, causing a few women's football teams to emerge in the early 1980s.[29] However, the body and the role of women in public space continued to be questioned. According to Goellner, if at the beginning of the century physical education for women served especially to prepare their bodies to generate good citizens, at the end of the 1970s a new stereotype was added about the feminine body: the eroticization.[30]

---

26. "Torcidas elegem sua rainha." (Fans elect their queen, translated title). *Jornal Vasco (Vasco Newspaper, translated title)*. Year XII, November, 1978. Edition 54, p. 6. Documentation provided by the Centro de Memória do Vasco da Gama (Vasco da Gama Memorial Centre).

27. MAGALHÃES, Lívia Gonçalves. **Com a taça nas mãos. Sociedade, Copa do Mundo e ditadura no Brasil e na Argentina [With the Cup in their hands. Society, World Cup and dictatorship in Brazil and Argentina, translated title]**. Rio de Janeiro: Lamparina, FAPERJ, 2014.

28. HOLLANDA, 2010. *Op. Cit.*

29. Cf. ELSEY, Brenda; NADEL, Joshua. **Futbolera. A History of Women and Sports in Latin America.** US: University of Texas Press, 2019.

30. GOELLNER, 2005. *Op.Cit.*

In this way, stadiums, gyms, and sporting competition venues came to be seen as places where there is an exhibition of the attributes expected from sporting women, such as beauty and sexuality.

In relation to the fan clubs, according to Leonardo Teixeira, as early as 1981, *ASTORJ—Associação das Torcidas Organizadas do Rio de Janeiro* (Association of Organized Fan Clubs of Rio de Janeiro, translated title) was created, the result of an attempt to expand the possibility of relations between representatives of rival clubs.[31] Founded by Armando Giesta, from *Young Flu,* the movement was led by leaders of different organized fan clubs in Rio de Janeiro who sought to reduce clashes between fans and build a force capable of proposing and obtaining a voice before the Rio de Janeiro Football Federation, FERJ.

Again according to Teixeira, ASTORJ, facing a new ticket price increase, included in its claims a new agenda: the request of half-entry for the female public. According to the *Última Hora* newspaper report on the fact, entitled "Tickets have increased," the request was promptly denied, using the argument that "everyone would become a woman."[32] Once again, the female presence is noted in a relevant way, since, even if one can make reservations about the request made, just the fact of its request already shows that there was a need for the demand.

It is also important to mention that throughout the 1980s, the aforementioned contest for the "Queen of the Fan Clubs" of Vasco da Gama fans, organized and run by supporters of several associations of the club, kept its editions. In 1984, as reported again by *Revista do Vasco,* another edition was held, coordinated by Iara de Barros, leader of the *Camisa 12* fan club, and with the participation of eighteen contestants representing several fan clubs.[33] The champion of this edition was Ana Lúcia, from *Renovascão*, a fan group founded by Dulce Rosalina, as already mentioned. It is also interesting to take into account that the presence of the girls from the *Camisa 12 fan club* was frequent in the games and in the stands. For being, in their majority, also club members, they had an easier access

31. TEIXEIRA, Leonardo Antonio de Carvalho. **Congregar, Congraçar e Unir: a atuação da Associação das Torcidas Organizadas do Rio de Janeiro (1981–1989) [To Congregate, to Harmonize and to Unite: The Work of the Association of Organized Fan Clubs of Rio de Janeiro (1981–1989), translated title]** Dissertation (Master's Degree in Social History)—Faculty of Teacher Training of São Gonçalo, State University of Rio de Janeiro, São Gonçalo, 2014.

32. "Aumentaram os ingressos." [Tickets have increased, translated title]. *Última hora*, June 28, 1983, p. 12.

33. "Ana Lucia. Queen of the fans." *Revista do Vasco*. No. 10, Oct., Nov., Dec. 1984, p. 27. Documentation provided by Centro de Memória do Vasco da Gama.

to the players and the technical commission, managing to keep contact with some players and members.

Being a Woman and a Supporter: The Different Ways of Being a Fan in the Brazilian Stands

Arlei Damo argues that the club identity, i.e., being a supporter of a specific football team, results in a feeling of belonging.[34] This belonging may be associated to neighborhood clubs, city clubs, or to bigger, better known clubs, whose fans may provide more grandiosity to the spectacle. This feeling of belonging and participating in a club can go beyond geographical borders. According to the author:

> This reinforces, in my opinion, the thesis that football mobilizes a series of national issues, including regional differences, causing fans from states whose clubs are less expressive from a performative point of view to opt for other clubs, from other states, but which guarantee the fan an effective, interested and successful participation in the national football scenario.[35]

However, this rooting, or belonging and club identity also vary according to gender. Women's belonging or liking for sports is questioned mainly due to the social construction made about women as the mistress of the home and domestic space, not of the football field, or of the stands, reaffirming the differentiations between those who should participate in the public and private space. As Damo points out:

> Rooting, or belonging, as they may wish, may vary, at least in the case of Brazilian football, according to gender relations. Among the representations of male fans, it is common to hear metaphors that approximate the love for the club to the love for a woman. Souza (1996) dedicates a chapter of her dissertation to the theme of sexuality in Brazilian football, disputing the claims that football is a "lesson in democracy." According to Souza, women are excluded from football as a subject to the extent that they themselves are the object of football discussions,

---

34. DAMO, Arlei. **Para o que der e vier: o pertencimento clubístico no futebol brasileiro a partir do Grêmio foot-ball Porto Alegrense [For Better or Worse: Club Belonging in Brazilian Football Through the *Grêmio Foot-Ball Porto Alegrense* club, translated title].** Dissertation presented to the post-graduation program in Social Anthropology of the Federal University of Rio Grande do Sul, 1998.

35. *Idem*, p. 38.

> metaphors and analogies. As a field reserved for the "symbol of masculinity," football would reinforce the "traditional male domination in Brazil."[36]

But after all, what is this gender determination in the stands? What differentiates the behaviour of men and women, and delimits that space as a masculine space?

The stands, considered for a long time as a *place for men,* ended up translating, or expecting to produce a defined enactment of masculinity, and reproducing a standard understood as masculine and heterosexual. According to João Moura, the very architecture of football stadiums contributes to the idea of being places of male belonging. As the author analyzes, "the circular space (as a rule) of football stadiums refers to the architecture of the great Roman Coliseum, in which, curiously or not, fighting spectacles that determined the masculine virility were staged."[37]

However, in addition to determining places of belonging, stadiums and stands specifically provide us some insights. As already mentioned, they allow producing and reproducing certain norms and forms of conduct considered as standard. Therefore, Bandeira states that stadiums exercise pedagogy. For him:

> Football stadiums can be thought of as a specific cultural context that teaches behaviours, values, "correct" or "adequate" forms of various practices through its architectural design, repeated chants and explicit performances. Stadiums constitute a cultural artifact, they are produced, they are made and they are carriers of pedagogies. Stadiums are concrete things, not only because they are made of concrete, but because they are constituted as artifacts, bearers of gender and sexuality pedagogies, among other cultural pedagogies. It is necessary to go through different learning processes so that subjects can be introduced into this cultural context. Being in a football stadium means going through different pedagogies. It is necessary to learn when to shout, when to be quiet, what to shout, what to be quiet, what and how to feel[38]

---

36. *Idem,* p. 61.

37. MOURA, João Carlos da Cunha. Joguem como Homens! Masculinidades, liberdade de expressão e homofobia em estádios de futebol no estado do Maranhão [Play Like Men! Masculinities, Freedom of Expression and Homophobia in Football Stadiums in the State of Maranhão, translated title]. Jundiaí, SP: Paco Editorial, 2019, p. 49.

38. BANDEIRA, Gustavo Andrada. Uma História do Torcer no presente. Elitização, racismo e heterossexismo no currículo de masculinidade dos torcedores de futebol [A History of Cheering in the Present. Elitism, Racism and Hetero-sexism in the Masculinity Curriculum of Football Fans, translated title]. Curitiba: Appris, 2019, 2019, p. 116.

Within this pedagogy of the stands, the heteronormative male standard is exalted, causing even some progressive groupings to try and fit within some sort of standard.

In Brazil, the role o f a football supporter is regulated by specific legislation, known as the *Estatuto do Torcedor* (Fan Statute), created under the aegis of the government of the current president of Brazil, Luíz Inácio Lula da Silva, in his first term in office, in 2003. According to such law, a "fan" is defined, in its second article, as: "every person who appreciates, supports or associates himself with any sporting practice entity in the country and follows the practice of this sport."[39] According to the law, therefore, a supporter is every person who identifies himself with a team or club and follows it, assiduously or not.

A first interesting observation to be made regarding the statute is that there is, in the body of the law, no mention or differentiated treatment of gender, whether thinking about the preservation of their physical integrity or their guaranteed access and permanence on match days and venues.[40] Therefore, there is no particular observance in the legislation of the presence of women and their own agendas in sporting events. I understand that this silencing may be analyzed in different ways. The first one is to believe that the non-differentiation aimed at avoiding the accusation of segregation of the feminine public, since the need for their own agendas could be questioned. This explanation empties itself, since it is the will and request of the women themselves that some measures prioritize their safety and comfort. The second explanation resides in the fact that the absence of specific guidelines for women is due to the fact that it is not believed that stadiums are environments widely frequented by women, and therefore, specific articles for women would not be necessary.

Many researches on fans and cheering have focused primarily on organized (male) supporters. However, as Bandeira already argued, in his doctorate research about *common* supporters of *Grêmio Foot-Ball Porto Alegrense* club, the fans considered common, who regularly attend the stadiums, but are not associated to any specific fan clubs, also embody several characteristics of cheering and

---

39. BRAZIL. Decree-Law No. 10.671, May 15, 2003. Available at: https://www2.camara.leg.br/legin/fed/lei/2003/lei-10671-15-maio-2003-496694-publicacaooriginal-1-pl.html. Accessed on March 15, 2023.

40. It can be argued that, in stadiums and sporting events, the female search is made by women, thus giving a gender highlight to female participation in these events. However, the bill establishing the search in sports events (PL 4627/16), determining that it must be made by persons of the same sex, is a general law, which refers to events of any nature. In other words, in the specific legislation for the case of sports—and football—such as the aforementioned Fan Statute, there is no determined gender specificity.

are also educated based on the pedagogy of the stadiums and stands, so that they may effectively participate in the belonging to that environment. According to the author:

> "The organized fans, seen as protagonists in the representations of cheering may generate a certain impression of homogeneity in the fan manifestations in football stadiums. However, many disputes for legitimacy take place, especially in the sectors of 'common fans.'"[41]

Among female fans, this dispute is no less true. It is still very common to hear that women understand football less than men because they do not practice it, although this statement has been questioned and criticized by sports fans and researchers, as is the case of the aforementioned sociologist Arlei Damo. Damo states that the understanding of a football match is the result of the communication established between the act and the reaction it provokes. Without underestimating the relevance of the experience, the author argues that, perceiving the game as a language and considering the players as senders and the fans as receivers, each kick would correspond to a code that needs to be deciphered by those in the stands.[42]

This being the case, a certain bid can be understood even by those not directly involved in it or even by those who have never participated in a similar event. It is enough to attribute a meaning to the event, and this is within the reach of any individual regardless of gender. As the years went by, the variety of fan groups which had more or less the same characteristics of the *youth fan clubs* of the previous decades increased, in addition to the presence of the original *youth fan clubs*, which exist until nowadays in the stands in Rio de Janeiro. This increased more and more the divisions in the stadiums and, thus, enabled the increase of the dispute among them. As already seen, the identity statement of a fan group is made, above all, in contrast with the other, the different, the rival. Even if this rival is a fan club of the same team.

Rosana Teixeira describes some of the organizational characteristics that define *youth fan clubs*—and organized groups in general that follow the same pattern—in Rio de Janeiro.[43] According to her, these associations have a nonprofit nature and are basically organized by means of a structure that comprises a president and vice

41. BANDEIRA, 2019, p. 85.

42. Damo (1998).

43. TEIXEIRA (2003).

president; council; several boards (financial, communication, banners and flags, drums) and their members who are responsible for the payment of the monthly fee that ensures, roughly speaking, the settling of expenses with the headquarters, employees, who are also supporters, and other expenses of the fan club.

The identification with these fans occurs through the use of shirts, the placement of flags and through the chants they sing during the games. Thanks to their protesting character, the organized groups often sing songs that offend or insult players, coaches, managers, or even other fans, often those considered to be their direct rivals, such as Flamengo and Vasco in Rio de Janeiro, for example.

The association of these fan clubs with violence in football is a theme that permeates the common understanding and is ratified by the press and much of the sports media. Of course, there are some journalists and sports commentators who still seek to relativize all the attribution of violence to these groups, considering that the violence attributed to the organized fan clubs is carried out by a minority belonging to them. The violence discourse was one of the arguments used and responsible for the creation of the new ways of cheering and fan groupings in Brazil as of the 2000s, as informed by Francisco Rodrigues.[44] This is the case of the so-called *Torcidas de Alento (Fans of encouragement)*, which began to spread across the country from the birth of the *Torcida Geral do Grêmio (General supporters of Gremio)*, founded in 2001.

These new forms of cheering are born in a moment considered to be a crisis of the organized fan groups, which suffered great restrictions in the 1990s, due to major episodes of violence, such as the known case of the *Guerra do Pacaembu (Pacaembu War)*, in São Paulo, which culminated in the expulsion or severe punishment of these groups. Or even at a time of greater commercialization of football, and the beginning of its elitism. Isabella Menezes, in a book resulting from her dissertation on two fan clubs of *Botafogo de Futebol e Regatas* states that she starts from the premise that "the modernisation of football enables/stimulates the emergence of transformations in the way of cheering."[45]

---

44. RODRIGUES, Francisco Carvalho dos Santos. **Amizade, trago e alento. A torcida Geral do Grêmio (2001–2011) da rebeldia à institucionalização: mudança na relação entre torcedores e clubes no campo esportivo brasileiro [Friendship, Drag and Encouragement. The General Supporters of Gremio (2001–2011) from Rebellion to Institutionalization: Change in the Relationship Between Fans and Clubs in the Brazilian Sports Field, translated title].** 2012. 140fls. Dissertation (master's degree)—Universidade Federal Fluminense (Fluminense Federal University), Instituto de Ciências Humanas e Filosofia (Institute for Humanities and Philosophy), Department of History.

45. MENEZES, Isabella Trindade. **Entre a Fúria e a Loucura: Análise de duas formas de torcer pelo Botafogo de Futebol e Regatas. (Between Rage and Madness: Analysis of Two Ways of Rooting for Botafogo de Futebol e Regatas)** Rio de Janeiro: Editora Multifoco, 2017, p. 76.

This new form of fan association had its first exponent in the *Grêmio* fan clubs, as already mentioned. According to Francisco Rodrigues, tired of the internal fights among *Grêmio's* fan clubs, supporters from *Torcida Jovem (Youth Fan Club)* decided to change their places on the stands and start watching the matches in the general area, a place that would later on give the name to a new fan club, and inaugurate a different way of cheering for their team.[46] Instead of the protesting spirit of the youth fan clubs, the emerging fan club took a stance of encouragement toward their players, proposing to support the team with songs of support throughout the game, giving no room for booing or complaints. According to Rodrigues:

> In that "new" space, they wanted to sing, fundamentally. To sing throughout the whole game for *Gremio*, for the team on the field, to change the mood of the players, demanding from them, in return, dedication and total delivery on the field. And it was no longer a matter of simply singing. His chants were called *Alentos*. An expression that represented what was necessary to be in that place, which did not demand formal requirements for its new adepts.[47]

It is thanks to this new way of cheering and singing, supporting and encouraging the players that these new supporters sought to differentiate themselves from the organized ones, which according to them only sang when the team scored goals. This fan club, in specific, still has other particular characteristics, such as the use of *rags,* old cloths where some image or news is painted, or even the realization of the so-called *avalanche* after *Grêmio* has scored a goal, where the fans from the upper levels go down the bleachers until they reach the stadium's railing. For Rodrigues:

> In a moment of rupture with other institutions, it was reinforced that the supporters present in the general seating area were not equal to those who they accused of being corrupt, profiteers of *Grêmio* and who did not encourage the club. The use of an old flag turned into a rag made those new supporters, an *anti-fan club*. The memory of the creation of this symbol is marked ritually as the passage of a group from being questioning people into being a new movement, a new fan club.[48]

46. RODRIGUES, 2012.

47. RODRIGUES, 2012. *Op. Cit*, p. 51.

48. RODRIGUES, *Op. Cit*, p. 53.

Still according to the author, the denomination of this fan club as a "*torcida de alento*" (*Alento fan club)* is due to the coat of arms of the new fan club, where the words: "Drag, friendship, encouragement (*alento)*" are written. For him, the extension of the nomenclature "*torcida de alento*" to other fan club associations such as the ones born in Rio de Janeiro, as of 2006, should be further studied. However, other authors, such as the already mentioned Isabella Menezes, make use of such classification for the fan clubs of Rio de Janeiro, a classification that will also be used here, as in Rio de Janeiro, one of the principles of these new fan clubs is also to unconditionally support the team, which makes possible the association between the support of the fan clubs from Rio de Janeiro and the encouragement used by the *Gremio* supporters.[49] Examples of such fan clubs in Rio de Janeiro are: *Guerreiros do Almirante* (Admiral's Warriors), of *Vasco da Gama* football club; *Movimento Popular Legião Tricolor* (People's Movement of the Tricolor Legion), from *Fluminense* Football Club; *Loucos pelo Botafogo* (Crazy for Botafogo), from *Botafogo* Football Club; and *Urubuzada* (Vultures), from *Flamengo* Football Club.

Some of these supporters groups take their inspiration in another way of cheering, widely used in South American countries, especially in Argentina and Uruguay, known as *barrabrava,* so much so that some *Carioca* fan clubs born through this new movement, identify themselves on their websites using the bars nomenclature, as is the case of *Loucos pelo Botafogo*[50] and *Guerreiros do Almirante*,[51] which in their own page on the social networking site *Facebook,* characterize themselves as such. This association with the same way of cheering as the *hermanos* should be, however, a little nuanced. Just like the supporters of the organized fan clubs in Brazil, the members of the South American bars are concerned with embellishing the spectacle, taking flags, vertical banners,

49. It is important to mention that I am aware of the debates about the extension or not of the term to the fan clubs in Rio de Janeiro, however, it is not the purpose of this work to create or counterpose new concepts about supporters and fans. This said, such denomination works for the purposes proposed by this research, which is, roughly, to understand the female position within these fan clubs. It is also important to mention that the fluidity between supporters and between the groupings themselves was not disregarded.

Gustavo Bandeira (2019), in his doctoral thesis, also makes use of the nomenclature *Torcida de Alento* to refer to the new Rio de Janeiro fan clubs. According to the author "Despite the imperative unconditional support appearing in supporters' chants (especially from the *General fan clubs*'s ethic/aesthetic of rooting for *Gremio*, in the same way as the *Popular fan club,* in the *Internacional* Football Club), what in Rio de Janeiro has been called torcida de *alento*..." (BANDEIRA, 2019, p. 55).

50. *Loucos pelo Botafogo* fan club page. Available at: https://www.facebook.com/LoucosPeloBotafogoOficial. ("The Facebook page is no longer used. To consult the group, consult your Instagram: https://www.instagram.com/loucosbotafogo/.") Accessed on March 9, 2023.

51 Guerreiros *do Almirante* Fan club page. Available at: https://www.facebook.com/gdavg/. Accessed on March 9, 2023.

musical instruments etc. But the association tends to stop there. The violence often associated with the South American bars is precisely what condemns the movements called *barras* in Brazil.

Two observations are important here. The first one is to highlight the fluidity of these supporters' groups and their members. As already stated throughout this work, belongings and identities are multiple and may vary. This multiplicity is what enables a supporter to be part of an organized fan club, then join a bar, condemning the principles of the organized fan clubs, and then return to take part in an organized fan club again, perhaps the one he previously took part in, or even another one. This idea of belonging to a certain grouping, although for some fans should be permanent and the exchange condemned, for others it is changeable and fluid. This mobility is also true within the groupings themselves: some which are born as fan clubs may become a movement or a bar, or even take an opposite path. What is important to highlight is that, despite the definitions made, neither the mentioned groupings nor their members are in a logic of fixity and immobility. On the contrary, both are and/or can be and carry out changes and flexibilities regarding their belonging as fans.

All explanations and demarcations made about the forms of association and fan clubs in Brazil include, of course, the female participation. As of the 2000s, the female presence in Brazilian stadiums has been increasing and, with it, the demands and claims raised by women from and in the stands.

So much so that a movement of female fans entitled *Mulheres de Arquibancada* (Women of the Stands) was created in Brazil. The movement, which unites female fans from different teams and clubs, including rivals, seeks to debate and propose improvements for themselves. Being a woman in the stands produces and exports a different belonging than being a man in the fan clubs. The gender demarcations and stereotypes mentioned in this work, which fell upon female fans throughout several decades in the 20th century did not magically disappear in the 21st century. In many cases, the stereotypes were updated and remodeled, but the gender issues and prejudices are still present in the stands.

So much so that the Women of the Stands movement, in 2017, organized an event, hosted by the Football Museum in São Paulo, in order to debate the situation of female fans in Brazil and, above all, to draw up agendas to be discussed, both within the fan clubs to which they belonged and by *ANATORG* (*Associação Nacional de Torcidas Organizadas* [National Association of Organized Fans]).

Before the end of the meeting, a letter of intentions was collectively drafted, containing the main proposals raised by the female fans during the meeting, seeking to be a fighting objective for the next meetings. The letter brought such propositions in the structure of topics, with a short introduction that will be transcribed here:

> The propositions below were gathered and elaborated based on the speeches made by the female fans present at the event. These suggestions contribute to the construction of more democratic, equitable and inclusive environment in football. It will also serve as a relevant documentary instrument in the record of women's participation in the history of Brazilian football, besides guiding the debate on problems and inequalities in the scope of fan clubs, collectives, football venues, public authorities, civil and military police officers, sports journalists and representatives of the State Sports Secretariat. As it is known, the organised football fan clubs occupy an important place in the social imaginary and in public opinion in general. It is understood that the indicators presented in this document may contribute to the discussion made by the media, as well as to the constitution of adequate public policies, taking into consideration the contribution of women who have been participating for years and assiduously in supporters groups, as well as those who attend individually the different environments dedicated to this sport.[52]

Thus, the document intended to synthesize the pleas and wishes of female fans inside and outside the stadiums, so that soon the stands and football could effectively be considered inclusive. Among the guidelines, the following stood out: attention to women's football; safety in the stadiums, especially through the implementation of a *Women's Police Department*, as well as the training of police officers to deal with female fans; the fight against structural sexism and the end of restrictions to women's clothing and accessories in the stadiums, as well as to their roles in the fan clubs; the improvement in the stadiums' structures to serve women; as well as the insertion of women in representative bodies such as *ANATORG*, among other demands.

Most of these demands have not yet been met; however, the importance of the event lies in the very fact of its existence. This demonstrates not only the

[52] Documento de proposições do 1° Encontro Nacional de Mulheres de Arquibancada [Proposal document of the 1st National Meeting of the Women of the Stands movement, translated text], 2017, p. 1. Available at: https://museudo-futebol.org.br/crfb/eventos/662830/. Accessed on March 10, 2023 (Document from author's personal collection).

presence of women in the stands in Brazil but also their fight for more equitable conditions for cheering.

Conclusion: A Woman's Place

They know what offside is. And you, do you know what respect is?[53]

In view of what was shown in this article, we can state that women's journey in the stands is perennial and constant throughout the 20th and 21st centuries. Just like the sport itself, the meaning of cheering and the ways of being and presenting oneself as a supporter have varied over time. However, the association of women with football—whether in the stands or on the pitch—has never ceased to exist.

As if to ratify the arguments presented here, especially that of the female presence regardless of having or not a partner in the stadium, and the estrangement of fans related to violence, recently, the supporters of *Coritiba*, a football club in *Paraná* state, were punished for violent acts and banned from going to the stadium in their team's subsequent match.

In view of this, the *Coxa-branca* women[54] took on a huge role and, often accompanied by their sons and daughters, filled the stands of *Major Couto Pereira* Stadium and delivered a beautiful spectacle, singing from beginning to end and making their voices heard from a distance in the surroundings of the stadium.[55]

This fact demonstrates two things. The first, already exhaustively pointed out in this article, is that the female presence is independent of the male. Women's appreciation for football and their team is true and is what brings them to the stadiums, not their companions.

The second point is the association between fan masculinity and violence. The punishment of the male fan club members occurred after an episode of violence in a derby. The fact that only women and children were allowed in

53. Phrase written on a poster by female supporters of Remo, which ended up being used by other supporters later, when they joined the #deixaelatorcer (Let Her Cheer) campaign. Available at: <https://gauchazh.clicrbs.com.br/esportes/noticia/2018/03/torcedoras-usam-a-hashtag-deixaelatorcer-para-pedir-respeito-as-mulheres-nos-estadios-cjeujrqaz03uq01p4nqbejxi8.html>. Accessed on March 16, 2023.

54. *Coxa-Branca* is the nickname given to the fans of Coritiba.

55. "Coritiba coloca apenas mulheres e crianças no estádio após punição por briga de torcidas" ["Coritiba puts only women and children in the stadium after punishment for fan fights", translated title). Available at: https://www.cnnbrasil.com.br/esporte/coritiba-coloca-apenas-mulheres-e-criancas-no-estadio-apos-punicao-por-briga-de-torcidas/. Accessed on March 16, 2023.

the subsequent games made it clear that the authorities associate the violence carried out to masculinity and to the male members of the fan clubs, especially the organized ones.

Another recent situation that rekindles the debates raised here concerns the bill by Member of Parliament Sâmia Bomfim, proposal 168/2023, which provides half-priced entry tickets to football matches for women.[56] The justification of the bill is due to the exclusion of women from football in Brazil, especially through the prohibition decree, which contributed to reaffirm the logic of football as a masculine space. However, this bill may, and I believe it will, if the discussion advances in the chamber, raise some debates. I will highlight two of them here.

The first concerns the intentionality of the project. As already pointed out in this article, in the 1980s a proposal for half-priced entry tickets for women had been mentioned, generating conflicting reactions. Of course, it is necessary to consider the change in mentality between that proposal and the new legislative proposal. However, I believe that statements of the same nature, alleging that everyone would want to be a woman, can be repeated in Brazilian society.

Besides, the proposal can also be interpreted in a paternalistic way, as if women needed to be encouraged somehow to go to the stadiums, or that they would only go if they did not have to pay for it. Still in this sense, assuming that Brazilian society still carries strong traces of misogyny and sexism resulting from the patriarchy, it is reasonable to assume that such a proposal will lead many male fans to disagree with the half-priced entry tickets, resulting in the most varied reactions, such as belittling the idea of the proposal or even trying to take advantage with the resale of the ticket.

In the meantime, a second point of analysis is related to the real need for half-priced entry tickets. The fact is that in different regions of Brazil, tickets for matches are becoming more and more expensive, especially in stadium arenas. However, the value of the tickets is much more a question of class than gender. I believe there would be much more value in a policy that aims at reducing the price of tickets or a way to subsidize some tickets for the low-income population. No doubt such a proposal would make much bigger steps toward making football what it originally was intended to be: a popular sport.

There are certainly many other points to be debated about the proposal, and they will certainly be debated in the bodies responsible for doing so, such as

56. BRAZIL, Câmara dos Deputados (Chamber of Deputies). PL 168/2023. Available at: https://www.camara.leg.br/proposicoesWeb/fichadetramitacao?idProposicao=2346893. Accessed on March 15, 2023.

the Chamber of Deputies. The presentation of the proposal here aims rather at starting a discussion rather than to answer them.

The female presence in the fan clubs, paraphrasing an analogy by Suely Gomes, presents itself as a rhizome.[57] Always there, even if scattered or small in quantity, or even if not always on the surface. Female fans, in Rio de Janeiro and in Brazil, have always been present in support of their favorite team.

REFERENCES

BANDEIRA, Gustavo Andrada. **Uma História do Torcer no presente**: elitização, racismo e heterossexismo no currículo de masculinidade dos torcedores de futebol [A History of Cheering in the Present. Elitism, Racism and Hetero Sexism in the Masculinity Curriculum of Football Fans, translated title]. Curitiba: Appris, 2019.

BOURDIEU, Pierre. **A dominação masculina**: a condição feminina e a violência de gênero [Male Domination. The Female Condition and Gender Violence, translated title]. Rio de Janeiro: Bertrand Brasil, 2019.

COSTA, Leda Maria. O que é uma torcedora? Notas sobre a representação e autorrepresentação do público feminino de futebol [What Is a Female Fan? Notes on the Representation and Self-Representation of the Female Football Audience, translated title]. In: **Esporte e Sociedade** *[Sport and Society, translated title]*, n. 4, Rio de Janeiro, 2006.

DAMO, Arlei. **Para o que der e vier**: o pertencimento clubístico no futebol brasileiro a partir do Grêmio foot-ball Porto Alegrense [For Better or Worse: Club Belonging in Brazilian Football Through the *Grêmio Foot-Ball Porto Alegrense* club, translated title]. Dissertation presented to the post-graduation program in Social Anthropology of the Federal University of Rio Grande do Sul, 1998.

ELSEY, Brenda; NADEL, Joshua. ***Futbolera****. A History of Women and Sports in Latin America.* Texas: University of Texas Press, 2019.

GOELLNER, Silvana Vilodre. Mulheres e futebol no Brasil: entre sombras e visibilidades [Women and Football in Brazil: Between Shadows and Visibilities,

57. GOMES, Sueli. "Onda, rizoma e 'sororidade' como metáforas: representações das mulheres e dos femininos" [Wave, Rhizome and 'Sorority' as Metaphors: Representations of Women and the Feminine, translated title] (Paris, Rio de Janeiro: anos 70/80 do século XX) (Paris, Rio de Janeiro: 70s/80s of the twentieth century, translated title). *InterThesis Magazine*, Santa Catarina, 2009.

translated title]. In: **Revista Brasileira Educação Física e Esporte**. São Paulo, v. 19, n. 2, pp. 143–151, abr./jun. 2005.

GOMES, Sueli. Onda, rizoma e "sororidade" como metáforas: representações das mulheres e dos femininos [Wave, Rhizome and "Sorority" as Metaphors: Representations of Women and the Feminine, translated title] (Paris, Rio de Janeiro: anos 70/80 do século XX) [Paris, Rio de Janeiro: 70s/80s of the Twentieth Century, translated title]. In: **Inter Thesis Magazine**, Santa Catarina, 2009.

HOLLANDA, Bernardo Buarque de. **O clube como vontade e representação**: o jornalismo esportivo e a formação das torcidas organizadas de futebol do Rio de Janeiro. [The Club as Will and Representation: Sports Journalism and the Formation of Organised Football Fans in Rio de Janeiro, translated title]. Rio de Janeiro: 7Letras, 2010.

HOLLANDA, Bernardo Borges Buarque de. A festa competitiva: formação e crise das torcidas organizadas entre 1950 e 1980 [The Competitive Party: Formation and Crisis of the Organized Fans Between 1950 and 1980, translated title]. In: HOLLANDA, Bernardo Buarque de.; MALAIA, João M.C.; TOLEDO, Luiz Henrique de.; MELO, Victor Andrade de. (orgs.). **A torcida Brasileira** [The Brazilian Fans, translated title]. Rio de Janeiro: 7Letras, 2012.

MALAIA, João. Torcer, torcedores, torcedoras, torcida (Bras.): 1910–1950 [Cheering, Fans, Female Fans: 1910–1950, translated title]. In: HOLLANDA, Bernardo Buarque de.; MALAIA, João M.C.; TOLEDO, Luiz Henrique de.; MELO, Victor Andrade de. (orgs.). **A torcida brasileira [The Brazilian fans, translated title]**. Rio de Janeiro: 7Letras, 2012.

MAGALHÃES, Lívia Gonçalves. **Com a taça nas mãos**: sociedade, Copa do Mundo e ditadura no Brasil e na Argentina [With the Cup in Their Hands. Society, World Cup and Dictatorship in Brazil and Argentina, translated title]. Rio de Janeiro: Lamparina, FAPERJ, 2014.

MENEZES, Isabella Trindade. **Entre a Fúria e a Loucura**: análise de duas formas de torcer pelo Botafogo de Futebol e Regatas [Between Rage and Madness: Analysis of two ways of rooting for Botafogo de Futebol e Regatas]. Rio de Janeiro: Editora Multifoco, 2017.

MOURA, João Carlos da Cunha. **Joguem como Homens!** masculinidades, liberdade de expressão e homofobia em estádios de futebol no estado do Maranhão [Play Like Men! Masculinities, Freedom of Expression and Homophobia in Football Stadiums in the State of Maranhão, translated title]. Jundiaí, SP: Paco Editorial, 2019, p. 49.

RODRIGUES, Francisco Carvalho dos Santos. **Amizade, trago e alento**: a torcida Geral do Grêmio (2001–2011) da rebeldia à institucionalização: mudança na relação entre torcedores e clubes no campo esportivo brasileiro. [Friendship, Drag and Encouragement. The General Supporters of Gremio (2001–2011) from Rebellion to Institutionalization: Change in the Relationship Between Fans and Clubs in the Brazilian Sports Field, translated title], 2012, 140fls. Dissertation (master's degree)—Universidade Federal Fluminense (Fluminense Federal University), Instituto de Ciências Humanas e Filosofia (Institute for Humanities and Philosophy), Department of History.

SCOTT, Joan. Gender: Uma categoria útil de análise histórica [A Useful Category of Historical Analysis, translated title]. In: **Revista Educação e Realidade** [Education and Reality Journal, translated title], Jul/Dec. 1995.

TEIXEIRA, Rosana da Câmara. **Os perigos da paixão**: visitando jovens torcidas cariocas [The Dangers of Passion. Visiting Young Carioca Fans, translated title]. São Paulo: Annablume, 2003.

TEIXEIRA, Leonardo Antonio de Carvalho. **Congregar, congraçar e unir**: a atuação da Associação das Torcidas Organizadas do Rio de Janeiro (1981–1989) [To Congregate, to Harmonize and to Unite: The Work of the Association of Organized Fan Clubs of Rio de Janeiro (1981–1989), translated title] Dissertation (master's degree in social history)—Faculty of Teacher Training of São Gonçalo, State University of Rio de Janeiro, São Gonçalo, 2014.

PART II

Contemporary Aspects of Women's Football Universe

CHAPTER 7

Women in the Brazilian Football Universe: An Overview from Theses and Dissertations in Social Sciences (2012-2022)[1]

Mariane Pisani

Introduction

Circumscribing, synthesizing, mapping, and representing are ideas that are linked to the action of delimiting, in a universe of possibilities, artifacts that make up a specific theme or subject. In the production of scientific knowledge, bibliographic reviews are often important instruments that can, for example, point out gaps and problems in an area of knowledge; indicate the formulation of new hypotheses and questions to be explored; suggest new methods and techniques for conducting research; and systematize articles, theses, and dissertations on a given subject or theme. It is also worth noting that bibliographic reviews are important resources for novice researchers to become familiar with the field they wish to research.

In the field of sports practices, and more specifically in the case of Brazilian football, several bibliographic reviews have been carried out over the last years. The mappings and representations are so diverse that they can be chosen, for example, from (i) area of knowledge, with the most common being those carried out in the humanities (Toledo, 2001; Gastaldo, 2010; Giglio and Spaggiari, 2010; Damo, 2016; Spaggiari et al., 2016; Toledo, 2021) and in Health Sciences (Melo and Genovez, 1998); or from (ii) specific themes, on women's football in physical education and history (Beirith et al., 2021; Goellner, 2013) or on fans and organized supporters (Sousa and Abrahão, 2022); and from (iii) comparisons between Brazilian productions and those hailing from other Latin American countries (Alabarces, 2004; Alabarces, 2011; Guedes, 2011).

[1] I am grateful to Felippe Cesar Chiella for his help with the careful translation of the manuscript.

As previously stated, mappings and representations of works produced from an area of knowledge can have different focuses. However, it is evident that there are some gaps when we look at bibliographic reviews on football in Brazil. Therefore, the present article aims to systematize academic works such as theses and dissertations published in the broad area of knowledge of Humanities and, more specifically, in the subareas of Social Sciences, Anthropology, Political Science, and Sociology, which address the presence of women in the universe of Brazilian football. Whether from the perspective of those involved in the sport as athletes, supporters, referees, managers, coaches, or journalists; or from the perspective of women who write and produce scientific knowledge about football.

Analyzing football in Brazil from a perspective of humanities and some of its sub-areas and together considering the presence or absence of women in this field allows us to understand how gender norms and standards create differences that enable exclusion, participation and/or recognition of women in this sport. It is through the theoretical and methodological contributions offered by Social Sciences, Anthropology, Political Science, and Sociology that we can examine in detail the institutional and political structures that guide the presence of women in football, whether as athletes, supporters, managers, coaches, journalists, referees, and/or researchers. These limitations and possibilities that emerge in practical experience and also in scientific work offer excellent data and indicators so that we can promote public policies aimed at gender equity and inclusion in football.

It is also noteworthy that in 2020, researchers Claudia Kessler, Leda Maria Costa, and Mariane da Silva Pisani organized and published a book collection entitled "*As mulheres no universo do futebol brasileiro*" (*Women in the Universe of Brazilian Football*) (2020) in Brazil. The material was initially published in ebook format (2020) and two years later printed (2022). The collection makes an allusion to DaMatta's work in its title and points out the absence of women in the 1982 work, either as researchers and except for the presence of Simoni Lahud Guedes, or as research interlocutors. The book (2020 and 2022) had seventeen academic articles and one interview, written by twenty-four authors from different areas of knowledge—Humanities, Health Sciences, and Applied Social Sciences—of which six were men and eighteen were women.

It was from the process of organizing the book (Kessler et al., 2020, 2022), and from daily contact with researchers who so generously contributed chapters and research data so that the work could be published, that we realized that discussing about the presence of women in the universe of Brazilian football, especially from Social Sciences is extremely important. Not only because the pioneer of football studies in Brazil was a woman (Guedes, 1977), but because sports, and more specifically football in Brazilian culture, is a socially and culturally widespread activity throughout the country. Thus, football played in Brazil still reflects and shapes power relations, norms, and values that prevail in Brazilian society.

In order to better circumscribe this objective, we imposed some necessary delimitations. The first one concerns the choice of publications to be taken into consideration. In this study, we chose to work with publications in the format of theses and dissertations: first, because we understand that these products are the result of larger research efforts, two and four years respectively; second, because they are works that usually have good bibliographic reviews and more critical details on the methodological procedures adopted during research.

It is worth noting that the non-inclusion of academic journal articles in this bibliographic survey has some valid reasons. First, it would be necessary to manage a long series of questions and reservations regarding the indexing and circulation processes of journals throughout the Brazilian national territory. That is, there is no standardization in the criteria of the main Brazilian indexers that dictate which journals may or may not be included. For this reason, on an indexer portal such as Scielo, a researcher is able to find a range of journals and articles; on the other hand, conducting the same search in another indexer portal, such as the Directory of Open Access Journals (DOAJ), may not yield the same results. This complexity of the publishing market makes it difficult to conduct an accurate bibliographic review.

The second delimitation of this study concerns the period of time allocated for the survey of theses and dissertations. We chose to work with publications made in a ten-year period, that is, from 2012 to 2022. This choice took into account the physical space, formatting, and ordering that must be followed when writing and producing an academic article.[2] Thus, dissertations and theses defended before 2012 and from the first semester of 2023 onward will not be counted in this bibliographic survey.

A third delimitation was made based on the subject matter worked on, that is, we gave priority to works that addressed—from different methodologies—the presence of women in the universe of Brazilian football. Which means that beyond works on athletes and football players, we included in this review works that

[2]. A Portuguese version of this article was submitted to the *Revista Brasileira de Informação Bibliográfica em Ciências Sociais (BIB)* (*Brazilian Journal of Bibliographic Information in Social Sciences*), which recommends to the authors of bibliographic reviews in different areas of knowledge time gaps of four or ten years.

discussed the presence of women in positions such as club managers, referees, and/or coaches, both in men's football and women's football. In the same way, we also sought to include works on football produced by women researchers, in order to show how knowledge is located (Haraway, 2009).

Consequently, this chapter is divided into three parts. In the first part, we will present how the searches for dissertations and theses were carried out answering: (a) which keywords were used in the searches; (b) which repositories were consulted; (c) if the works are easily accessible; among other questions that concern the ways in which this bibliographic survey was carried out. In the second part, we will discuss how the presence of women in the universe of Brazilian football was presented from selected works. At this point we resort to four guiding axes: (i) women's football in Brazil; (ii) women fans in organized fan clubs and Brazilian football stadiums; (iii) women who work in Brazilian football; (iv) women researching men's Brazilian football. And finally, in the third part, we present our final considerations that point out some paths that can still be taken to increase women's participation in the universe of Brazilian football.

Reviewing Theses and Dissertations on Women in the Brazilian Football Universe

The Consulted Websites

In order to achieve the objective proposed in this chapter, it was necessary to start searching different online portals for dissertations and theses defended between 2012 and 2022 from three specific subareas of the Social Sciences, namely: Anthropology, Political Science and Sociology. The chosen portals were the *Portal Brasileiro de Publicações e Dados Científicos de Acesso Aberto* (Brazilian Portal of Open Access Scientific Publications and Data); the *Biblioteca Digital Brasileira de Teses e Dissertações (BDTD)* (Brazilian Digital Library of Theses and Dissertations); and finally, the *Catálogo de Teses e Dissertações da CAPES* (CAPES's Catalog of Theses and Dissertations).

The Brazilian Portal of Open Access Scientific Publications and Data,[3] or *Oasisbr*, is a site maintained and fed by the *Instituto Brasileiro de Informação em Ciência e Tecnologia (IBICT)* (Brazilian Institute of Information in Science

3. https://oasisbr.ibict.br/vufind/

and Technology) that provides free access to a large amount of scientific and academic material produced in Brazil and other Portuguese-speaking countries. The site allows users to search a wide collection of scientific journals, theses, dissertations, books, and other types of academic publications. In addition, it also offers advanced search resources, including filters by author, title, subject, and type of publication.

The Brazilian Digital Library of Theses and Dissertations *(BDTD)*[4] is part of an initiative fostered and maintained by the Brazilian government to democratize access to the scientific production of Postgraduate Programs throughout the country. The site provides free access to theses and dissertations produced in Brazilian universities in various areas of knowledge. Like *Oasisbr*, *BDTD* also allows the search for theses and dissertations from filters such as author, title, keyword, and university.

Finally, the CAPES's Catalog of Theses and Dissertations *(CTDC)*[5] is a site maintained by the *Coordenação de Aperfeiçoamento de Pessoal de Nível Superior (CAPES)* (Coordination for the Improvement of Higher Education Personnel), a Brazilian government agency responsible for coordinating and developing stricto sensu postgraduate courses (master's and doctorate) in the country. The site allows free access and research on information about theses and dissertations defended in Brazilian postgraduate programs recognized by *CAPES*. The catalogue contains information on works produced in various areas of knowledge and, like the other platforms used in this work, offers an advanced search that allows research by various criteria such as title, author, advisor, institution, year of defense, and keyword. It is worth noting that the site provides detailed information on each work, including summary, abstract, keywords, concentration area, and author data, and, invariably, has an external link that allows us to access the material of each work in full.

Keywords

After delimiting the portals and sites to be consulted for the development of this study, it was necessary to establish which keywords would be necessary to carry out the search. The steps described in this subsection of the text were replicated in

4. https://bdtd.ibict.br/vufind/

5. https://catalogodeteses.capes.gov.br/

all three portals chosen for research. In a first stage, we started the bibliographic search by writing the word *"Futebol"* (Football) in the search engine. *Oasisbr* showed us 12,217 works—including theses, dissertations, books, and articles; *BDTD* presented a set of 2701 theses and dissertations; and *CTDC* generated 2133 results. It is evident that it would be almost humanly impossible to review the more than 17,000 results shown by the three portals.

Therefore, it was necessary to refine the search. The second stage concerns the next attempt to refine the search results; for this purpose, we added the keyword *"Futebol"* to the keyword *"Mulher"* (Woman). Thus, *Oasisbr* showed us 501 results; *BDTD* 128 results; and CAPES's Catalog of Theses and Dissertations twenty-five results. Still in this stage, we chose to also search from the junction between "*Futebol" AND "Mulheres"* (Women), opting for the plural of the noun *Mulher* precisely to highlight any changes in the results presented. We came across the following survey: on the one hand, *Oasisbr* and *BDTD* continued to show the same data, 501 and 128 materials respectively; on the other hand, *CTDC* presented sixty-six works, that is, forty-one more results than when the keywords were "*Futebol" AND "Mulher."* A third stage consisted of carrying out a similar movement but replacing one of the keywords. We then searched for "Futebol" allied with *"Feminino"* (Feminine). Thus, *Oasisbr* provided 720 results; *BDTD* 126 results; and *CTDC* sixty-eight results.

In all three portals it was possible to refine the searches from indicators—which are usually available in the sidebar of the sites, such as: Human Sciences, Social Sciences, Anthropology, Sociology, Political Science, and/or period from 2012 to 2022. The results presented in the next subsection were the published works found on these search systems.

Published Works Found

A total of nineteen master's theses and four doctoral dissertations were found, totaling twenty-three works defended and published in the period from 2012 to 2022, in the broad area of human sciences, and more specifically in the subareas of anthropology, political science, social sciences, and sociology (Tables 8.1–8.6). Anthropology was responsible for conveying six dissertations and three theses; social sciences for nine dissertations and one thesis; sociology for two dissertations; and political science for two dissertations; The materials found on *Oasisbr*, *BDTD*, and *CTDC* is presented in two divisions: (a) by subarea, i.e., how many and which were the works defended in the subareas of Anthropology, Political Science, and Sociology; (b) by the type of material published, whether thesis or dissertation. In the next section of this chapter, we discuss the material found. Except for Figueiredo's complete work (2017), which could not be found, all theses and dissertations listed in this article are possible to find online.

Table 8.1 Master's Theses in Anthropology—Period from 2012 to 2022

Author	*Title*	*Year*	*Institution*
Pisani, Mariane da Silva	PODEROSAS DO FOZ: trajetórias, migrações e profissionalização de mulheres que praticam futebol.	2012	Universidade Federal de Santa Catarina (UFSC)
Almeida, Caroline Soares de	"Boas de bola": Um estudo sobre o ser jogadora de futebol no Esporte Clube Radar durante a década de 1980	2013	Universidade Federal de Santa Catarina (UFSC)
Oliveira, Valleria Araujo de	Periguetes, sapatões e mulherzinhas: (des)construindo o que "ser mulher" no campo de futebol	2014	Universidade Federal de Goiás (UFG)
Figueiredo, Tiago Sales de	Processo de Institucionalização do Futebol Feminino no Brasil e no Uruguai: Perspectivas comparadas, feminismos e políticas públicas	2017	Universidade Federal Fluminense (UFF)
Mandelli, Mariana Carolina	Allianz Parque e Rua Palestra Itália: práticas torcedoras em uma arena multiuso.	2018	Universidade de São Paulo (USP)
Leite, Ana Daniella Fechine	FUTEBOL DE MULHERES: Um estudo feminista nos campos e nas arquibancadas be João Pessoa/PB	2021	Universidade Federal Da Paraíba (UFPB)

Source: PISANI, Mariane (2023).

Table 8.2 Doctoral Dissertations–Period from 2012 to 2022

Author	*Title*	*Year*	*Institution*
Kessler, Claudia Samuel	Mais que Barbies e ogras: uma etnografia do futebol de mulheres no Brasil e nos Estados Unidos	2015	Universidade Federal do Rio Grande do Sul (UFRGS)
Pisani, Mariane da Silva	"Sou feita de chuva, sol e barro": o futebol de mulheres praticado na cidade de São Paulo	2018	Universidade de São Paulo (USP)
Almeida, Caroline Soares de	DO SONHO AO POSSÍVEL: projeto e campo de possibilidades nas carreiras profissionais de futebolistas brasileiras	2018	Universidade Federal de Santa Catarina (UFSC)

Source: PISANI, Mariane (2023).

Table 8.3 Master's Theses in Political Science–Period from 2012 to 2022

Author	*Title*	*Year*	*Institution*
Fernandes, Hevilla Wanderley	NÃO É APENAS UM JOGO: a questão nordestina no futebol	2020	Universidade Federal da Paraíba (UFPB)
Cerreira, Nathalia Borges	AS TORCIDAS ANTIFASCISTAS NO BRASIL: um estudo sobre o ativismo online nas eleições presidenciais de 2018	2020	Universidade Federal do Estado do Rio de Janeiro (Unirio)

Source: PISANI, Mariane (2023).

Table 8.4 Master's Theses in Sociology—Period from 2012 to 2022

Author	*Title*	*Year*	*Institution*
Alves, Cristina Cordeiro	"Posso morrer pelo meu time": A construção social da rivalidade clubística entre Grêmio e Internacional e a sua	2013	Universidade Federal do Rio Grande do Sul (UFRGS)
Vale, Ana Hilda Lima do	"NÃO É SÓ FUTEBOL": relações de sociabilidade e identidade na torcida Esporão do Galo em Teresina-PI	2019	Universidade Federal do Piauí (UFPI)

Source: PISANI, Mariane (2023).

Table 8.5 Master's Theses in Social Sciences—Period from 2012 to 2022

Author	*Title*	*Year*	*Institution*
Almeida, Ana Letícia Canegal De	Entrando em campo: a "pelada organizada" no Aterro do Flamengo	2012	Pontifícia Universidade Católica Do Rio De Janeiro (PUC-RJ)
Corteze, Kessia Costenaro	O JOGO QUE NUNCA ACABOU: a permanência do Maracanaço no imaginário dos brasileiros	2015	Universidade Federal de Santa Maria (UFSM)
Raposo, Clarissa Carramilo	COBERTURA MIDIÁTICA DAS OLIMPÍADAS RIO 2016: construção da imagem da jogadora de futebol pela imprensa no Brasil e nos Estados Unidos	2018	Universidade Federal do Maranhão (UFMA)
Maltez, Juliana Campos	DAS ARQUIBANCADAS DOS ESTÁDIOS ÀS PISTAS DA CIDADE: um estudo sobre torcedores organizados de Salvador, Bahia	2018	Universidade Federal da Bahia (UFBA)

Silva, Mariana Schade Da	O Canto do Galo da Vila no Espírito Santo: a Trajetória do Atlético Itapemirim e o Seu Processo de Profissionalização	2018	Universidade Federal Do Espírito Santo (UFES)
Khayat, Stella Valentini	JOGO DE FUTEBOL OU FUTEBOL DO JOGO? A CPI do Futebol (2015) como ilustração da dinâmica política do futebol Brasil	2020	Pontifícia Universidade Católica de São Paulo (PUC-SP)
Ziviani, Larissa Nunes	CONSUMO, FUTEBOL E IDENTIDADES: uma abordagem etnográfica do circuito futebolístico da cidade de Araraquara-SP	2020	Universidade Estadual Paulista Júlio De Mesquita Filho (Araraquara)—UNESP
Ferrari, Nathallie Matos	INTERfeminista: as mulheres na gestão do futebol brasileiro	2021	Universidade Estadual De Maringá (UEM)
Andrade, Marianna Castellano Bar	Para além da arquibancada: Uma etnografia sobre as "Gaviãs" da Fiel	2022	Universidade Federal De São Paulo (Unifesp)

Source: PISANI, Mariane (2023).

Table 8.6 Doctoral Dissertations in Social Sciences—Period from 2012 to 2022

Author	*Title*	*Year*	*Institution*
Dantas, Marina De Mattos	Cartografias de um campo invisível: os anônimos jogadores do futebol brasileiro	2017	Pontifícia Universidade Católica de São Paulo (PUC-SP)

Source: PISANI, Mariane (2023).

Possible Discussions from the Material Found

Women's Football in Brazil

From the collected material we were able to perceive that of the twenty-three publications, between theses and dissertations, nine specifically address women's football (Pisani, 2012; Almeida, 2013; Oliveira, 2014; Kessler, 2015; Figueiredo, 2017; Almeida, 2018; Pisani, 2018; Raposo, 2018; Leite, 2021). Most of this material was produced in southern Brazil, with UFSC contributing with three works in the subarea of Anthropology (Pisani, 2012; Almeida, 2013; Almeida, 2018), and UFRGS contributing one work also produced in Anthropology (Kessler, 2015). Regarding the second region that published the most on the subject, we have a tie between the southeastern region, with one work defended at USP (Pisani, 2018) and another at UFF (Figueiredo, 2017), both in the subarea of Anthropology; and the northeastern region, with one work defended at UFPB (Leite, 2021) in the subarea of Anthropology and another at UFMA (Raposo, 2018), in the subarea of Social Sciences. The midwest region contributes only one work on the subject defended at UFG (Oliveira, 2014), also in Anthropology. And the north region does not appear with any contribution on the subject.

From this bibliographic review we can observe that the subarea that researched and published the most about women's football in Brazil was Anthropology. We can also highlight that the Federal University of Santa Catarina was the institution that had the most publications on the subject, with three published works (Pisani, 2012; Almeida, 2013; Almeida, 2018); all of which were supervised by anthropologist Carmen Silvia Rial. Furthermore, within the research period from 2012 to 2022 only two researchers carried out both theses and dissertations on the subject. This is the case of both Pisani (2012 and 2018) and Almeida (2013 and 2018).

Regarding the content of the reviewed works, some researchers dedicate an entire chapter or subchapter to discuss part of the continuities and discontinuities that cross the practice of women's football in Brazil. In Pisani's thesis (2012), there is a subtopic to discuss about the prejudices experienced by women football players based on analytical categories such as gender, sexuality, and bodies; in Almeida's thesis (2013), there is an entire chapter dedicated to the history of the sport, pointing out how it was banned by law for more than thirty-five years in Brazil.

Based on the data found during the research, conducted from two ethnographies, one with players from the Brazilian state of Paraná (Pisani, 2012) and another with players from Rio de Janeiro (Almeida, 2013), the authors show how Brazilian women football players have been subverting institutional and political structures that have excluded and prevented women from being present on the fields. It is widely known and shared among these and other authors who make up this systematization (Kessler, 2015; Pisani, 2018; Almeida, 2018; Raposo, 2018; Leite, 2021) that Decree-Law No. 3.199, instituted in 1941 and revoked in 1979, was a limiting element of Brazilian women's rights regarding access to certain sports practices such as football, for example.

Oliveira (2014) begins her thesis by carrying out an important epistemological reflection on the possibilities of producing science from the place of an anthropologist-player. In this manner, the author shows us the academic knowledge located from bodies, corporeality and also sports practices. The objective of Oliveira's thesis (2014) is to demonstrate the ways in which the players of her ethnography construct multiple gender identities, thus exposing how players perform identities linked to the notions of "periguetes" (hoochie), "sapatão" (butch/dyke) and "mulherzinhas" (femme), thus conferring other possibilities of "being a woman" in the football environment.

Kessler's dissertation (2015) is innovative in this scenario by evoking an explanatory effort and proposing a replacement of the expression *"futebol feminino"* ("Feminine football," chiefly used in Brazil) by "futebol de mulheres" ("Women's football"). The author justifies this by saying that the term women's football would encompass other possibilities of bodies and corporealities, evidencing the subjectivities of subjects from a non-neutral, abstract, and/or universal perspective (Kessler, 2015). Kessler's work is also innovative in proposing a comparative ethnography, based on the professionalization processes, between women's football practiced in Brazil and in the US.

In this sense, it is from Almeida's dissertation (2018) that it is possible to perceive a presence and deepening of the theme of professionalization of women's football initially addressed in Pisani's thesis (2012) and again later by Kessler (2015). Almeida goes a step further by systematizing the stages of professionalization of women's football, pointing out how Brazilian footballers are involved in social and power relations networks that (re)formulate the athletes' trajectories, life projects, and careers.

Pisani's doctoral dissertation inaugurates an academic discussion on women's football from an intersectional perspective (Collins and Bilge, 2021) by showing how the concepts of gender, race/ethnicity, and sexualities cannot be dissociated in the analysis of this sport practice. Based on ethnography with football teams from the peripheries of the city of São Paulo, the author also shows how football can become a space for exchanges and support, especially among women that are black, lesbians, bisexuals and belong to the working classes.

The movements of comparison between Brazilian and North American women's football are carried out once again in Raposo's thesis (2018), where the author investigates the production of journalistic discourse from the *UOL Online* and Fox News websites on the coverage of women's football during the Olympic Games held in Rio de Janeiro in 2016. The author highlighted differences in the ways in which Brazilian and North American presses portray women's football. While in the US more women journalists write about women's football, in Brazil most of the reports were produced by male journalists. Raposo attributes this phenomenon to the absence of female representation in the press, football and fan clubs (2018).

The last thesis that appears in this subtopic is conducted and published in 2021 by Leite. The author develops research from a feminist and gender perspective, evidencing the occupation by women in important spaces of football in João Pessoa, Paraiba. Thus, she divides her material into two moments: the first where she presents the occupation of women in football practice; and the second moment when she talks about women fans. The author states that despite the daily violence faced by players and fans, "the ball keeps rolling and women continue to seek their place to speak out about gender oppression and the difference between categories in sports" (Leite, 2021, p. 103).

It is possible to highlight, from the works listed in this subtopic that deal with women's football in Brazil, that there is a recurrence of themes that are addressed, namely: Gender Identities and Violence, Professionalization, Sports Trajectories, Migration and Media Discourses. Finally, a last issue that deserves attention is the fact that the three dissertations produced on women's football (Kessler, 2015; Pisani, 2018; Almeida, 2018) broaden the variety of themes, bringing to the debate issues of race/ethnicity and sexualities. In the specific case of Pisani (2018), as mentioned earlier, the categories of gender, race/ethnicity, and sexualities are articulated from the concept of intersectionality (Collins and Bilge, 2021).

Finally, many of the researchers who make up this section (Kessler, 2015; Pisani, 2018; Almeida, 2018) discuss from their work how women's football in Brazil can be understood as a field with very different logics and means of operation from men's football; therefore it is not possible or even appropriate to compare them from an academic-scientific perspective. Women's football in Brazil becomes a fruitful space for studying changes, impermanence and upheavals existing in Brazilian society regarding gender relations and combating sexism and machismo. Similarly, the authors point out that because it is a dynamic space, women's football becomes an area with infinite possibilities for conducting new research.

Women Fans in Organized Fan Clubs and Brazilian Football Stadiums

From the bibliographic survey, we were able to perceive that there were two works produced, specifically, on women supporters, one thesis in Anthropology (Leite, 2020), defended at UFPB; and another in Social Sciences (Andrade, 2022), defended at Unifesp. It is worth noting that Leite's dissertation (2020) approaches the theme of football from two perspectives, the first being women players and the second being women supporters. Therefore, her work was discussed in the previous subtopic and will be again addressed here.

Regarding the similarities of these works, we can observe a discussion of gender relations, youth, ways of supporting and sociability. Both authors focus on the sociability processes of young female supporters of two male football teams, one develops her research in the city of São Paulo and the second conducts hers in the city of João Pessoa. It is also worth noting that while Leite produced her work based on *Botafogo da Paraíba* supporters, Andrade worked with *Sport Club Corinthians Paulista* supporters. It is interesting to note that the authors start from the same concept of sociability developed by Georg Simmel (1983).

The research results found are also quite similar to each other, especially with regard to gender inequalities in organized football supporters. In Leite's thesis (2021), the author states that all women supporters who participated in her research had something in common. At some point in their lives, they have suffered some form of discrimination or violence because they are women. And in the space of the supporters' group, it would not be different. Leite (2021) even states that she witnessed some scenes of sexism and misogyny against female supporters during the research. However, the author points out that even in the face of violence, these women do not give up supporting their teams and continue to compete strategically for spaces in the stands through feminist practices and actions of resistance.

Andrade's thesis (2022) focused on the culture of Brazilian organized football supporters, pointing out how these groups can be full of conflicts and inequalities, especially in the relationships established between male and female supporters. For Andrade (2022), the organized supporters' group *Gaviões da Fiel* operates in a constant tension between political progressivism and gender conservatism. However, despite the many interdictions imposed by patriarchal structures that dominate the environment of supporters' groups, *Gaviões da Fiel*'s female supporters are gradually conquering their space and defending their demands around supporting. Andrade's research (2022) concluded by affirming that women are following a path of counterhegemonic struggle in the space of supporting.

Both Leite and Andrade affirm, based on their research experiences, that Brazilian organized supporters' groups are still places where it is possible to experience and witness the reproduction of gender stereotypes and, consequently, numerous inequalities that cross the experiences of women supporters. Andrade makes an even more virulent criticism by pointing out that despite some supporters' groups claims of being progressive or even anti-fascist, they continue to be places for the reproduction of numerous gender-based violence against women. Regardless of the difficulties faced daily in the act of supporting, both authors emphasize that women supporters are increasingly achieving a prominent place in the participation of organized supporters' groups, not allowing sexism and misogyny to be impediments to their presence (Leite, 2020; Andrade, 2022).

Women in Brazilian Football

For the composition of this bibliographic review and during the retrieval of theses and dissertations in the area of Human Sciences and its subareas Social Sciences, Anthropology, Political Science, and Sociology, we were able to find some works on the presence of women in the universe of Brazilian football, especially from two perspectives: that of athletes and fans. Interestingly, none of the works found specifically addressed the role of women as coaches, referees, or journalists. Nevertheless, we highlight that the theses of Kessler (2015), Almeida (2018), and Pisani (2018) have some passages, albeit brief, about the presence and actions of these characters in the space of women's football.

Regarding the survey on women in Brazilian football from these other areas of activity, only one work has been published on women in management positions. This is the case of the thesis by Ferrari (2021), defended in the Post-Graduate

Program in Social Sciences at the *Universidade do Estadual de Maringá* [State University of Maringá]. Thus, we consider the research and material presented to be unprecedented, when we take into account the perspective of the knowledge area in which it is located. Ferrari inaugurates, in the Social Sciences, the discussions about women's participation in a deliberative council of a men's football team (2021).

Ferrari's thesis addresses how women's participation in football politics, especially in management spaces, occurs; and presents the case of women who make up the Deliberative Council of *Sport Club Internacional*, located in the city of Porto Alegre, Rio Grande do Sul. Thus, based on the fan collective called *INTERfeminista*, Ferrari developed her master's research (2021). Based on the data obtained, the author concludes that more and more fans of various Brazilian clubs have been organizing themselves around Collectives and Political Movements with the aim of conquering space in the football environment (Ferrari, 2021).

Women Researching Brazilian Football

In this subtopic we highlight the works produced by Brazilian women researchers who have dedicated themselves to the theme of football. After searching the portals and repositories consulted, we realized that for this section we can highlight eleven theses and one doctorate dissertation. The southeastern region appears with most of the productions, with six theses and one dissertation (Almeida, 2012; Khayat, 2015; Danta, 2017; Mandelli, 2018; Silva, 2018; Cerreia, 2020; Ziviani, 2020). The northeastern (Maltez, 2018; Vale, 2019; Fernandes, 2020) and southern (Alves, 2013; Corteze, 2015) regions contribute respectively with three and two theses.

Another fact that deserves attention is in the thematic choices. Of the eleven theses, six are about fans, organized fans, consumption and sociabilities, with different methodological and empirical approaches such as: the rivalry between the fans of *Grêmio* and *Internacional* in Rio Grande do Sul (Alves, 2013); new ways of cheering for fans of *Sociedade Esportiva Palmeiras* in São Paulo after the reconfiguration of *Arena Allianz Parque* (Mandelli, 2018); practices and representations of organized football fans in Salvador, Bahia (Maltez, 2018); fan practices of *Torcida Esporão do Galo* in Teresina, Piauí (Vale, 2019); cyberactivism of organized fans during the *#EleNão* movement (Cerreia, 2020); circuits, consumption and identity construction processes of *Ferroviária S/A* fans in Araraquara city in São Paulo (Ziviani, 2020).

I also emphasize that some of the aforementioned researchers indicated in their texts that being women and studying a field permeated by masculinities made them face and dodge situations of harassment and machismo coming from interlocutors-fans (Mandelli, 2018; Maltez, 2018; Vale; 2019; Cerreia, 2020). Other authors highlighted the occurrence of situations of racism and homophobia perpetrated by fans and witnessed by them during the conduct of their research (Alves, 2013; Maltez, 2018; Cerreia, 2020). Despite the difficulties faced by researchers, Mandelli (2018) points out a path by discussing the possibility of critical thinking based on Haraway (2009). That is, there are privileges in the partial perspective in research conducted by a woman among organized supporters, directing the issue of science and scientific production for feminism.

The other five theses that make up this subtopic address various themes, for example: describing how *peladas* (leisure) matches played at *Aterro do Flamengo* are configured as leisure spaces, sociability and, in turn, also help in the reconfiguration of urban space in Rio de Janeiro city (Almeida, 2012); analyzing how the two most significant defeats of Brazil's men's football team, *Maracanaço* (match between Brazil and Uruguay at the 1950 World Cup) and *Mineiraço* (match between Brazil and Germany at the 2014 World Cup), were compared by Brazilian fans and press (Corteze, 2015); an analysis of the trajectory of *Atlético Itapemirim*, a football club from southern Espírito Santo state, and its process of professionalization (Silva, 2018); an examination into the patrimonialist and conservative structure of Brazilian football through the Parliamentary Inquiry Commission (CPI) on Football in 2015 in the Brazilian Federal Senate (Khayat, 2020); understanding how football guides and crosses the constitution of a "northeastern issue" (Fernandes, 2020).

The only dissertation found during the searches on portals was the work "*Cartografias de um campo invisível: os anônimos jogadores do futebol brasileiro*" [Cartographies of an invisible field: anonymous players in Brazilian football] by Marina de Mattos Dantas (2017). Similarly, the author was the only researcher to conduct interviews with male football players and contextualize the perspective of "anonymous" athletes, who are, in the author's words, "athletes without access to major clubs, [who] live closer to the border between being and not being professional and are constantly remaking this choice [of being a football player]" (Dantas, 2017, p. 229). From the interviews, Dantas problematizes professional football and its effects on subjectivity production in the football player profession.

Final Considerations…or, on Paths and Possibilities for Women in the Brazilian Football Universe

The objective of this study was analyzing how women are inserted in the universe of Brazilian football from theses and dissertations produced and published between 2012 and 2022 in the area of Human Sciences and some of its subareas. Using sites that catalogue such works—*Portal Brasileiro de Publicações e Dados Científicos de Acesso Aberto*; *Biblioteca Digital Brasileira de Teses e Dissertações*; and finally, Catálogo de Teses e Dissertações da Capes—we came across nineteen master's dissertations and four doctoral theses, totaling twenty-three published works. The material was analyzed and debated based on four topics: (i) women's football in Brazil; (ii) women fans in organized fan clubs and football stadiums in Brazil; (iii) women who work in Brazilian football; (iv) women researching Brazilian football.

We now point out some future perspectives that aim to ensure, more and more, the presence of women in the universe of Brazilian football. The first issue we would like to bring up concerns the fact that, for most of the works discussed here, football still constitutes itself as a space that encourages the maintenance of violent masculinities and also the propagation of macho, homophobic and racist attitudes and actions. Almost all authors pointed out having witnessed or even heard reports of some scene, situation, or passage where the aforementioned violences were perpetrated. They emerge from distinct research contexts, and it becomes urgent to think about actions and strategies that can make football increasingly safe, fair, ethical, and respectful to everyone who is part of its universe.

A second issue we would like to point out concerns the promotion of public policies to encourage the insertion and permanence of girls, young women, and women in different spaces of football, whether as athletes, fans, coaches, technicians, referees, journalists, managers, or researchers. These public policies should provide for investments in sports facilities aimed at women, training and competition programs, policies of salary equality and recognition for women athletes, and campaigns to promote women's participation in physical activities. These measures would help mitigate the barriers that many Brazilian women have faced and still face regarding their participation in the universe of football and perhaps in other sports modalities.

The third and final issue we would like to point out concerns the research gaps that still persist in this field. Only one of the reviewed works focused on the presence of women in Brazilian football from leadership positions in clubs and federations. Similarly, there is a lack of work on coaches, referees, club managers, and sports journalists. It is evident that until recently, they were not allowed to occupy such professions, but currently it is possible to find more and more women occupying these prominent positions.

Another gap that appears in this bibliographic review is the few works dedicated to discussing women's participation in football competitions and tournaments, based on national and international championships. By proposing new studies in this direction, it can be debated how the development of these competitions, such as the difficulties that women faced to participate in them and how the most recent achievements of women's football reveal the historical difficulties that women had to face and overcome to participate in sports.

We also highlight that none of the works carried out between 2012 and 2022 analyzed the life trajectory of Brazil's main players such as Sisi, Meg, Formiga, Cristiane, and Marta, among many others. Therefore, it is urgent to develop research on Brazilian women's football players, including their trajectories in sports, achievements and influence on the football scene. In this sense, the absence of research addressing football played by transgender and transvestite women is also noteworthy.

REFERENCES

Alabarces, P. Veinte años de ciencias sociales y deportes, diez años después (Twenty Years of Social Sciences and Sports, Ten Years Later). In: *Revista da ALESDE*, v. 1, n. 1, pp. 11–22, 2011.

Alabarces, P. Veinte años de ciencias sociales y deporte em América Latina: un balance, una agenda (Twenty Years of Social Sciences and Sports in Latin America: An Assessment, an Agenda). In: *BIB*—Revista Brasileira de Informação Bibliográfica em Ciências Sociais. São Paulo: v. 1, n. 58, pp. 159–179, 2004.

Almeida, Ana Letícia Canegal de. *Entrando em campo*: a "pelada organizada" no Aterro do Flamengo (Taking the Field: The "Organized Pickup Games" at Flamengo Park). Rio de Janeiro: Dissertação de Mestrado em Ciências Sociais/PUC-Rio, 2012.

Almeida, Caroline Soares de. *"Boas de bola"*: um estudo sobre o ser jogadora de futebol no Esporte Clube Radar durante a década de 1980 ("Good at Ball":

A Study on Being a Female Football Player at Esporte Clube Radar During the 1980s). Mestrado em Antropologia Social. Universidade Federal De Santa Catarina, 2013.

Almeida, Caroline Soares de. *Do sonho ao possível*: projeto e campo de possibilidades nas carreiras profissionais de futebolistas brasileiras (From Dream to Possibility: Project and Field of Possibilities in the Professional Careers of Brazilian Female Footballers). Florianópolis: Tese de Doutorado em Antropologia Social, 2018.

Alves, Cristina Cordeiro. *"Posso morrer pelo meu time"*: a construção social da rivalidade clubística entre Grêmio e Internacional e a sua relação com as violências no futebol ("I Can Die for My Team": The Social Construction of Club Rivalry Between Grêmio and Internacional and Its Relation to Violence in Football). Porto Alegre: Dissertação de Mestrado em Sociologia/UFRGS, 2013.

Andrade, Marianna Castellano Barcelos de. Para além da arquibancada: uma etnografia sobre as "Gaviãs" da Fiel (Beyond the Stands: An Ethnography of the "Gaviãs" of Fiel). São Paulo: Dissertação de Mestrado em Ciências Sociais/ UNIFESP, 2022.

Beirith, Mariana Klauck, Araldi, Franciane Maria e Folle, Alexandra. produção científica relacionada ao futebol de mulheres em teses e dissertações brasileiras na área da educação física (Scientific Production Related to Women's Football in Brazilian Theses and Dissertations in the Field of Physical Education). Movimento [online]. 2021, v. 27 [Acessado 1 Maio 2023], e27064. Disponível em: <https://doi.org/10.22456/1982-8918.113239>. Epub 07 Jan 2022. ISSN 1982-8918. https://doi.org/10.22456/1982-8918.113239.

Cerreia, Nathalia Borges. As Torcidas Antifascistas No Brasil: Um Estudo Sobre O Ativismo Online Nas Eleições Presidenciais De 2018 (Antifascist Supporter Groups in Brazil: A Study on Online Activism During the 2018 Presidential Elections). Mestrado em Ciência Política. Universidade Federal do Estado do Rio de Janeiro, 2020.

Collins, Patricia; Bilge, Sirma. *Interseccionalidade* (Intersectionality). São Paulo: Boitempo, 2021.

Corteze, Kesia Costenaro. O Jogo Que Nunca Acabou: A Permanência Do Maracanaço No Imaginário Dos Brasileiros E Suas Reatualizações Contemporâneas (The Game That Never Ended: The Permanence of the Maracanazo in the Brazilian Imagination and Its Contemporary Reinterpretations). Mestrado em Ciências Sociais. Universidade Federal de Santa Maria, 2015.

DaMatta, Roberto. Universo Do Futebol: Esporte E Sociedade Brasileira (The World of Football: Sport and Brazilian Society). Rio de Janeiro: Pinakotheke, 1982.

Damo, A. Posfácio. Novas abordagens sobre o esporte em ciências humanas no Brasil (Postface: New Approaches to Sport in Human Sciences in Brazil). In: SPAGGIARI, E.; MACHADO, G. M. C.; GIGLIO, S. S. (orgs.). Entre jogos e copas. Reflexões de uma década esportiva. São Paulo: Intermeios; Fapesp, 2016, pp. 325–353.

Dantas, Marina De Mattos. Cartografias De Um Campo Invisível: Os Anônimos Jogadores Do Futebol Brasileiro (Cartographies of an Invisible Field: The Anonymous Players of Brazilian Football). Doutorado em Ciências Sociais. Pontifícia Universidade Católica De São Paulo, 2017.

Fernandes, Hevilla Wanderley. Não É Apenas Um Jogo: A Questão Nordestina No Futebol. Mestrado em Ciência Política e Relações Internacionais (It's Not Just a Game: The Northeastern Question in Football). Universidade Federal Da Paraíba, 2020.

Ferrari, Nathallie Matos. Interfeminista: As Mulheres Na Gestão Do Futebol Brasileiro (Interfeminist: Women in the Management of Brazilian Football). Mestrado em Ciências Sociais. Universidade Estadual De Maringá, 2021.

Figueiredo, Tiago Sales De Lima. Processo De Institucionalização Do Futebol Feminino No Brasil E No Uruguai: Perspectivas Comparadas, Feminismos E Políticas Públicas (The Institutionalization Process of Women's Football in Brazil and Uruguay: Comparative Perspectives, Feminisms, and Public Policies). Mestrado em Antropologia. Universidade Federal Fluminense, 2017.

Gastaldo, Edison. Estudos sociais do esporte: vicissitudes e possiblidades de um campo em formação (Social Studies of Sport: Vicissitudes and Possibilities of a Field in Formation). In: *Logos: Comunicação e Universidades*, v. 17, n. 2, 2010.

Giglio, S. S; Spaggiari, E. A produção das ciências humanas sobre futebol no Brasil (1990–2009) (The Production of Human Sciences on Football in Brazil (1990–2009)). In: *Revista de História,* n. 163, pp. 293–322, 2010. Dossiê "História e Futebol."

Goellner, S. V. Gênero e esporte na historiografia brasileira: balanços e potencialidades (Gender and Sport in Brazilian Historiography: Assessments and Potentialities). In: *Revista Tempo*, v. 17, n. 34, pp. 45–52, 2013. Dossiê "Uma história do esporte para um país esportivo."

Guedes, S. L. Os estudos antropológicos dos esportes no Brasil: perspectivas comparativas com a América Latina (Anthropological Studies of Sports in Brazil: Comparative Perspectives with Latin America). In: *Antropolítica,* n. 31, pp. 31–43, 2011.

Guedes, Simoni Lahud. O futebol brasileiro: instituição zero (Brazilian Football: Institution Zero). Dissertação (Mestrado)—Programa de Pós-Graduação em Antropologia Social. Universidade Federal do Rio de Janeiro, Rio de Janeiro, 1977.

Haraway, D. Saberes Localizados: A Questão Da Ciência Para O Feminismo E O Privilégio Da Perspectiva Parcial (Situated Knowledges: The Question of Science for Feminism and the Privilege of Partial Perspective). In: *Cadernos Pagu*, n. 5, pp. 7–41, 2009.

Kessler, Claudia Samuel. Mais Que Barbies E Ogras: Uma Etnografia Do Futebol De Mulheres No Brasil E Nos Estados Unidos. Doutorado em Antropologia Social (More Than Barbies and Ogres: An Ethnography of Women's Football in Brazil and the United States). Universidade Federal Do Rio Grande Do Sul, 2015.

Kessler, Claudia; Costa, Leda Maria; Pisani, Mariane Da Silva. As Mulheres no Universo Do Futebol Brasileiro (Women in the Universe of Brazilian Football). Santa Maria: Editora Ufsm, 2020 (Ebook) E 2022 (Impresso).

Kessler, Claudia; Pisani, Mariane Da Silva. As Mulheres no Universo Do Futebol Brasileiro: Resgatando O Gênero (Women in the Universe of Brazilian Football: Rescuing Gender). In Revista Conexões, Campinas: Sp, V. 20, 2022.

Khayat, Stella Valentini. Jogo De Futebol Ou Futebol Do Jogo? A CPI Do Futebol (2015) Como Ilustração Da Dinâmica Política Do Futebol Brasileiro (Football Game or Game of Football? The Football Parliamentary Inquiry (2015) as an Illustration of the Political Dynamics of Brazilian Football). Mestrado em Ciências Sociais. Pontifícia Universidade Católica De São Paulo, 2020.

Leite, Ana Daniella Fechine. Futebol De Mulheres: Um Estudo Feminista Nos Campos E Nas Arquibancadas De João Pessoa/PB (Women's Football: A Feminist Study on the Fields and Stands of João Pessoa/PB). Mestrado em Antropologia. Universidade Federal Da Paraíba, 2021.

Maltez, Juliana Campos. Das Arquibancadas Dos Estádios Às Pistas Da Cidade: Um Estudo Sobre Torcedores Organizados De Salvador (From the Stadium Stands to the City Streets: A Study on Organized Supporters in Salvador). Mestrado em Ciências Sociais. Universidade Federal Da Bahia, 2018.

Mandelli, Mariana Carolina. Allianz Parque E Rua Palestra Itália: Práticas Torcedoras Em Uma Arena Multiuso (Allianz Parque and Rua Palestra Itália: Fan Practices in a Multi-Purpose Arena). Mestrado em Ciência Social, concentração em Antropologia Social. Universidade de São Paulo, 2018.

Melo, V. A.; Genovez, P. F. Bibliografia brasileira de história da educação física e do esporte (Brazilian Bibliography on the History of Physical Education and Sport). 1. ed. Rio de Janeiro: Editora da Universidade Gama Filho, 1998. v. 1.

Oliveira, Valleria Araujo de. Periguetes, Sapatões E Mulherzinhas: (Des)Construindo O Que "Ser Mulher" No Campo De Futebol. Mestrado em Antropologia Social ("Flirts, Lesbians, and Little Ladies": (De)Constructing What It Means to "Be a Woman" on the Football Field). Universidade Federal De Goiás, 2014.

Pisani, Mariane Da Silva. Poderosas Do Foz: Trajetórias, Migrações E Profissionalização De Mulheres Que Praticam Futebol (The Powerful Women of Foz: Trajectories, Migrations, and Professionalization of Women Who Play Football). Mestrado em Antropologia Social. Universidade Federal De Santa Catarina, 2012.

Pisani, Mariane Da Silva. Sou Feita De Chuva, Sol E Barro': O Futebol De Mulheres Praticado Na Cidade De São Paulo. Doutorado em Ciência Social, concentração em Antropologia Social (I Am Made of Rain, Sun, and Mud": Women's Football Played in the City of São Paulo). Universidade de São Paulo, 2018.

Raposo, Clarissa Carramilo. Cobertura Midiática Das Olimpíadas Rio 2016: Construção Da Imagem Da Jogadora De Futebol Pela Imprensa No Brasil E Nos Estados Unidos (Media Coverage of the Rio 2016 Olympics: The Construction of the Image of Women Football Players in the Press in Brazil and the United States). Mestrado em Ciências Sociais. Universidade Federal Do Maranhão, 2018.

Silva, Mariana Schade Da. O Canto Do Galo Da Vila No Espírito Santo: A Trajetória Do Atlético Itapemirim E O Seu Processo De Profissionalização No Futebol' (he Song of the Galo da Vila in Espírito Santo: The Trajectory of Atlético Itapemirim and Its Professionalization Process in Football). Mestrado em Ciências Sociais. Universidade Federal Do Espírito Santo, 2018.

Simmel, Georg. Sociabilidade: Um Estudo De Sociologia Pura Ou Formal (Sociability: A Study of Pure or Formal Sociology). In: Moraes Filho, E. (Org.). Sociologia. São Paulo: Ática, 1983.

Sousa, Cleyton Batista; ABRAHÃO, Bruno Otávio de Lacerda. Estudsos sobre os torcedores de futebol: uma revisão sistemática (Studies on Football Fans: A Systematic Review). In: *FuLiA/UFMG*, v. 7, n. 1, pp. 82–103, 2022.

Spaggiari, E.; Machado, G. M. C.; Giglio, S. S. Apresentação. Por uma (nova) agenda de pesquisa sobre práticas esportivas. In: SPAGGIARI, E.; MACHADO, G. M. C.; GIGLIO, S. S. (orgs.). Entre jogos e copas. Reflexões de uma década esportiva. São Paulo: Intermeios; Fapesp, 2016. pp. 9–31.

Toledo, Luiz Henrique. Futebol e teoria social: aspectos da produção acadêmica brasileira (1982–2002) (Football and Social Theory: Aspects of Brazilian Academic Production (1982–2002)). Revista Brasileira de Informação Bibliográfica em Ciências Sociais, v. 52, 2001.

Toledo, Luiz Herique. Balanços bibliográficos e ciclos randômicos: o caso dos futebóis na antropologia brasileira (Bibliographic Reviews and Random Cycles: The Case of Football in Brazilian Anthropology). In: *Revista Brasileira de Informação Bibliográfica em Ciências Sociais,* São Paulo, n. 94, pp. 01-32, 2021.

Vale, Ana Hilda Lima Do. "Não é só Futebol": Relações De Sociabilidade E Identidade Na Torcida Esporão Do Galo Em Teresina-PI ("It's Not Just Football": Sociability and Identity Relations in the Esporão do Galo Fanbase in Teresina-PI). Mestrado em Sociologia. Fundação Universidade Federal Do Piauí, 2019.

Ziviani, Larissa Nunes. Consumo, Futebol e Identidades: Uma Abordagem Etnográfica Do Circuito Futebolístico Da Cidade De Araraquara-SP (Consumption, Football, and Identities: An Ethnographic Approach to the Football Circuit in the City of Araraquara-SP). Mestrado em Ciências Sociais. Universidade Estadual Paulista Júlio De Mesquita Filho, 2020.

CHAPTER 8

Women's Football in *Placar* Magazine 1983–2023: A Story of Belated Acceptance

David Wood

The fortieth anniversary of the 1983 legal and institutional framework that allowed for the practice of women's football came shortly after the fiftieth anniversary of *Placar*, Brazil's most popular sports magazine, which has consistently focused its coverage on the nation's footballing landscape.[1] The convergence of these events gives cause to reflect on the magazine's treatment of women's football as part of that picture and how coverage may have changed over decades of significant developments in terms of the position of women in Brazil. Indeed, the publication in November 2019 of the first edition of *Placar* devoted to women's football, as well as an apology a few months earlier for its previous coverage of the women's game, had highlighted the magazine's poor treatment of women's football—in quantitative and qualitative terms—over recent decades.

Given that women's football was illegal in Brazil until December 1979, it is perhaps no surprise that coverage in the first decade of the magazine's existence was limited. However, as has been widely demonstrated (Rigo et al., 2008; Costa, 2017; Ribeiro, 2018; Bonfim, 2019), women played football throughout the era of prohibition and *Placar* did discuss and illustrate this reality during the 1970s, although such coverage as there was reinforced what Connell describes as "emphasised femininity" (Connell, 1987, p. 183), whereby conventionally feminine features are highlighted for an assumed heterosexual male gaze. Once the ban was lifted, it would take another four years for the infrastructure that would allow for women's football to be practiced in Brazil, and by 1983:

[1] Almost all editions between 1970 and 2010 can be accessed via a digital catalogue, and, most recently, a *Placar* app. The catalogue can be accessed to view most of the various articles and images discussed in this study via https://books.google.co.uk/books?id=QXW27JKseFQC&redir_esc=y (accessed April 5, 2023).

> *Placar* had already delegitimised it by representing women in traditional gender roles in which the female body is constituted as the site of natural physical attributes associated with femininity and motherhood that render the female body an object of heterosexual male desire rather than as a form of physicality that results in agency or movement for the women themselves. (Wood, 2021)

This study will build on the analysis of the magazine's coverage of women's football prior to 1983 (Wood, 2021) and develop consideration of the practice in relation to works that have a more specific temporal focus (Saldanha, 2009; Saldanha and Goellner, 2013; Salvini and Marchi Júnior, 2013a, 2013b, 2016; Silva, 2015).

1983–1995: Women's Football on the Pitch, But Rarely on the Page

The recognition and regulation of women's football by Brazil's sporting authorities had little impact on its presence in *Placar* over the following twelve years. A note in the April 1983 edition of the magazine declared that "The Ball is (Also) for Women" and gave brief details of the National Sports Council's official recognition of women's football, together with the different rules for the women's game. The nature of these rules (matches to last 70 minutes, lighter balls and smaller pitches) speaks to assumptions around women's lesser physical capabilities while the caption for the small photo of women players highlights a key consideration for the readership: that swapping shirts will not be permitted (April 8, 1983, p. 68).

Despite the fact that the magazine had published interviews and letters that attested to the existence of women players and teams since 1971 (Wood, 2021), its first significant item on women's football after April 1983 came almost a year later via an announcement on a front cover that "Women's Football Exists," immediately underneath another announcement proclaiming "Aldine Muller, fan of Internacional," while the main headline (and full-page photo) featured Socrates (February 24, 1984). The three-page article "Women's Football: the Charm of the Conquest," revealed that there were "at least four good women's teams in Brazil" (*ibid*: 42), with Radar of Rio de Janeiro the only team not representing a club based around a professional men's team.

The author comments briefly on the players' ability and the results of their teams, but much of the text is devoted to the age and physical appearance (height, weight, eye and hair color) of selected players, and the article opened with a description of how the players spend hours in front of the mirror to look their best before a match. The story closed with the observation that "women's football is a cheerful reality, made up of goals and charm" (*ibid*: 46), the players' emphasized femininity and sexual allure highlighted by a two-page photo of a well-known soft porn actress lying behind a goal, "with only a football shirt between her and nudity" (*ibid*: 49).

Similar strategies are found a few months later in the first edition to feature women's football as the front cover of *Placar*: the main headline of "Women's Football: 3,000 teams and 45,000 Women on the Pitch" is accompanied by the image of a young black woman in a changing room, wearing a football shirt but no shorts as she lifts one leg onto a bench to wrap her calf with a bandage, her foot next to her other boot as well as a makeup palette and some lipstick (July 13, 1984; see image below).

The table of contents told the reader that "Women Invade the Pitch—3,000 teams," the choice of verb clearly flagging the unwelcome nature of their presence in this domain, at least for the magazine. The article itself (July 13, 1984, pp. 24–27), written by a woman reporter, gave serious coverage to the topic, but the text was undermined by the images that illustrated the story: Bel, a player for Internacional, is shown from behind in a football shirt and very short, tight shorts, in front of a mirror putting on lipstick, described in the caption as "the great muse of beautiful Inter" (*ibid*: 25).

Another changing-room photo of the player from the front cover was accompanied by a description of her as "a slender mulatta who wears carefully applied make-up and a showy earring every time she goes onto the pitch" (*ibid*: 26). The repeated feminization and sexualization of women players via such images and captions, presumably selected by male copy editors and editors, undermined efforts by female journalists to present their subjects' serious intent and ability as footballers to the Brazilian public. More recently, Bel has reflected on the tensions between the repeated use of her image to promote women's football in the 1980s and her desire to be known for her prowess and achievements on the pitch. Her moving comment that she "saw a different woman in the mirror" (Goellner and Cabral, 2022, pp. 161, 166), after surgery for breast cancer and subsequent radiotherapy, reveals the extent to which the sexualized media representations of women footballers could shape their sense of self during and well beyond their playing careers.

The next substantial piece, a three-page discussion of the outstanding Radar team, written six months later by another female journalist, carried alongside the story of their achievements a short description of each player that included their age, height, weight, bust and shoe size,[2] with a subheading declaring that "with these measurements the champions of Rio and Brazil want to beat the world" (February 1, 1985, p. 26). The textual and visual depictions of women football players considered here are part of a strategy—consciously developed or not—of feminizing women's football during the years after its official recognition in Brazil, thus simultaneously maintaining established modes of representation for women and minimizing the challenge that their participation in football provided to traditional gender roles.

[2] The preoccupation with shoe size may be attributed to "scientific" concerns, dating from the 1920s, that the feet of women who play football will grow bigger. The players' shoe sizes, ranging from 33 to 39, may reassure readers that they are not "sapatão," a derogatory term for a lesbian whose literal translation is "big foot."

During the second half of the 1980s and the early 1990s, women's football was almost completely absent from the pages of *Placar*, appearing very occasionally as a sexualized spectacle featuring models and actresses from national television (April 8, 1988, p. 53). This absence was also starkly evident in the "Historic Edition" that celebrated hundred years of football in Brazil (October 1994), with features on the greatest players, the greatest teams, the best managers, the national team, fans, and referees, among others. Among such a panoramic landscape, the solitary handful of references to women are as fans. The section on Atlético Mineiro exemplified the fans' love for the club in its early days through an elderly woman who was "a fanatical supporter who personally made the kits for all the players," while the section on Santos is illustrated by a young woman with long blonde hair holding a child in front of a club flag (October 1994, p. 14), both conforming to the representations of women in the realm of sports as "beautiful, maternal and feminine" (Goellner, 2003).

The chronology of Brazil's footballing centenary that runs along the bottom section of each page also systematically omitted women, whose key dates and players were not mentioned once; the resulting male-only history of the national sport constituted a clear example of a practice that was an "invented tradition" (Hobsbawm and Ranger, 1983).

1995–1999: Football, Sex and Rock 'n' Roll

In January 1995 *Placar* announced a relaunch with the subtitle "Football, Sex and Rock 'n' Roll" in an attempt to appeal to a younger male audience. This initiative was led by Juca Kfouri, long-term editor of *Placar* and, at the time, also director of the Brazilian edition of *Playboy* magazine as part of the Editora Abril portfolio. This phase of *Placar*, which lasted four years, saw the overt sexualization of women football players, and of women in general, as the magazine moved closer to its stablemate *Playboy* by including items that often depicted models in various stages of undress as they supposedly prepared to play football, as well as a naked model on the back cover.

In addition, a regular "Goddess" section featured a seminaked model with a loose connection to a (men's) football team, while "The Tastiest Reader" section consisted of photographs sent in by scantily clad young women conforming to the hegemonic sexualized representation of women in the realm of football. Women in football (or rather models in football kit) were present as never before, the subject of four front covers between August 1995 and March 1997, although in each case they were heavily sexualized via clothing, posture, and makeup; furthermore, photographs tended to show the "players" from the knees up, omitting their feet as the key to football success but always including thighs, waist and breasts to signify their status as sexualized football objects rather than subjects (e.g., March 1997, pp. 22–29).

Even when women's football appeared as a serious sporting practice the coverage was undone by the prevailing narrative of the time: after narrowly losing out on a medal at the Los Angeles Olympic Games, a "dossier" on the situation for women's elite football in Brazil repeatedly discussed homosexual scandals among players while highlighting the beauty and femininity of others, all following a six-page feature on "Goddess" Susana Werner (September 1996, pp. 40–45, 46–50). The "Football, Sex and Rock 'n' roll" era, undoubtedly the most lamentable in terms of *Placar's* representation of women's football, came to end in December 1998 as the magazine announced that it was changing "to increase its coverage of football" (December 1998, p. 22), resulting in the discontinuation of the "Goddess" section and of "The Tastiest Reader" feature. This change was entirely the result of commercial considerations as the magazine sought to recapture its more traditional readership, for it continued to publish images of seminaked young women in adverts, as well as a regular full-page ad for Playboy.[3]

1999-2014: Enduring Feminization vs. Serious Consideration

Despite excellent results in the Women's World Cup (third place in 1999 and runner-up in 2007) and the Olympic Games (silver medals in 2004 and 2008), women's football was the subject of substantial coverage in just 6 of the 457 editions of *Placar* that were published in the first decade of the new millennium (Salvini and Marchi, 2013a, p. 57). The overt sexualization of women's football was largely replaced by coverage (such as there was) that instead feminized both the practice of women's football and its players. The table of contents of the edition published ahead of the Sydney Olympics announced a feature article "The women's national team earns the status it deserves" under the title "Only in Little Shoes" (May 2000, p. 7), highlighting the tensions evident in much coverage

3. Cristina Veit, personal communication.

of the period and echoing the previous hegemonic discourses around "sapatão" that portrayed women's football as a sexually abnormal practice.

The article itself wrestled with these same tensions, opening with: "Candidates for a medal in Sydney, the girls of the national team fight for their femininity and celebrate unimaginable conquests, like made-to-measure kit," the use of "girls" for players aged between 16 and 33 a practice that repeatedly reduces their agency as athletes. The players' "emphasised femininity" (Connell, 1987, p. 183) marks a contrast with the situation of previous times "when the sport used to be associated with homosexuality" (May 2000, p. 57). This femininity is illustrated through the nine photographs that accompany the article, more than half of which show the players in traditionally gender-appropriate roles (applying makeup, knitting, painting their nails, drying recently washed clothes).

One photograph in particular entered into dialogue with the article's title ("Only in Little Shoes") via a juxtaposition of the largest and smallest football boots used by the players, 41 and 34 respectively, revealing ongoing anxieties in relation to the impact of women's participation in football on their "feminine" bodies and on their sexuality. In addition to these features that implicitly reassured the reader that these football players are also women according to traditional constructions of femininity, the author stated explicitly that things are changing and that the younger players, whose boyfriends are discussed, "are at peace with their femininity [...] burying the reputation for this being Sapatão Football Club" (*ibid*: 57).

At the other end of the decade, the Beijing Olympic Games saw recognition of the women's football team as a candidate for the gold medal, portraying them as representatives of the nation in a way that was unimaginable even a decade earlier (December 2007, pp. 40–41), the same issue carrying a report on women's beach football in Santos as a sport rather than a sexualized spectacle (*ibid*: 28). In the aftermath of the Games, *Placar* reflected on the medals in football (silver for the women, bronze for the men) and concluded that "the women's tournament is more interesting than the men's" (September 2008, p. 88) because all of the world's best players were there, with no restrictions on age; matches were more evenly contested; and the players embodied the Olympic (amateur) spirit more than their highly paid male counterparts.

Despite this, however, the author stated that he would not go to watch a women's match outside the Olympic Games, which he saw as normal because "people don't exactly like women's football. What they like is to see Brazil fighting for a medal" (*ibid*: 89). It is this prospect of a medal that is apparently the only reason behind the author's appeal for more investment in the women's game in Brazil. To improve women's football, he makes five recommendations: reduce pitch sizes; reduce match duration; play with lighter balls; make the goals smaller; and oblige Brazil's clubs to develop women's teams (*ibid*: 88). With the exception of the last point, effectively implemented by CONMEBOL a decade later, the others derive from a view of women's physical frailty in comparison to men that was expressed in articles from the 1970s (Wood, 2021), and even in the reasoning behind the introduction of the ban on women's football in 1941 (Franzini, 2005).

There is little doubt that the achievements of the women's national team during the first decade of the 21st century ensured that their activities on the international stage were taken seriously, but *Placar*'s scant coverage also revealed that underlying stereotypes and prejudices had changed far less and were still significantly informed by narratives and codes that the magazine had established decades before.

The years before *Placar*'s fiftieth anniversary saw a marked shift in the magazine's representation of women's football. Paradoxically, Brazil's hosting of the 2014 (men's) World Cup had provided public spaces for the promotion of women's football in the country: Marta was one of six FIFA football ambassadors for the tournament and shortly before it began she inaugurated Rio de Janeiro's Football for Equality Plaza, where a multimedia exhibition "Women on the Pitch" explored almost hundred years of women's football in Brazil. Another exhibition, "Exposição Futebol e Mulheres no País da Copa 2014," was simultaneously held in Porto Alegre and later that year *Placar* published a feature about a team of women photographers who had spent two years capturing stories of women's football across the country for an exhibition—and book—from which sexualized representations were absent (November 2014, pp. 48–52).

In 2015, the Museu do Futebol in São Paulo hosted a major exhibition "Visibility for Women's Football," which subsequently toured other cities, and in 2016 the nationwide cultural organization SESC (Commercial Sector Social Services) held the exhibition "Twenty Years of Women's Football at the Olympic Games."

This unprecedented public visibility for women's football, with the support of highly respected national (and international) institutions coincided with *Placar* being sold in June 2015 to Editora Caras, which also published several of the country's leading women's magazines (Sacchitiello, 2015). A few months later, six pages were devoted to coverage of the women's national team and their victory in the Natal International Tournament, which rounded off "a good year for women's football, with **our athletes** winning their sixth title" under the header "Seleção principal" (January 2016, p. 98, my bold emphasis). Describing the women players as "our athletes" marked a significant shift away from the use of "girls," while the use of "our" and "Seleção principal" signified acceptance of the women's team as representatives of the nation via the "deixis of little words" (Billig, 2010, p. 94) that constitutes an integral part of banal nationalism.

Furthermore, an extensive report on the tournament focused exclusively on the action on the pitch and players' achievements, with no references to shoe size, sexual orientation, or makeup and the only mention of beauty coming in the description of the best goal of the tournament (January 2016, pp. 98–103). Similarly, the images and their captions referred exclusively to key moments on the pitch, to preparations for matches and to the award of medals, trophies and prizes. Women's football featured again the following month via a serious and supportive article about another photographic exhibition on women's football at the Museu do Futebol in São Paulo (February 2016, p. 33), the same edition also featuring other Brazilian women athletes at the top of their chosen sport. The celebration of women for their achievements as elite athletes, consonant across both textual and visual references, marked a long overdue change in the representation of women's football in *Placar*, reflecting broader social changes and the creation of a National Women's League in 2013, as well as the various initiatives around the 2014 World Cup.

Published to coincide with the Rio Olympic Games, the August 2016 edition of *Placar* featured on its front cover Marta and Neymar to symbolize the hopes of Brazil's first ever gold medal in the Olympic football tournament. The players were both pictured wearing the famous No. 10 shirt of the national team, both were wearing the captain's armband and both were depicted walking forward with their arms by their sides, faces relaxed.

A study of Marta in *Placar* concluded that her football ability, recognized in the award of FIFA World Player of the Year on five consecutive occasions (2006–2010, and again in 2018), meant that media discussion of her football activity was similar to that found in relation to some male players (Salvini and Marchi, 2013b, p. 312). The parity of treatment with Neymar on the cover above suggests that such treatment continued well beyond the period analyzed in that study; indeed, that she appears on the left of the image and that her name comes before that of Neymar in the headline suggests that she enjoys primacy as a national football icon, a radical change from the ways in which women's football was represented at the Olympic Games in Peking or Sydney, discussed earlier.

Despite a poor start to the tournament for the men's team and outstanding performances by the women's team, it was Neymar who scored the winning penalty to secure the country's first gold medal in football while the women's team lost their semifinal against Sweden on penalties, having beaten the same opponents 5–1 in the group stages. Under the title "Two Sets of Tears, One Gold Medal," the September 2016 edition of *Placar* carried a full-page photo of Neymar as he took the decisive penalty, with a small image of a tearful Marta on the floor after their defeat (September 9, 2016, p. 83). The challenge thrown down by the style of play of the women's team, which "delighted the world and deserved to win" (*ibid.*, p. 83), had ultimately been seen off by the men's team, which had initially disappointed but had ultimately reclaimed their place as representatives of the nation.

2016-2020: *Placar* Turns 50

Soon after the Rio Olympics, *Placar*, along with several other titles, returned to Editora Abril, which had stopped publishing the Brazilian edition of *Playboy* in December 2015 because of falling circulation (April 2016), thereby breaking the connection between the two magazines that had been evident in shared advertising and—in the early 1990s—shared editorial leadership that resulted in the consistent sexualization of women in the realm of football. After the showcasing and celebration of women's football during the fifteen months that *Placar* was published by Editora Caras, the return to Editora Abril resulted in far less coverage as women's football again became almost invisible.

The award of FIFA's player of the year title to Marta in 2018, for a record sixth time, led to her reappearance on the front cover alongside Modric as the winner of the men's title, the format echoing the cover of August 2016 with both players in their national team's kit, each wearing the iconic No. 10 shirt and the captain's armband. Marta again appeared on the left-hand side of the image, granting her visual primacy, this time as the sole representative of Brazil's prowess as the nation of football, and she was also named before Modric under the front-page headline "The Best in the World." This representational prioritization of Marta and, through her, of women's football was, however, undone over the pages that followed: coverage of her achievements occupied two pages (one page of text and a full-page action photo) that followed the six-page report (two pages of text and four pages of photos) on Modric (October 2018, pp. 8–13, 14–15). The remainder of the sixty-six pages of that issue were devoted entirely to the global and Brazilian stars of men's football under various categories: the international recognition of Marta and her football ability opened a space of exceptionalism for her alone in this consideration of the greatest players in Brazil and the rest of the world.

The international dimension also played an important role in the edition of July 2019, which was devoted to ranking the best 100 male players and the best 20 female players of the 21st century, a historic departure for *Placar* in terms of inclusivity. All the more striking was that of the twenty-star players who appeared on the front cover, the photograph at the top left-hand corner was that of Marta, again occupying what is visually the dominant position to which the eye is drawn according to conventions around reading in western culture.

Unlike the edition of October 2018, discussed above, on this occasion the foregrounding of women's football continued beyond the symbolism of the front cover as the table of contents page was dominated by a photograph of Marta and several teammates as she celebrated a goal at the 2019 Women's World Cup. The caption drew attention to the fact that her goals in France made her the top scorer in World Cup history, and a text box entitled *In Search of Equality* apologized for the paucity of coverage that women's football had received in the magazine, and for the quality of that coverage: "In the 1980s and 1990s we looked on women's football in the wrong way, almost objectifying women players."

We are sorry for that period of ignorance and seek to improve' (July 2019, pp. 4–5). There is no doubt that the objectification of women players is entirely absent here, the focus being exclusively on their skill and achievements, but the quantity of coverage for the women's game leaves room for further improvement: 50 pages were devoted to the best 100 men and 5 pages to the best 20 women, men's football thus receiving exactly twice as much space as women's football per player.

For the section devoted to women's football, which followed the coverage of men's football to occupy the final pages of this edition, it is also striking that on deciding to include women players *Placar* came to realize "the extent of our ignorance," admitting that "*Placar* does not cover women's football enough to be able to provide a reliable ranking" (*ibid*: 61), leading to a partnership with the website Planeta Futebol Feminino to be able to do so.[4] The anonymous authors of the article excused their ignorance by explaining that "in some ways, our magazine is a reflection of the behaviour of the media and of society, concentrating our coverage of women's football around major events" (*ibid*: 61), thereby overlooking the influence that the media can have on public perceptions and also the systematic delegitimization of the women's game in which the magazine had engaged since its foundation.

Although they claimed to have taken various measures to include women's football among their themed monthly issues, this was exemplified solely in the 2018 cover shared by Marta and Modric, discussed earlier. Furthermore, by flagging the success of the 2019 Women's World Cup in "reintroducing" the profile of the women's game to the media and revealing interest among male and female audiences alike, the author(s) were clearly behind the curve on issues such as unequal sponsorship for male and female players and gender equality more broadly. In this regard, it is revealing that the previous month's issue (*Placar*, No. 1452, June 2019) was devoted entirely to the forthcoming (men's)

[4] Their website, which provides excellent coverage of women's football in Brazil and beyond, can be consulted at https://planetafutebolfeminino.com.br/ (accessed April 12, 2023).

Copa América and included not a single reference to the Women's World Cup that was about to take place in France over the same period, to be watched by a global television audience in excess of one billion people.[5]

Four months later, almost fifty years since the magazine was launched, *Placar* published its first ever edition devoted to women's football (see front cover shown here), working in partnership with four organizations already active in the field,[6] to produce articles on the Women's World Cup and women's football in Brazil, as well as a number of features on and interviews with leading figures in the women's game in Brazil.

5. https://www.fifa.com/tournaments/womens/womensworldcup/france2019/news/fifa-women-s-world-cup-2019tm-watched-by-more-than-1-billion (accessed April 12, 2023).

6. In addition to Planeta Futebol Feminino, a key partner in producing the ranking of the best twenty women players for the July 2019 issue, *Placar* drew heavily on the expertise of Jogamiga, Elas no ataque, and Jogadelas.

The editorial celebrated the media success of the recent Women's World Cup and other achievements within Brazil in what it describes as "one of the best years for women's football," while also claiming that "*Placar* is correcting little by little its past errors in its treatment of women's football" (November 2019, p. 4). Readers are reminded of the magazine's public apology, in the July 2019 edition, "for our machista past," and the coeditors here go further by stating that previous editor Juca Kfouri, the man behind the "Football, Sex and Rock 'n' Roll" era, confirmed that its coverage had not been "almost always sexist in its objectification of women," but had simply "always" been so.

One of the coeditors of the special issue subsequently stated that it was "a starting point and we hope to continue giving space to women's football in 2020" (Cardim, 2019), although the sporadic coverage of women's football since then suggests that this aspiration seems to have been lost as editorial control of the magazine passed to the team of sportswriters of *Veja* from the start of 2020 (Paraizo, 2020). Known for its political conservatism (Gomes and Alencar, 2019) and for its traditional representations of women (Giordano, 2017), the involvement of *Veja* seemed unlikely to result in the ongoing promotion of women's football: *Veja* previously traced the origins of the women's game in Brazil to 1981 and suggested that the first teams were founded in gay nightclubs (Flores, 1996), thereby ignoring the previous sixty years of women's football in the country while simultaneously delegitimizing it as a sexually transgressive practice. However, the inclusion of an interview with Pia Sundhage in her role as the new coach of the women's national team (October 2020, pp. 26–27), which draws attention to recent positive developments in Brazil and to the ongoing inequalities in the resourcing of football for men and women, offered hope that *Placar* would continue to represent women's football in sporting—rather than feminized or sexualized—terms.

Beyond Fifty Years: 2020-2023

Toward the end of the year that marked the magazine's fiftieth anniversary, *Placar* featured ex-star player Robinho on its front cover as the former star player of the national team was accused of rape during his time in Italy. Alongside the photo, the magazine declared that "Brazil no longer accepts with impunity rape culture," adopting the discourse of feminist organizations in a marked change of tone. In addition to coverage of the trial, which found Robinho guilty and sentenced him to nine years in prison, a lengthy article by Martha Esteves, who was a journalist at *Placar* during the 1980s, reflected on the sexist treatment and negative experiences she endured at the magazine during that decade.

Furthermore, the editorial went well beyond the public apology of the July 2019 edition in what the magazine's website described as a "mea culpa," focusing in particular on the "Football, Sex & Rock 'n' Roll" period of the late 1990s and describing the magazine's coverage as being "somewhat irresponsible, without realizing the discomfort and trouble it could cause" (November 2020).[7] The editorial closed with a powerful affirmation of the magazine's changed attitudes, whereby women in football are "ever more present and active —on the pitch, in refereeing, with a microphone in hand and wherever else they wish, without being inconvenienced or insulted, without simply being objects of the male gaze."

Since the watershed of the November 2020 issue, *Placar*'s coverage of women's football has focused on the achievements of Brazil's leading players and teams, with occasional features on developments in the women's game elsewhere. The front cover of the December 2021 edition, which features "Images of a Special Year," includes a photo of the dominant Corinthians women's team alongside the top men's teams, while the February 2023 "Edition of Champions of 2022" carries two photos of women players (from Palmeiras and Corinthians, respectively) among the seven champions of the previous year.[8] Further coverage of women's football is now provided via a dedicated section of the *Placar* website,[9] which features regular stories about Brazilian women's teams, players at home and abroad and the international women's game. Such developments stand in marked contrast with the situation a decade earlier, when women's football was largely ignored by the magazine—and by the Brazilian media more widely—but coverage remains at a far lower level than the men's game, to which entire editions are regularly dedicated to discuss forthcoming championships and tournaments, both at home and abroad.

7. Available online at https://placar.abril.com.br/placar/arquivo-caso-robinho-foi-tratado-em-capa-com-mea-culpa-de-placar/ (accessed April 11, 2023).

8. Palmeiras won the Copa Libertadores Femenina and Corinthians won the Campeonato Brasileiro Feminino for the third consecutive year.

9. See https://placar.abril.com.br/tudo-sobre/futebol-feminino (accessed April 11, 2023).

Conclusion

The ways in which women's football in Brazil has been portrayed and discussed in *Placar* have changed significantly over the last fifty years, as has the women's game itself. Throughout its existence, *Placar* has undergone several relaunches and changes in format for primarily commercial reasons, seeking to increase the magazine's appeal to a wider readership. The magazine's public apologies for its previous representations of women explained the sexualization and objectification of women as being the result of different times and while such an explanation may be seen to avoid assuming responsibility for such actions it is nonetheless worth considering the shift in public perceptions vis-à-vis the representation of women.

A nationwide survey conducted in December 2015, the same month that Editora Abril stopped publishing *Playboy* because of falling circulation, found that participants consistently felt that "women are hyper-sexualized across the board" (*Cinema and Society*: 18), while 74% of those surveyed thought that there was "too much nudity and sex in media," with only 16% disagreeing (*Cinema and Society*: 14). The magazine's move toward coverage of women's football that focuses on sporting achievement rather than on a sexualized spectacle has coincided, then, with a desire among Brazilians for fewer sexualized representations of women in the media. All of this came at a time, of course, when other initiatives, such as the Law of Femicide, Ni Una Menos, and Ele Não,[10] brought gender inequality and gender-based violence to public attention as never before, especially via the use of electronic and social media.

Furthermore, the readership of *Placar* changed with the move to a multiplatform mode of delivery in 2016 following the break of the connection with *Playboy*: from 92% of its readers being male in 2008 (Saldanha, 2009, p. 17), 24% of readers via the dedicated website were female in 2024 (Similarweb, 2024), a significant shift away from the overwhelmingly male gaze for which the magazine catered in previous decades. In recent years, *Placar* has acknowledged the broader significance that women's football has as part of this political domain via reporting on Marta's campaign for equality in the 2019 Women's World Cup (July 2019, p. 61), in acclaim for the recent introduction by the CBF of equal

[10] The Law of Femicide was signed into action by President Dilma Rousseff in March 2015; the first mass demonstration in Brazil under the #NiUnaMenos banner took place in October 2016; #EleNão arose in September 2018 as a movement against the election of Jair Bolsonaro to the country's presidency.

pay for the men's and women's national teams, and in positive reporting on the appointment of women to leadership positions in the women's game in Brazil (October 2020, p. 26).

During the period of the ban on women's football, occasional references to the practice of the game by women in Brazil and Europe routinely emphasized the players' femininity and overtly sexualized them, while the presence in the magazine of women as wives and girlfriends of well-known male footballers conformed to traditional gender roles whereby women were "beautiful, maternal and feminine" (Goellner, 2003). These features, which delegitimized women's football as a sporting practice between 1970 and 1983 (Wood, 2021), continued to underpin the "symbolic annihilation" (Duncan and Messner, 1998, p. 171) of women's football in *Placar* over the next two decades. They were foregrounded as never before from 1995 when the magazine was relaunched in a new format that explicitly brought together football and sex, always assumed to be heterosexual and from the perspective of a male reader/viewer.

This phase, which saw the consistent and blatant sexualization of women football players, and of models posing as football players, was replaced at the end of the decade by an emphasis on the feminization of women's football, exemplified in the report in May 2000 on the women's team that would compete at the Olympic Games in Sydney. Less overtly damaging than the sexual objectification of women's football during the late 1990s, this phase nonetheless sought to locate women footballers within a framework of traditional gender roles, thereby minimizing the potential challenge of women's football to a male-dominated field.

The success of the women's national team at international sporting mega-events in the first decade of the new millennium resulted in a move toward coverage that focused more on the sporting action than on the players' appearance, although ongoing tensions with the established narratives surrounding women's football continued to be in evidence. This same period also witnessed the rise to international prominence of Marta, who would go on to achieve iconic status on the international stage, as well as becoming the scorer of the most goals both at the World Cup finals and in the shirt of the Brazilian national team.[11]

Her unrivalled position in the women's game in Brazil and beyond, and the global recognition of her achievements, has resulted in her appearing on the cover

[11]. Marta has scored 17 goals at World Cup Finals (cf. Germany's Miroslav Klose, with 16) and 118 goals for the *seleção* (cf. Neymar and Pelé, both with 77).

of *Placar* no fewer than five times between 2016 and 2020. The frequency with which she is represented serves also, however, to highlight the space of exception that she occupies amid the continuing relative invisibility of other outstanding women players in the media more widely.

Placar is, of course, only part of the story in relation to the representation of women's football in Brazil, but, as the country's leading sports magazine over the last fifty years, it has played an important role in establishing the textual narratives and visual codes through which women's football has been variously ignored, ridiculed, sexualized, and feminized, before coming finally to occupy a space in which it receives qualitative, if not quantitative, parity with the men's game, at least in terms of the national team and its star players. The changing representation of women's football has undoubtedly reflected changes in Brazil more broadly, but such influences are not unidirectional, for "how we are seen determines in part how we are treated; how we treat others is based on how we see them; such seeing comes from representation" (Dyer, 1993, p. 1).

A century after the first documented women's match in Brazil, over half a century since the first edition of *Placar* and forty years since the introduction of official structures for women's football in Brazil, its representation has belatedly come to be that of football played by women who are seen—as they have long seen themselves—as equal subjects in the country of football.

REFERENCES

"Abril retoma títulos transferidos a Caras," ("Abril Recovers Titles Transferred to Caras.") *meioemensagem* October 10, 2016 (consulted online at https://www.meioemensagem.com.br/home/midia/2016/10/10/abril-retoma-titulos-transferidos-a-caras.html; accessed April 12, 2023).

Billig, Michael. *Banal Nationalism* (London: Sage, 2010 [1995]).

Bonfim, Aira. "Football Feminino entre festas esportivas, circos e campos suburbanos: uma história social do futebol praticado por mulheres da introdução à proibição (1915–1941)." (Women's Football between sports festivals, circuses, and suburban fields: A social history of football played by women from Its Introduction to its prohibition (1915–1941)). unpublished MA dissertation, Fundação Getúlio Vargas CPDOC, 2019. Available online at https://hdl.handle.net/10438/28563 (accessed April 12, 2023).

Cardim, Maria Eduarda. "Revista Placar ganha primeira edição dedicada ao futebol feminino em 50 anos," ("Placar Magazine Releases Its First Edition Dedicated to Women's Football in 50 Years.") Elas no ataque, November 30, 2019. Available online at https://blogs.correiobraziliense.com.br/elasnoataque/revista-placar-novembro-2019/ (accessed April 12, 2023).

Cinema and Society: Shaping our Worldview Beyond the Lens. Investigation on the Impact of Gender Representation in Brazilian Films (Geena Davis Institute on Gender in Media, no date. Available online at https://geenadavisinstitute.org/research/investigation-on-the-impact-of-gender-representation-in-brazilian-films/#:~:text=in%20Brazilian%20Films-,Investigation%20on%20the%20Impact%20of%20Gender%20Representation%20in%20Brazilian%20Films,identity%20in%20our%20latest%20study (accessed April 12, 2023).

Connell, Raewyn W. *Gender and power* (Cambridge: Polity Press, 1987).

Costa, Leda Maria da. "O futebol feminino nas décadas de 1940 a 1980," ("Women's Football in the 1940s to 1980s.") *Revista do Arquivo Geral da Cidade do Rio de Janeiro*, No. 13 (2017), 493–507.

Duncan, Margaret Carlisle and Michael A. Messner. "The Media Image of Sport and Gender," in L. A. Wenner (ed.), *MediaSport* (London: Routledge, 1998), 170–185.

"Flores do campo," *Veja* October 30, 1996: 72–73.

Franzini, Fábio. "Futebol é "coisa para macho"?: Pequeno esboço para uma história das mulheres no país do futebol," (Is Football "a Man's Thing"? A Brief Outline for a History of Women in the Country of Football). *Revista Brasileira de História* (São Paulo), 25 (2005), 315–328.

Giordano, Verónica. "Derechas, neoliberalismo y estereotipos de género. La revista *Veja* de Brasil, 1989–1999," ("Right-Wing Politics, Neoliberalism, and Gender Stereotypes: Brazil's Veja Magazine, 1989–1999"). Nuevo Mundo Mundos Nuevos [online], Colloques, October 02, 2017. Available online at http://journals.openedition.org/nuevomundo/71292 (accessed April 12, 2023).

Goellner, Silvana Vilodre. *Bela, maternal e feminina: imagens da mulher na Revista Educação Physica* (Beautiful, Maternal, and Feminine: Images of Women in Educação Magazine). (Ijuí: Unijuí, 2003).

Goellner, Silvana Vilodre and Juliana Ribeiro Cabral. *As pioneras do futebol pedem passage: conhecer para reconhecer* (The Pioneers of Women's Football

Demand a Place: Knowing to Recognize). (Porto Alegre: Universidade Federal do Rio Grande do Sul, 2022).

Gomes, Emanoel Pedro Martins and Claudiana Nogueira de Alencar. "A mídia como ator político: uma análise de textos da Revista *Veja* sobre casos de corrupção política," The Media as a Political Actor: An Analysis of Veja Magazine Texts on Political Corruption Cases"). Alfa, revista linguística (São José Rio Preto), vol. 63, N0. 1 (2019), 81–111. Available online at http://www.scielo.br/scielo.php?script=sci_arttext&pid=S1981-57942019000100081&lng=en&nrm=iso (accessed April 12, 2023).

Hobsbawm, Eric and Terence Ranger (eds.). *The invention of tradition.* Cambridge and New York: Cambridge University Press, 1983.

Paraizo, Danúbia. "Placar se reposiciona e passa a ser editada pelos jornialistas de Veja," *Propmark*, ("Placar Repositions Itself and Starts Being Edited by Veja Journalists"). January 23, 2020. Available online at https://propmark.com.br/midia/placar-se-reposiciona-e-passa-a-ser-produzida-pelos-jornalistas-de-veja/ (accessed April 12, 2023).

Similarweb (consulted online at https://www.similarweb.com/website/placar.uol.com.br/#demographics; accessed January 6, 2025).

Ribeiro, Raphael Rajão. "Futebol de mulheres em tempos de proibição: o caso das partidas Vespasiano x Oficina (1968)," ("Women's Football in Times of Prohibition: The Case of Vespasiano vs. Oficina Matches (1968)"). *Mosaico* (Rio de Janeiro), 9, No. 14 (July 2018), 48–69.

Rigo, Luiz Carlos; Flávia Garcia Guidotti, Larissa Zanetti Theil and Marcela Amaral. "Notas sobre o futebol feminino pelotense em 1950: um estudo genealógico," ("Notes on Women's Football in Pelotas in the 1950s: A Genealogical Study"). *Revista Brasileira de Ciências do Esporte*, 29, No. 3 (May 2008), 173–188.

Sacchitiello, Bárbara. "Abril vende 7 revistas e investe em branded content," ("Abril Sells 7 Magazines and Invests in Branded Content"). *meioemensagem* June 2, 2015. Available online at https://www.meioemensagem.com.br/home/midia/2015/06/02/abril-vende-7-revistas-e-investe-em-branded.html (accessed April 12, 2023).

Saldanha, Renato Machado. "*Placar* e a produção de uma representação de futebol moderno," ("Placar and the Production of a Representation of Modern Football"). unpublished MA dissertation, Universidade Federal do Rio Grande do Sul, Porto Alegre, 2009.

Saldanha, Renato M. and Silvana V. Goellner. "Futebol, sexo e rock and roll: o futebol moderno na revista *Placar*," ("Football, Sex, and Rock and Roll: Modern Football in Placar Magazine"). *Revista Brasileira de Ciências do Esporte*, 35, No. 2 (2013), 281–296.

Salvini, Leila and Wanderley Marchi Júnior. "Velhos tabus de roupa nova: o futebol feminino na revista Placar entre os anos de 2000–2010," ("Old Taboos in New Clothes: Women's Football in Placar Magazine Between 2000 and 2010"). *Praxia,* 1, No. 2 (2013a), 55–66.

Salvini, Leila and Wanderley Marchi Júnior. "O futebol de Marta na revista Placar: recortes de uma história," ("Marta's Football in Placar Magazine: Snapshots of a Story"). *Espaço Plural,* No. 29, 2 (2013b), 298–313.

Salvini, Leila and Wanderley Marchi Júnior. "Registros do futebol feminino na Revista *Placar*: 30 anos de história," ("Records of Women's Football in Placar Magazine: 30 Years of History"). *Motrivivência,* 28, No. 49 (2016), 99–113.

Silva, Giovana Capucim e. *Narrativas sobre o futebol feminino na imprensa paulista: entre a proibição e a regulamentação (1965–1983)* (Narratives About Women's Football in São Paulo Press: Between Prohibition and Regulation (1941–1983)). MA Dissertation. Faculdade de Filosofia, Letras e Ciências Humanas da Universidade de São Paulo, São Paulo, 2015.

Wood, David. "Fifty Years of Women's Football in *Placar*: From Disallowed Goals to Winning at Home?" *Revista Movimento*, v. 27 (Jan–April, 2021), p. e27002 (https://doi.org/10.22456/1982-8918.109870).

CHAPTER 9

Supporters' Club: Conceptual Aspects of Women Soccer Fan Groups in Brazilian Stadiums

Carolina Moraes

This chapter aims to present a master's study conducted in 2018 in the Multidisciplinary Program in Culture and Society at the Federal University of Bahia, titled "Women want to have the right to support their football clubs." This study aimed to investigate the participation of women in supporter clubs. To achieve this objective, the methodology of participant observation was employed, involving the researcher's immersion in the social spaces frequented by the female supporters' group of the two largest fan groups in the state of Bahia, called Bamor and Os Imbatíveis, the supporters' group of Esporte Clube Vitória.

Through this approach, the study seeks to understand how the presence of women in supporters' groups can influence and modify cultural, gender, and football-related aspects, considering the construction of national identity, masculinity, and identity. Negotiation is a central concept employed in this study, enabling the identification of the potential transformative impact that the presence of female supporter groups can have on organized fan groups. Therefore, this research proposes an interdisciplinary analysis of the relationships between culture, gender, and football, with an emphasis on the presence and role of the women supporters group.

Introduction

My emotional connection with football, from childhood to adolescence, both as a player and a fan, sparked my desire to investigate the presence of the female supporters group. Football is deeply intertwined in our society and provides fertile ground for analyzing social, cultural, and political issues in Brazil. This chapter, therefore, aims to share in general terms the research conducted in 2018 in the Multidisciplinary Program in Culture and Society at the Federal University of Bahia, titled "Women Want (to be able to) Cheer." This study investigated the presence and role of women in supporter clubs in Brazil, addressing aspects of sociability, identity, and resistance. The chosen methodology for the research was participant observation (Brandão, 1999), which involved an accompanying women supporter group in the social spaces that encompass the lifestyles of fan groups. Based on this, the study was organized into three main parts:

1. "The Place of Women in the National Passion" explored the contradictions and challenges faced by women in the "Country of Football." This section discusses the relationship between football, culture, and national identity, examines how football is an important part of Brazilian culture, and analyzes the presence and space of women in this context.
2. "Women Want to Cheer" delved into understanding the trajectory and experience of female football fans and their relationship with the social spaces of football. It addressed the challenges and achievements of women in supporters' groups and how their presence changes the social dynamics of these groups.
3. "Does My Presence Bother You?" reflected on the discomfort caused by the presence of women in the stands and the negotiations necessary to gain and maintain space in these environments. This section discusses possible conclusions and future paths for the presence of women in support clubs.

Throughout the research, stories, trajectories, and perspectives of the fans "Bamor" from Esporte Clube Bahia and "Os Imbatíveis" from Esporte Clube Vitória were presented, as well as accounts and observations from female fans who are part of the stands, stadiums, headquarters of fan groups, and bars, including my own experiences as a fan. Contact was made with female fans who participated in the I National Meeting of Women in the Stands, held on June 10, 2017, at the Auditorium of the Museu do Futebol, located in the Pacaembu Stadium in the city of São Paulo, SP. In addition, interactions from an exclusive WhatsApp group created after the event were considered.

Me, a Female Fan

My familiarity with the theme of football originated in my childhood, when I started participating in games with boys in the condominium where I lived in São Bernardo do Campo, SP. In this context of my daily involvement in sports, I quickly realized that my presence in that environment was not accepted because I was the only girl who frequented that court. To establish my visibility, I had to respond promptly, not only by participating in football but also by understanding the fundamentals and nuances of the sport. Over the years, what was initially just a playful activity has turned into a serious pursuit. With the unconditional support of my mother, I began to explore different training locations dedicated to women's football, dedicating approximately a decade of my life to football practice.

Quitting was not a choice, but a circumstance imposed upon me. Due to family matters, I had to give up playing football and start working since that period, only allowed for school and sports. Unfortunately, this brief history is not unique to me but rather a common experience for the majority of women who play football in the country. Despite no longer playing, I have always been a loyal fan of my favorite club. For me, like many football enthusiasts, the club is not just a badge but also has a name and a home, which happened to be my uncle's house. It did not take much time to win me over. I eagerly awaited joining family gatherings to watch matches. With some new jerseys and cherished old ones, I started being invited to go to the stadium with my uncle and cousin. That is how I had my second encounter with football—the fan experience. I can still recall the first moments of walking around the stadium, the captivating chants, the symbolic sense of belonging, and the excitement that made my heart race, just like when my club scored a goal. Accompanied by the men in the family, I had limited mobility as that space was not entirely "mine" either. As time passed, during my teenage years, I gained more freedom to attend the stadium and consequently joined an organized fan group.

This study holds significance in my personal journey, not only for the potential professional opportunities that university life can offer but also for the belief in the importance of the sense of belonging that football has provided me, making me an enthusiast of this sport. By reconnecting these feelings with the experiences of female fans, I am not only fulfilling an ethnographic obligation but also positioning myself once again as an integral part of this context.

Through these recent experiences, I always leave the stadiums with the certainty that change is possible, even in an unassumed way. Today, given the challenges in football, my evaluation is more conscious and critical, yet no less passionate. Being a part of, feeling a part of, and being a fan of a football team may seem unusual. For those who have never been to a football stadium, all I can say is going.

The Place of Women in the National Passion

Football, as a cultural phenomenon (Franco Júnior, 2014), plays a fundamental role in the construction of national identity in many countries. In Brazil, this bond is even stronger. Passion for sports transcends the boundaries of the field and infiltrates various aspects of society, shaping traditions, customs, and values. In this sense, Brazilian football has become a symbol of pride and belonging (Damo, 2014) and is closely tied to our history and way of life. The achievements of international competitions, combined with the unique and creative style of play, have contributed to the consolidation of a national identity that celebrates the talent, joy, and resilience of the Brazilian people. Thus, football is not just a sport. It is a cultural expression that reflects and strengthens a nation's identity, bringing together people from different backgrounds, beliefs, and realities around a common passion.

The statement "We are the Country of Football," whether it is a sentence, achievement, or destiny, is claimed as a privilege in our country. Hypothetically, if this is true, it is undeniable that we are the country of men's football (Braga, 2015; Goellner, 2014; Moraes, 2018). According to Rosenfeld (2007), football is a symbol of masculinity in Brazil, a country in which patriarchal culture values virile power and literary-rhetorical eloquence. However, it is undeniable that women increasingly assert themselves as active and passive participants in sports. They challenge the notion that football is exclusively a male space and confront fears and anxieties associated with femininity in the context of this sport (Eco, 1984; Guedes, 1982; Noronha, 2016).

The construction of national identity and its link to masculinity in Brazilian football are complex and multifaceted topics. For decades, women have been excluded from sports such as football due to social concerns about the "masculinization" of those who play football and how it may deviate from the imposed standards of femininity. However, women's participation in football is not new despite the challenges they face. There is a pursuit of equality and recognition, but the presence of women remains unsettled. What can be observed is that women have been fighting to find their space and be heard in this context, facing social and cultural barriers that often reinforce gender inequality. By challenging these norms and asserting their right to fully participate in the national passion for football, women contribute to the deconstruction of sexism and the creation of a more inclusive and equal environment in sports.

Female Fans, Their Clubs, and Fan Groups

The word "torcer" (to support) originated from the action of women from wealthier classes who attended matches and "twisted" their gloves in anxiety for a goal (Malaia, 2012). The presence of women in stadiums was seen as a way to enhance spectacle and demonstrate the family friendly nature of the event. However, the presence of women also led to reflections on the occupation of public spaces and inclusion of women in society.

Once the intrinsic connection between symbolism underlying the act of cheering and the role assigned to women in the social structure is understood, it becomes imperative to acquire a deeper understanding of the act of cheering itself, along with its multiple manifestations and symbolic representations. As the phenomenon of football spreads, women enter the spaces of football clubs where matches occur. However, to better understand this issue, it is essential to examine the process of selecting football clubs for support. The answer to this question may initially seem obvious, especially due to the frequent accounts of fans claiming they were "born" supporting Esporte Clube Bahia or that they have been fans of Esporte Clube Vitória since childhood. These expressions, in a way, support the idea that this "choice" is constructed within the family sphere, in proximity to friends, neighbors, and acquaintances, as emphasized by Damatta (1982), Damo (1999), and Reis (1998).

The supporters' club is a choice made by a group in which both male and female fans assimilate the patterns of attitudes and behaviors adopted by the fan group itself, as pointed out by Carlos Máximo Pimenta (2000). On the other hand, there is the figure of the female fan who attends matches and supports her club but does not engage in an associational way with an organized group, as highlighted by Heloisa Baldy dos Reis (1998). This distinction exists between those who are part of a fan faction with an independent organizational structure from the club they support, in contrast to uniform fans who express their preference for the club by wearing the team's shirt (Reis, 1998, p. 6).

Currently, women's choice to attend football stadiums no longer causes astonishment in society. However, the decision to participate in a supporters' club still seems to generate discomfort. The inclusion of women in supporters' groups does not reflect an immediate connection because the information disseminated about these fan groups is aligned with societal expectations regarding women, which, from a Bourdieusian perspective, does not relate to the feminine habitus as a fan.

The choice of a football club to support is often influenced by factors such as family upbringing, as in my case, proximity to friends and neighbors. This choice is a cultural construction that involves the creation of emotional bonds, and is imbued with personal stories and trajectories.

In the early 20th century, football gained popularity in Brazil, with fans increasingly appearing in the local press in São Paulo and Rio de Janeiro. The clubs Esporte Clube Bahia and Esporte Clube Vitória were founded during this period, each with its own stories and trajectories. During a turbulent period in Brazilian politics due to the 1930 coup d'état, Esporte Clube Bahia was born in Salvador on January 1 of the same year, with colors representing the state of Bahia, reinforcing the premise of identity and regional pride. As presented by Paulo Roberto Leandro (2015), Esporte Clube Bahia emerged from the merger of two of the city's top clubs: Associação Atlética da Bahia and Clube Bahiano de Tênis.

According to the author, these two clubs could not withstand the pressure from the football department and eventually closed their doors due to opposition to the presence and participation of black workers in a football club in Salvador. On the other hand, Esporte Clube Vitória was founded on May 13, 1899, making it one of the oldest clubs in the country, born within the racist upper bourgeoisie of Salvador (Leandro, 2015). Initially, the club used black and white colors and paid homage to Corredor da Vitória, one of the most expensive areas in Salvador, where its nineteen founders resided at the time. The club later adopted red and black colors due to its sympathy for Clube de Regatas do Flamengo, and football activities began in 1902 (Sampaio, 2011).

The Bamor supporters' club is the largest organized fan group of Esporte Clube Bahia, with approximately 1468 members, including hundred members from the female subgroup called "Bonde Feminino." The female fans of Bahia who participate in the Bamor supporters' club are between the ages of 17 and 33, with the highest concentration between 21 and 23 years. The Bamor Fan group is divided into four zones within the capital of Bahia and is represented in other states. Bamor's Bonde Feminino was officially founded in 2005, providing an exclusive space for female fans.

The "Os Imbatíveis" supporters' club is the largest organized fan group of Esporte Clube Vitória, with approximately 1300 members. Among them, forty-four belong to the "Comando Feminino" (Female Command), and in total, about 120 women are football supporters. Female fans of Vitória range from 16 to 30 years of age, with the highest concentration being between 21 and 23 years of age. The Comando Feminino is a specific part of a fan group composed exclusively of women, and members can choose to be part of this subgroup.

It is evident that this configuration represents progress by providing female fans with their own space, acknowledging, and promoting their active participation in the world of fan groups. However, it is important to address the issues arising from this perspective. By establishing a space exclusively dedicated to female fans, a challenge arises to avoid creating segregation or distinction between genders, especially considering that there is no district or command equally dedicated to male fans. Therefore, it is crucial to strive for a balance that promotes the inclusion of all fans regardless of gender, thus avoiding the reproduction of gender stereotypes and ensuring equal opportunities and participation in the context of fan groups.

In recent decades, there has been a significant increase in women's participation in public spaces, including football stadiums. Despite social advancements and a greater presence, women still face stereotypes and prejudices regarding their role as fans. Leda Maria da Costa (2007) identifies the true fan as someone who unconditionally supports their beloved club, contrasting them with those who see football as a pastime. Women's participation in football stadiums raises discussions about the stereotypes imposed upon them and the issues that arise as a result of their paths as fans.

The growing presence of women in football stadiums no longer surprises Brazilian society. However, their participation in supporter clubs still generates discomfort. The inclusion of women in these groups does not occur immediately, as the information disseminated about organized fan groups aligns with the expected societal standards for women, which does not correspond to the feminine habitus. Roger Chartier (1988) states that understanding the social realm involves intentionality and strategies, indicating that the choices made by supporters' clubs to keep women at a distance are mechanisms to preserve the organization and exalt masculinity.

When analyzing the participation of women in supporters' clubs, it becomes apparent that the expressions associated with football stadiums do not fit the societal expectations placed upon women. This can generate fear of the division of space and the loss of identity among men. However, with the increasing presence of women, some male fans have started trying to better understand and strengthen their discourse to support women.

During the ethnographic research conducted with the Bamor and Os Imbatíveis fan groups as well as other participating female fans, observations and dialogues were established with various women engaged in this context. It is important to highlight that, specifically regarding the mentioned fan groups, there was evidence of active participation of women in the daily activities of football supporters, including decision-making processes and organizing celebrations in the stands, such as the use of large flags and drumming, among other elements. However, it is worth noting that not all fan groups follow this dynamic.

During the National Meeting of Women in the Stands, there were situations in which some female fans did not have access to the material resources mentioned earlier, nor did they actively participate in organized fan groups. Female fans face difficulties in accessing the assets of supporter clubs, such as large flags and drumming. Despite this, some female fans took on responsibilities, such as creating shirts in tribute to players and organizing birthday celebrations. Although the participation of female fans in traditionally male-dominated activities, such as using large flags and playing in drumming groups, is still limited, their attempts to enter these spaces have resulted in significant progress and changes in the dynamics of organized fan groups. However, it is important to mention that some of the interviewed female fans reported experiences of sexism and prejudice, which created discomfort regarding their presence in these contexts.

The Role of Negotiation in the Lives of Female Football Fans

Using the concept of negotiation to explore the relationships that shape the football universe is not common, and research linking "negotiation" with "football" often tends to focus on player negotiations or issues of identity in football, such as national identity. In my quest to understand the relationships between football, fandom, and female fans, I dared to explore negotiation as a crucial element in the presence and actions of the female supporter group.

The word "negotiation" originates from Latin and is formed by the roots "neg" and "otium," which literally mean without leisure or without rest (Pereira, 2012). In the consulted dictionaries, the definitions refer to acts of making agreements, dealing with, conversing, and the act or effect of negotiation. Maria Ester de Freitas (1994), in her article "Organization: a space of negotiation," refers to Dean G. Pruitt's (1981) concept to define negotiation as:

> "making concessions and compromises to achieve a mutually acceptable solution. The negotiation process involves active communication, understanding the different perspectives and needs of each party, and finding a common ground to address conflicting interests. by making concessions and seeking new alternatives that offer greater mutual benefits" (Pruitt, 1981, p. 14).

Freitas highlighted that the negotiation process involves social conflicts, as there are opposing interests at stake, but also possibilities for resolving these conflicts, as negotiations require the exposure and analysis of alternatives to build an agreement that repositions the relationship. Dean Pruitt (1981) also elaborates on the functions of negotiation, such as developing specific agreements, long-term policies, and mediating social change.

In football, negotiations usually address transfers and identities; however, in this case, the focus is on the presence and involvement of female fans. Thus, negotiations involve social conflict and the pursuit of agreements that can mediate social change. Interactions between women, fan groups, and clubs are strategies and demands for space within the supporters' club, a "territory" marked by the status quo. These negotiations often involve gaining access to spaces within fan groups, sometimes by creating specific sections for the women supporters' group, allowing for closer bonds and strengthening relationships among female fans. Male dominance is explained by Bourdieu (2002) as the result of a series of everyday, predominantly symbolic forms of violence exerted by the dominators and legitimized by the dominated. This domination, based on the biological differences between men and women, is perpetuated by both men and women, as the historical structures of male dominance are incorporated in the form of habitus, an unconscious form of perception that determines which attitudes are appropriate for each gender. The presence of women in football stadiums generates tensions and negotiations, as it challenges established habitus and necessitates adjustments to a new context.

In this research, testimonies were gathered from female fans about their struggles for the right to wave the fan group's flag and play in the drum section, highlighting the need for female empowerment. Other accounts highlight the barriers imposed on women, such as the prohibition of travel to matches considered dangerous or to carry fan group materials. However, female fans who face these challenges and assert their rights contribute to opening up space and inspiring other women to do the same. The discussion emphasizes the importance of analyzing and problematizing gender negotiations and hierarchies within football supporters, aiming for the equality and representation of women.

Final Remarks

This chapter allowed us to revisit the essential aspects of the work, recognizing that academic studies should be evaluated and referenced considering the historical period in which they were produced. It is important to highlight that a ten-year interval can be considered negligible in terms of historical, cultural, and social changes.

During the research period, one aspect caught my attention, which I referred to as "Considerations: Resilience and Adversity—Why are they there?" At that time, the country's political landscape progressed with the election of President Dilma Rousseff, who became the first woman to lead Brazil. After two terms by President Luiz Inácio Lula da Silva (2003–2006 and 2007–2010), Brazil experienced significant advancements in social, cultural, and economic spheres.

However, everything began to change after the impeachment of President Dilma Rousseff in 2016, followed by the government of Michel Temer and, subsequently, the election of Jair Messias Bolsonaro in 2019. Many changes have occurred, and in football, as in society, progress and setbacks often go hand-in-hand. Today, we can observe positive changes in the participation of women in football, whether as players in the field, in courts, or working as reporters, journalists, commentators, or coaches, among other roles in various spaces. Despite the difficulties they face, women occupy, resist, and remain redefining spaces previously dominated by men.

In the case of supporters' clubs, it is essential to highlight their lifestyles (Toledo, 1996), a space filled with contradictions, experiences, and prejudices. In this debate, some female fans demonstrate the need to discuss their right to be fans. In our conception, this right should go hand in hand with the advancements experienced by women in society (Goellner, 2021).

Studying female supporter groups requires tolerance, care, and complicity. Tolerance is needed to build trust, care is necessary to preserve the safety of female fans, and complicity ensures the relevance of work. Organized fan groups are spaces of diversity and contradictions. The right to become a fan should align with the advancement of women in society. The experiences of female fans in the stands deserve admiration for their persistence in occupying that space.

This emphasizes the importance of addressing the specificities of football supporters and recognizing the need for a sensitive and empathetic approach when studying female fans. Furthermore, it highlights the significance of valuing the courage and determination of women who face challenges in occupying fan spaces.

Despite these difficulties, female fans have a deep sense of belonging. The legitimacy of women as fans is constantly questioned in spaces that are still predominantly male. Stadiums, traditionally seen as places of leisure, are often considered exclusive to men. Our research aims to determine why women cannot share these moments.

The involvement of women in supporters' clubs is analyzed, identifying the persistence of stereotypes associated with the private sphere. However, it is important to highlight the remarkable advancements achieved by the women's support group. They seek space and assert their needs, facing challenges driven by their love for the club and passion for the fandom. Despite adversity, they feel part of something greater. The word "love" is frequently used to describe their presence in the stands.

The quest for a "space of their own" may indicate a fear of loss. Female fans challenge symbols and meanings shared by male fans. The choice of how to express passion is constantly judged. Our hope is to contribute to a change in this stance, strengthen the struggles of female fans, and allow them to cheer in the way they desire.

This revision highlights the struggle of female fans in their pursuit of recognition and space while emphasizing the importance of breaking down existing stereotypes and prejudices. It also emphasizes the need to strengthen the fights of female fans and promote freedom of expression in fandom, regardless of gender.

Football stadiums have become spaces where certain behaviors are accepted and normalized (Daólio, 2005), even though these behaviors may be questioned outside the stands. However, currently, we can observe some examples of "favorable winds, albeit timid." Considering that football is considered a male-dominated domain (Dunning and Maguirre, 1997), it is interesting to reflect on what is at stake.

This adaptation acknowledges the ongoing struggle faced by female fans while highlighting the changing tides and the importance of examining power dynamics in football as a traditionally male-dominated space.

Considering that the stadium is seen as a space of the "permissible," fans—organized or not—turn it into their leisure time, where acts of violence, insults, and profanity are glorified and accepted. However, as many of these actions may cause unease, we need to question why female fans in supporter clubs cannot share these moments, just like men. Perhaps it is because they expect to embody stereotypes of what is considered feminine in our society, such as nurturing, affection, grace, emotional instability, vanity, and fragility, among others.

Ultimately, what seems to be at stake is the fear of losing a "space of their own." As women share this space, men may feel a sense of "loss." Why do they experience this fear? This may be because they contribute to the maintenance of symbols that male fans share, which are not necessarily shared by female fans. The struggle to maintain this exclusive space can be observed in other contexts, as mentioned previously.

REFERENCES

BOURDIEU, P. **Masculine Domination**. Rio de Janeiro: Bertrand Brasil, 2002.

BRAGA, Harian Pires. **The Sweet Memory of What I Lived:** The Formation of National Identity in Football (1938–1950). 2015, p. 184. Dissertation (Master's in Physical Education and Society)—Universidade Estadual de Campinas—Unicamp, Faculty of Physical Education, Campinas, 2015.

BRANDÃO, Carlos Rodrigues (Org.). **Rethinking Participatory Research**. São Paulo: Brasiliense, 1999.

CHARTIER, Roger. **Cultural History Between Practices and Representations**. Trans. Maria Manuela Galhardo. Lisbon: Difusão Editorial, 1988, p. 244. (Series "Memory and Society," coordinated by Francisco Belhencourt and Diogo Ramada Curto, vol. 1).

COSTA, Leda Maria da. **What Is a Female Fan?** Notes on the Representation and Self-Representation of Female Football Audiences. Esporte e Sociedade, v. 2, n. 4, Nov/2006–Feb/2007. Available at https://periodicos.uff.br/esportesociedade/article/view/48008. Accessed on April 1, 2023.

DAMATTA, Roberto (Org.) and others. **Universe of Football: Sport and Brazilian Society**. Rio de Janeiro: Pinakotheke, 1982.

DAMO, Arlei Sander. **Ah! I'm a Gaucho! The National and the Regional in Brazilian Football**. Historical Studies. Rio de Janeiro, FGV. v. 13, n. 23, 1999, p. 87–117.

DAMO, Arlei Sander. **Spectacles of Identities and Alterities**. In: ALFONSI, Daniela; CAMPOS, Flávio de (Org.). Football: An object of human science. São Paulo: Leya, 2014.

DAÓLIO, Jocimar (Org.). **Football, Culture and Society**. Campinas: Autores Associados, 2005.

DUNNING, Eric; Maguirre, Joseph. "**Gender Relations in Sport.**" Revista de Estudos Feministas, IFCS/UFRJ, Rio de Janeiro, 1997, vol. 5, n. 2, pp. 321–348.

ECO, Umberto. **Journey in Everyday Unreality**. Rio de Janeiro: Nova Fronteira, 1984.

FRANCO JÚNIOR, Hilário. **Football, Society, Culture:** Notes for a Conclusion. In: ALFONSI, Daniela; CAMPOS, Flávio de (Eds.). Football as an Object of Human Sciences. São Paulo: Leya, 2014.

FRANCO JÚNIOR, Hilário. **The Dance of the Gods: Football, Society, and Culture**. São Paulo: Companhia das Letras, 2007.

FREITAS, Maria Ester de. **Organization: Space for Negotiation**. Revista de Administração de Empresas. São Paulo, v. 34, n. 5, pp. 13–20, 1994.

GOELLNER, Silvana Vilodre. **Women and Football in Brazil: Discontinuities, Resistance, and resilience**. Movimento (Porto Alegre), v. 27, e27001, January–December 2021. Available at: https://seer.ufrgs.br/Movimento/article/view/110157. Accessed on March 30, 2023. DOI: https://doi.org/10.22456/1982-8918.110157.

GUEDES, Simoni Lahud. **Suburb: A Cradle of Soccer Stars.** In: DAMATTA, R. (Ed.). The World of Football: Sport and Brazilian Society. Rio de Janeiro: Pinakotheke, 1982.

GUEDES, Simoni Lahud. **Gift and Identity Dialogues of the FIFA World Cups in Brazil**. In: ALFONSI, Daniela; CAMPOS, Flávio de (Org.). Football: An Object of Human Sciences. São Paulo: Leya, 2014.

HOLLANDA, Bernardo Borges Buarque de; MALAIA, João Manuel Casquinha; TOLEDO, Luiz Henrique de; MELO, Victor Andrade de. **A Brazilian Fan Base**. Rio de Janeiro: 7 Letras, 2012.

LEANDRO, Paulo Roberto. Negô! Baêa! **Invention of the Bahian Fan Base**. Salvador: EDUFBA, 2015.

MALAIA, João M.C. **Supporters' Club, Female Supporters' Group (Brazil)**: 1910–1950. In: A Brazilian Fan Base. Rio de Janeiro: 7 Letras, 2012.

MÁXIMO, Pimenta Carlos Alberto. **Violence Among Supporters' Clubs**, São Paulo Perspec. [online]. 2000, vol. 14, n. 2, pp. 122–128.

MORAES, Carolina Farias. **Female Fans Want (to Be Able to) Cheer**. 2018, p. 157. Dissertation (Master's in Culture and Society)—Institute of Humanities, Arts, and Prof. Milton Santos Sciences, Federal University of Bahia, Salvador, 2018.

NORONHA, Marcelo Pizarro. **Football is for Women. An Ethnographic Study on the "Feminine" Place in Club Football**. 2010, p. 233 Thesis (Ph.D. in Social Sciences), Universidade do Vale do Rio dos Sinos, UNISINOS, School of Humanities, São Leopoldo, 2010.

NORONHA, Marcelo Pizarro. **(De)constructing Identities: Ambiguities, Stereotypes, and Political Struggles in Women-Football Relations.** In: KESSLER, Cláudia Samuel (Ed.). Women on the Field: Gender, Diversity, and Inclusions in Football. Porto Alegre: UFRGS, 2016.

PEREIRA, Maria do Mar. **Gender at Recess: Gender Negotiation in School Spaces**. Lisbon: ICS. Imprensa de Ciências Sociais, 2012.

PRUITT, D. G. **Negotiation Behavior**. New York: Academic Press, 1981.

REIS, Heloisa Helena Baldy dos. **Football and Society: Fan Manifestations**. 1998, p. 164. Thesis (Ph.D. in Physical Education), Universidade Estadual de Campinas, Unicamp, Faculty of Physical Education, Campinas, 1998.

ROSENFELD, Anatol. **Black people, Macumba, and Football**. Petrópolis: Perspectiva, 2007.

SAMPAIO, Aurino Cesar Freire. "**Ba-VI—The Passion of Soteropolis**" Social History of Football in Bahia (1986–2010), Salvador. Instituto de Ciências Humanas da Universidade Católica do Salvador, 2011.

TOLEDO, Luiz Henrique. **Supporters' Club**. Campinas, SP: Autores Associados/Anpocs Publishers, 1996. (Collection of Physical Education and Sports).

CHAPTER 10

Pathways and Experiences of Female Organized Supporters in Rio de Janeiro[1]

Rosana da Câmara Teixeira

Introduction

The present text brings some reflections based on an initial reflection from a set of interviews conducted from 2019 to 2022 with ten female fans belonging to organized fan clubs in Rio de Janeiro.[2] During the fieldwork research on young female fans from Rio de Janeiro carried out in 1997, during my master's degree, I had great difficulty to get in touch with them. Thus, the female participation was characterized based on the views of men. In general, they like to emphasize the presence and importance of the female fans. However, in their statements it was evident that they evaluated it in a different way when compared to the performance of men.

This difference would be related to a certain difficulty of women in doing this activity, "not feeling comfortable in leadership roles," or yet, for considering that they are not as united as they are, being more subject to disagreements among themselves, as there have been recurring conflicts and gossip that required intervention (Teixeira, 2004, p. 57). Therefore, through the interpretation of these

1. This study was funded by CNPQ—National Council for Scientific and Technological Development. Process number 421784/2021-0.

2. Three female fans from *Torcida Jovem do Flamengo* (TJF); one from *Torcida Jovem do Botafogo* (TJB); two female fans from *Força Jovem do Vasco* (FJV); two from *Young Flu* (YF); one from *Fúria Jovem do Botafogo* (FJB); and one from *Loucos pelo Botafogo* (LB), to whom I would like to thank for their availability and trust. The youth fan clubs were created between the end of the 1960s and the beginning of the 1970s, initiating a new pattern of sociability characterized by a critical and defensive position and by festive performances in football stadiums. *Fúria Jovem do Botafogo*, a dissident derivative of *Torcida Jovem do Botafogo*, which emerged in 2001, aligned with this style of cheering. *Loucos pelo Botafogo*, on its turn, founded in 2006, inaugurates another model of supporters inspired by the South American bars, defending the unconditional support to the team and seeking to distinguish itself from the bellicose character that historically guides the actions of the Youth.

interlocutors, "the fans' conviction and loyalty to the fan club would not be so intense, defining themselves much more by the relationship they keep with the others—boyfriends, brothers, friends" (Teixeira, 2004, p. 57).

I observed, then, the existence of a symbolic and affective hierarchy, because according to these leaders, the passion of the female fan did not carry the same weight and value as demonstrated by their male counterpart, and was therefore often disqualified.

The obstacles encountered in surviving in this field of research at the time, due to mistrust and existing rivalries, made it impossible for me to advance toward a discussion on gender issues. However, I cherished this project over the years. The opportunity to make it come true came in the second half of 2019, when I reencountered, in a group of organized fans on WhatsApp, a female fan I had met in 2014, at a meeting held by the Federation of Organised Fans of Rio de Janeiro (FTORJ)[3] at *Fundição Progresso.*[4] As soon as I was added, she greeted me enthusiastically. Her participation was remarkable, giving her opinion on various themes and controversies, which led to heated discussions on numerous occasions, most of the time with the male members, who were in the majority.

After a while, I got excited and decided to send a private message proposing a chat. She was very receptive, and we scheduled it for the following week. The interview lasted about 2 hours, in a café in the city center. After that, she invited me to visit the headquarters of the fan club, which is located in the same street where we were. There I took some photographs, and we finished our conversation. Very motivated by the success of this exchange, I decided to get in touch with other members of fan clubs I have known for a long time (some former leaders) presenting the idea and asking for their mediation in approaching the women. Along the way I was also given referrals by a female fan I interviewed and by a master's student who is developing their research on youth fan clubs. Step by step, the network of speakers was being formed.

This research fills a gap concerning the debates about gender in the inaugural studies and allows me to revisit my own work, opening new perspectives. On this

[3] The purpose of the meeting was to discuss the situation of the organized affiliation, which was punished and therefore banned from attending stadiums. *FTORJ* was created in 2008, gathering the main organized fan clubs from the four major football clubs in Rio de Janeiro (Botafogo, Flamengo, Fluminense, Vasco). Among its objectives, the constitution of cooperative relations between rival groups stands out, giving a truce to their historical disagreements; and the definition of a claims agenda to fight in the public space (Hollanda and Teixeira, 2017).

[4] Cultural center and show house located in the Lapa neighborhood, in the central region of the city of Rio de Janeiro.

journey, I highlight the timely dialogue with research developed in recent years by scholars on the history of female fans in the stands (Costa, 2007) and, more specifically, those dedicated to address the role of women in organized fan clubs (Andrade, 2022; Campos, 2010; Moraes, 2018; Silva, 2016). Another aspect to be highlighted refers to the increasingly expressive presence of female fans in public arenas to fight for social recognition, for the right to cheer in the stands, to get involved and cooperate in the fan clubs without the tutelage, monitoring, criticism, and harassment of men.

Through the narratives of organized female fans in Rio de Janeiro, it was intended, therefore, to know the meanings attributed to this social experience. This chapter is organized into three sections. The first one deals with the context of the interviews, presents information on the profile of the interviewees, the issues addressed and some theoretical and methodological issues. In the "Trajectories and Narratives of Female Fans" section, I analyze some selected excerpts, focusing on two dimensions: (1) the initiation into the world of football and (2) membership of the fan club. In the final considerations, I return to some main points discussed here in order to continue the work.

The Interviews: Some Theoretical and Methodological Observations

As mentioned earlier, ten life-story interviews were conducted between 2019 and 2022. The age range of female fans varied from 31 to 58 years. They joined the associations in the period from 1973 to 2006. Six live in the North Zone, two in the South Zone, one in the municipality of *São Gonçalo*, and one in the State of *Espírito Santo*. With regard to the professional occupation, a quite diversified scenario was found: physical education teacher/administrative assistant; retired primary school teacher; housewife (she has worked as a secretary and a saleswoman previously); salesperson; cultural animator/cruise ship crew member; housewife/father's caregiver (she has previously worked in a gym, office, in a cleaning company, in a football club); supermarket cashier; secretary; nursing technician; and sales representative.

From different generations, these female fans have experienced different sociocultural, political, and economic circumstances, as well as several professional football scenarios and the situation of their clubs in the competitions and of the associations to which they belong. All of them exercised administrative functions within the fan clubs, some in management positions. Many collaborated in the constitution, organization, coordination, or reactivation of the women's group.

The interviews lasted an average of 2 hours based on a semistructured script organized around the following topics: age/schooling/profession/marital status; parents/family relations/neighborhood; initiation as football supporter; entrance and coexistence in the fan clubs; female groups; sexism, prejudices and opinions about the future of the fan clubs. The idea was to propose an itinerary that would guide the reconstruction of the paths traveled over time, with emphasis on the events, knowledge and learning they had.

The first two interviews, face-to-face (one on the street, in a bar, and the other, in the cafeteria of a bookstore, in a mall in the south zone of Rio), occurred in the second half of 2019. However, in March 2020, the outbreak of the coronavirus disease 2019 (COVID-19) pandemic[5] created a scenario of numerous uncertainties, characterized by the requirement of social distancing, sanitary protocols and the expectation of production and distribution of vaccines. In view of this, the **interviews** were interrupted, being resumed months later, in December 2020. At that time, we lived another moment in the pandemic scenario, we already had more information about the spread of the virus, the vaccination scheme was in progress and the control and safety protocols (the use of masks and the use of alcohol gel), widely and massively disseminated by the media.

In this context, the interaction mediated by technologies had gained strength and spread. For this very reason, the other eight interviews took place online, through the *google meet* platform, and most accessed it through the use of mobile phones. Anyway, I feared that without the face to face contact, the exchange would become a little artificial and cold. But, to my surprise, they all readily accepted the invitation and the communication flowed very well.[6]

The interviews, more than a qualitative method of obtaining data through questions and answers, compose a central dimension in the continuous and incessant training of anthropologists and their craft. It is a singular mode of communication, whose success depends on the willingness to dialogue, on the synergy that is established. It is, therefore, in the way I see it, a particular method of encountering and of sociability.

---

5. Caused by the new coronavirus SARS-CoV-2.

6. Undoubtedly, the openness found for dialogue is also due to the fact that I have a public track record in the study of football fan clubs. Being close to the associations, in debates in the public arena, as well as being identified, many times, as someone who supports them in the fight for rights, favored their acceptance.

The set of stories told shows that despite the heterogeneity in terms of social origin, occupational distribution, ethno-racial and generational diversity, the co-existence in the associations, sharing values, ideals, symbols, languages, body techniques, forms of interaction and action, enabled them to share a certain definition of reality, moving through the same province of meaning (Velho, 1994, p. 17).

Through the remembrance, stimulated by my questions, they were weaving connections and meanings between the several phases of their experience as a female fan. In the process of analyzing the statements collected, I tried to be attentive both to the singular aspects of life trajectories and to recurrences. Such strategy was intended to build some totality, from this plurality, and not just accumulate details that do not talk among themselves. We will consider these issues in depth in the next section.

Trajectories and Narratives of Female Fans

> The narrative, which for so long flourished in a artisan's milieu, in the fields, at sea and in the city, is itself, in a certain sense, an artisan's form of communication. It is not interested in conveying the 'pure in itself' thing that was narrated as an information or a report. It immerses the thing in the life of the narrator and then draws it out of him. Thus the narrator's imprint is projected on the narrative, like the potter's hand on the clay of the vase. (Benjamin, 1994, p. 205)

Before turning to the statements of female fans, I would like to underline that I do not consider them as "testimonies proving an experience" to be unraveled. The stories, points of view, and interpretations gathered here need to be situated in the field of interested "conversations." This means that when I invited them to this "chat" I had in mind a set of doubts and concerns. Thus, the itinerary followed directions and recommendations that were impossible to anticipate due to the very dynamics of the act of narrating. There is something happening there, in that circumstance in which that "telling" unfolds. That is, the images of the past do not remain preserved in the galleries of thought, needing only to be adequately activated to manifest themselves. In fact, it is in society that they find the indications to be reconstructed (Halbwachs, 1990).

Therefore, remembering implies following reference points, from the present to the past, from links with family, neighborhood, religion, work, to country.

From this perspective, memory is a social fact, a cultural attitude. The narrator draws from experience the memories he shares, his own or that reported by others (Benjamin, 1994, p. 201). By handcrafting his raw material, which is experience, he relies on temporal and spatial references, feeling free to interpret moments and situations that gain their own design. For Pollak (1992, p. 204), events, people/characters, and places are constitutive elements of individual or collective memory and its organization suffers the influence of the subject's concerns the moment they build it, highlighting or excluding consciously or unconsciously certain aspects.

This reasoning leads us to another. There is a close relationship between memory and sense of identity, the image constructed for oneself and for others. Consequently, every act of remembering is situated in relation to other addressees and interlocutors. Memory and identity are, therefore, "disputed values in social and intergroup conflicts" (Pollak, 1992, p. 205).

The manufacturing of self-image does not escape the relations of alterity and occurs, therefore, in its clashing with the Other. Finally, one cannot neglect that being the discontinuous past, remembering implies selecting and chaining episodes and situations. When trying to give coherence to the path taken, one also draws possible futures, indicating intentions and dispositions to reach them. As Gilberto Velho (1994, p. 101) points out: "They are retrospective and prospective visions that place the individual, their motivations and the meaning of their actions, within a life conjuncture, in the succession of phases of their trajectory." These ideas will be resumed in light of the female fans' narratives.

From the Initiation Into the World of Football[7] to the Discovery and Engagement in the Organized Fan Clubs

As some studies have already shown (Andrade, 2022; Damo, 2012; Teixeira, 2004), family ties are important in the association with the football club. The following statements attribute to the father an important role in this initiation:

> As I told you, my family on my mother's side are all Italian. And as you can see, my house, back here, everything is *tricolor*. I always asked my father to take

[7] To preserve the identity of the interviewees, in the excerpts selected for analysis, I chose to mention the initials of the association to which they belong and their age.

> me to the games, I was always like that. I always wanted to see Fluminense and so on. (YF, 58 years old)

> My father played for Flamengo, but then he was hired to work in a bank, the *Banco do Estado de MG*. His sister did athletics there, my aunt Dilha. My mother was already a Flamengo supporter, as well as my father. At that time we lived in *Pinto beach*, the favela. He jumped over the wall of the Flamengo training grounds and ended up being called to play. Soon after he left, he played and worked for the bank. (TJF, 57 years old)

> My father was a die-hard Flamengo and Salgueiro fan. People say that I am Flamengo because of my father, but it's not true. If it were for my father I would be Salgueiro, because the intensity to which he lived for Flamengo, he lived for Salgueiro. But I'm Mangueira. The feeling emerged in me in the final of the 81 World Cup, when my father took me to a snack bar to watch the game on television. It was in that World Cup that all this awakened in me. I cried so much, I was so excited about Flamengo's World Cup, I was a child, but I remember every detail of the game perfectly. I was 12 years old. (TJF, 52 years old)

> I always had a connection with him (my father), a very strong connection. I used to spend holidays at his house. He's the Vasco fan in the family, the one who made me a Vasco fan. My mother is too, but he was the one who encouraged me. But my greatest relationship has always been with my mother, she is my friend, sister, partner. (FJV, 32 years old)

While it is widely thought that a passion for football is inherited, passing on from parents to daughters and sons, this does not constitute a rule. In many accounts, other mediators come into play in the definition of club belonging.

> My father says he lost me to Túlio, to the '95 Cup. In fact, he has three daughters, he is a die-hard Vasco fan, and I was the only one who had this taste for football from a very young age. And we always watched football together, any game of any team. And he was into Vasco, but I wasn't, I'm Botafogo. I think that in the beginning there was that thing of opposing, being against him, I can't explain it because I was very young, but there was a little bit of this. [...] My mother already said she was Botafogo, because her father was Botafogo, I started to say

> "I'm Botafogo." I am totally the Túlio generation, I fell in love, I cut out photos from the newspaper, pasted them, made an album. (LPB, 34 years old)

Despite the influence of her Botafogo mother, idolization emerges as an indisputable fact when the fan states her condition of being a fan of the player Túlio: "my father lost me to Túlio," "I am totally the Túlio generation, I fell in love." The feeling of passion triggers the practice of collecting, which in turn strengthens the association.

In general, to explain "how it happened," the adherence to the club, facts and characters are used. Friends and neighbors appear as central characters in going to the stadium:

> Like, I don't have this thing about my father taking me to the games and so on, because my father is a Flamengo fan. So, the first game I went to was with friends, it was Flamengo and Botafogo, at the Maracanã. So I did not inherit this black-and-white passion, because my father was a Flamengo fan. (FJB, 32 years old)
>
> [The neighbor] was a die-hard Fluminense fan, from the street. Then he came up to my mother and said 'Can you let her go to the Maracanã with me?' To watch the final Fluminense-Bangu, in 1983. It was my first time at the Maracanã, I had never been there. Then she said, 'don't you dare lose my daughter there.' My mother had a feeling something was going to happen. 115 thousand people [...]. Cement stands, when they threw the white powder, we could trip and fall, you know what I mean? I did not know what a crowd of fans was. Then I got there and we stayed in the white part of the crowd. Until then I didn't know it was the *Young Flu*, it hadn't even crossed my mind. It was very crowded, it was difficult for us even to shake our arms. [...] Everyone was leaving and did he remember to take me with me? No, he left me on the stands. I left in the middle of the crowd and thought 'I will stop here,' I was small and skinny. Then I stopped at a white door, sat down and waited. The people were leaving and nothing, leaving and nothing...Then a man arrived and said, 'I need to open the door.' I said, 'this door here?' He said, 'Yes, because I'm going to put the flags there.' 'Are you waiting for someone?' I said, 'I'm lost.' 'Where do you live?' I said, 'I live in *Bonsucesso.*' 'You're lost, didn't you come with someone to the Maracanã?' I said, 'I came with my neighbor, but he disappeared.' He said: 'I live in *Vicente de Carvalho*, I can take you home.' I said: 'You're not taking me home. I'm going to call the police because my mother told me not to leave

> with anyone. If anything happens, don't go away with anyone.' Then he said, 'But I'm responsible, I'm head of the YF crowd here. My name is Armando Giesta, I'll take you home. I'm going to tell your mother and your neighbor off, because he should have been holding hands with you.' Then I said, 'OK.' But I cried and cried. Then they put away the flags and everything and he took me to *Bonsucesso*. When we got there he told my mother off. Then I got it in my head…'Young Flu, Young Flu…' (YF, 49 years old)

The incident, described in a jocular tone, describes the cathartic atmosphere of the cement stands of Maracanã in the 1980s. And, despite being "lost" at the end of the game, a situation that generated apprehension and fear, the experience was crucial to establish a link between the club and its fans. Especially because it was precisely the fan club leader who found her and took her home.

However, there are cases in which cheering for the club and joining the fan base occurs through family relationships:

> I'm 37 years old. I come from a Portuguese family, but I was born in Brazil, and I think that explains a lot about why I support Vasco da Gama and consequently my love for the *Força Jovem do Vasco* fan club. I started in the fan club very young (1993), very small, skinny, at the age of 13, influenced by my brother, who was 3 years older. We used to go to the games, and we used to stay in the section for the fan clubs, but we weren't official supporters. We always passed by a bar where there were a lot of Vasco fans watching the games, and they used to put up flags before the game. For example, the game started at 4pm, but at 9am people were already in this bar with flags, letting off fireworks and we always passed by this bar, there in Rio Cumprido. One fine day people called my brother, who was already a supporter, and they asked: 'Is she your sister? Take her to the fan club too!' (FJV, 37)

> When I joined the fan club, she (my mother) joined as well. She became an official member. As time went by she withdrew, nowadays it's rare when she goes to a game. I go a lot more. But she was a fan. […] Then during a match, we said we were going to join *Força Jovem* and a boy told us to look for G, who was responsible for the women's family. We looked for her and never stopped. But from the beginning my mother went with me. I was 17 years old. It was in 2007. (FJV, 32 years old)

The decision is a result of observations, assessments, relationships established in the neighborhood, in the stadium, and/or contacts in social networks. The enchanting exhibition of the fans in the stands and the desire to be part of that collective, in addition to the welcoming and encouraging nature of leaders and colleagues become defining aspects.

The next recollection highlights the receptiveness with which the leader welcomes the newcomer, who starts working with him to rebuild and strengthen the fan club. The bond of trust that is established between the two ensures that she acts jointly in the management of the association, having even created the slogan that made it famous:

> Then I stayed there, but I was charmed by *Young*. The rowdiness, I liked the rowdiness, the drumming. Then I went to *Young*, when I arrived at *Young* in 73, more or less, *Young* was very small, *Young* was almost bankrupt. Then I met Armando. He said, 'Well, look how *Young* is doing? Nobody wants to take *Young*, but I will. I'm going to lift this fan club up.' [...] I said, 'but how are you going to do it?' He had a firm in *Pilares*, so the headquarters of the fan club moved to *Pilares*. I met him at Maracanã. I think I was around 16, 17 [...] Then he said, 'We're going to lift this fan club up.' We started making t-shirts, everything at the headquarters. I always worked, my father always taught us that we had to start working early. I studied and worked. Then he said, 'Look, my company is more than broke.' I said, 'My God, the fan club's broke, the company's broke.' He said, 'Do you have a check?' I said, 'Yes.' Then he said, 'Then we'll buy everything with your check.' Then I put my hands on my head and said, 'Oh my God, what's going to happen?' He said, 'We'll find a way. We'll find a way to pay.' Mr. Armando had a company in *Pilares*. It was an aniline company. He made things for carnival, but it was already going bankrupt. So what happened was that we bought everything, but when it came time to pay, we couldn't cover the check. And I spent a long time without being able to buy anything. Then as time passed [...] And the crowd was growing little by little. Then there was a basketball game at the *Maracanãzinho*. He said, 'Daughter, you're like my daughter [...] I want you to create a slogan for the fans. Everyone has a slogan, only my fans don't.' [...] Then I was watching a basketball game, and suddenly I said: 'Young Flu, a passion to cheer. Does that work?' He said, 'Yes, that's the one.' And that slogan is still used today. (YF, 58 years old)

The following accounts highlight a very frequent idea: the decision to join the group as an individual choice:

> I joined the fan club totally on my own. There is always someone you end up meeting. I never had many Botafogo friends, that's a fact, at school it was me and two others. At college there was a friend of mine, but he didn't go to all the games. So I was always trying to bring a friend, trying to take someone with me. I always liked to go to all the games, not only to the finals. I think that's why I joined the fan club, because you get there and you know everyone. There is no longer this thing of having to go with someone. I joined in 2007. I joined the *Loucos*. Actually, it was the final of the Guanabara Cup in 2007. [...] Then I saw a boy who studied with me at the *Pedro II* high school, but he was that person you'd never talked to, that you'd just say 'hello.' I arrived, said, 'hello, so-and-so.' Then I made friends. He was with two other friends of his, and he asked if I was alone, I said I'd lost my friend, then he said 'stay here with us, come with us.' (LPB, 34 years old)

> It's what I said, I am very objective, if I want that I want that. I'm not one of those, 'I'll only go if someone else goes,' that doesn't interest me, better alone than in bad company, you know. I went, it was the first time that I'd seen those flags, [...] the big flag, then I said, 'That's what I want.' Then I started to participate in the (social media) groups from Orkut, there was no WhatsApp, there was MSN [...]. They used to meet on Fridays, at *Ponta da Areia*, in *Niterói*. I took advantage of the fact that I was studying in Niterói, I left college and went there to meet the people. I think they were intimidated, because the women there were so-and-so's wife, so-and-so's girlfriend, there were no independent woman the way I went. There were guys there, 'ah, I will call so-and-so, she is also from Botafogo, she wants to join the supporters group, but there are no women.' Then I said, 'then call her, come on,' and we started to form a little female group inside the 'kennel.' [...] I was chosen by the *Fúria* and it is the flag which I defend until today, I never wore a shirt of another fan club. Despite all the difficulties that the fan club has had, I never abandoned it, I was always present, I always carried the banner of the fan club to other states, at the allied parties, and I am still there today. (FJB, 32 years old)

In recalling her arrival to the fan club, she emphasizes the strangeness caused in the members of the organization for being an "independent woman," who took the initiative to go alone, without the intermediation of another man, a rare fact, as she noted. But, instead of this posture being recriminated, it was seen positively, and could even stimulate other women. In this way, she quickly ends up assuming the function of organizing "a little female crew." And she concludes, reaffirming her fidelity to "the flag" she chose to represent and defend, in spite of the adversities.

The two stories below contribute to understanding that the affiliation to the fan club is also the result of a process. First they report the relationship with another supporter of the club. However, the coexistence, the welcoming and the friendships originated in the caravans, occasions in which several fan clubs traveled together, influenced the decision to change clubs.

> It was passion at first sight. I used to go to the stadium with two friends, but they watched the games with *Raça*. I was always watching *Jovem*, I don't know why. From there I made friends, everyone spoke to each other, on the trips I met people…I first went to *Raça*, then to *Força Independente* […]. Then, on a trip to Belo Horizonte, I started to make friends with people, everyone travelled on the same bus. *Independente* and *Jovem*. There were two buses, we went with them. From there I started to make friends, I met Hercules, who became my boyfriend, and from there I jumped. (TJF, 57 years old)

> I started going alone in 1986, when I joined *FlaPonte*, João welcomed me, he looked after me. I always went. I spent about two years going with the *FlaPonte*, all the time. Then there was a Flamengo and Palmeiras game at the Morumbi, and João didn't organize a bus. And I really wanted to go, it would be my first game outside of Rio, and that's when I went with *Torcida Jovem do Flamengo*. […] Then I went on that trip, and Cemir called me. There I said, 'I think I've found myself, it's *Torcida Jovem*.' One day he talked about the trip to São Paulo, he asked if I wanted to go, and I said, 'I do.' I went to that match, Flamengo won, and when I came back I went to *Atofla* and said, 'Captain Léo, I want to get my card, I want to join *Jovem*.' At the time, the *Jovem* room was inside Gávea, there was an association of organized fan clubs inside Gávea. (TJF, 52 years old)

These and other explanations indicate that in the 1980s, there was more openness for women to participate in the trips, privileged opportunities for initiation into organized fan clubs and an important stage of socialization into this style of cheering.

From the 1990s on, an agonistic logic was established in the relationship between the organized fan clubs in Rio de Janeiro, with the intensification of rivalries and an increase in physical confrontations and deaths. The escalation of intergroup violence seems to be among the factors responsible for the prohibition of women to go in caravans to games considered dangerous.

> I love *Torcida Jovem*, it was my life story and I learned a lot. I learned to be human, I learned to respect, I learned everything about Flamengo in *TJF*. I didn't have any problems when I joined, on the contrary, I was very well accepted, the boys looked after me, I was never banned from going to any games. And nowadays there is all this nonsense about 'women not being allowed to go to such and such a game.' Why should I be part of a fan club then?

Many complain about this attitude, they do not accept the justifications that they are physically more fragile, and their presence on these trips would leave the fans more vulnerable, as the leaders claim that they would have to protect them.[8]

This argument of "fragility" is contested by those who understand that by joining the fan club they know the risks they are exposed to and want the right to choose.

> I am very respected, but I am also very disrespected. I am not an exception. Everyone at some point suffers some prejudice, some disrespect, some hostility. Women are gaining more space and a bigger voice as fans. Like it or not, women have their importance. Women have already gained a lot of space in the fan clubs. In my 15 years I've seen a lot of things change, but I think still a lot has to change. […] The big problem is that men disrespect women a lot, and also they need to stop seeing women as the weaker sex that will get in the way of a fight, when many times women help. As I told you, some women get really involved in fights. I've been involved in fights. Obviously there will be some concern, but not because I'm a woman. This concern has to be with everyone. This issue of respect has to change a lot. (FJV, 32 years old)

[8] There is no consensus on this issue. There are female fans who agree with the men, positioning themselves against the presence of women in matches in other states, where there is a risk of conflict.

In the above evaluation, it is noted that despite the fact that women have conquered more space in recent years, and that they consider themselves respected, they still suffer hostility and experience disrespectful situations. The fact is that they have to deal with sexist behaviors. Besides the suspicion that they may also become romantically involved with adversaries and thus reveal plans, strategies, and internal affairs of the group. However, getting romantically involved with members of their own fan club may also be frowned upon. Thus, implicit or explicit codes about the expected conduct of female fans promotes stigmatizing views and actions, generating indignation:

> There is still a lot of prejudice. As it is a very masculine environment, and I say that it was my only place of distraction, of leisure, my leisure was going to the games, the fan club parties, so, you end up having relationships within the fan clubs. A woman can't have a relationship with one, then another, because then so-and-so is a whore. They say that she is only in the fan club looking for a man. But not the guy, the guy is 'the man,' he's right to get with a lot of women. For a long time my friendships were only within the fan club, so then logically my romantic relationships will also be within the fan club. But for women this is still very badly seen. (FJV, 32 years old)

> I suffered, and still suffer today from sexism, but I take all this sexism and turn it into strength. Just like there are wrong women, there are also wrong men, but nobody goes there and confronts a man the same way they confront a woman. Men don't have a logical argument when they confront women, we say 'you did this, you did that,' but men don't point out the woman's mistake, they just say, 'ahh, you are a bitch, you are this, you are that,' but they don't point out the mistake. I say, 'OK, I'm a bitch, but what was my mistake here within the fan club? Come on, let's start.' And there isn't, if there was they didn't say anything. They only know how to name-call. But I had a lot of prejudice, a lot of sexism. Part of the sexism we suffered was that women couldn't go in a caravan. And I'll tell you, here in Rio, the fan clubs are more flexible towards women than supporters from outside. (FJB, 32 years old)

As Carolina Moraes (2018, pp. 60–61) points out, even if the organized female fans have been acquiring greater visibility for their requests "they remain in a limbo of eternal arrangements and negotiations for the performance of their act and/or way of cheering." Restrictions and prohibitions trigger clashes, negotiations and, in some cases, "disobedience," when for instance, they decide to travel on their own.

> This business of women not being allowed because it is dangerous, I know this, if it was not dangerous I would have gone to *Loucos*, I would have become *Loucos*, I would have become *Botachopp* or I would have stayed at home. I know the risks that entails being part of the *Fúria*, and I want to travel, I am of age. That is what I say to the girls, you are joining the *Fúria Jovem do Botafogo*, this is not Disney where you can get a lollipop and play fan club. This is serious business and you have to take this into your life. There have been times when I took my little backpack and went to the bus station alone, when I got there the guys freaked out when they saw me, but I couldn't accept being banned from traveling. (FJB, 32 years old)

Concluding Remarks

A point I would like to emphasize is that making these life stories of these organized female fans visible does not mean to take them as evidence that can be generalized for the participants of such associations. Here, we start from the assumption that the category "female fans" does not constitute a fixed and immutable identity and the shared experiences should not be essentialized, but historicized and understood in its diversity and inequality. According to Scott (1991), if we consider that subjects are constituted through experience, this becomes:

> not the origin of our explanation, not the authorized evidence (because seen or felt) that grounds knowledge, but rather that which we seek to explain, that of which knowledge is produced. To think of experience in this way is to historicize it, as well as the identities it produces. (Scott, 1991, p. 27)

An initial balance of the set of narratives presented enables the formulation of some interpretations. A clue to be pursued and confirmed indicates that, despite the problems faced in the 1970s and 1980s in Rio de Janeiro, female fans seemed to enjoy more freedom and autonomy in the fan club dynamics, despite the existing prejudices and sexism. Even though these are spaces markedly male dominated, those who joined them were absorbed in the daily life of the fan clubs, even engaging themselves in organizational tasks in different spheres. In retrospective views, the emotional tone stands out when they mention the circle of friendships built, the learnings, the shared moments and the impact of the fan clubs on their lives.

> It is one of the most incredible experiences I have had in my life. Within a fan club you get to know the good and the bad, you create enemies and many friendships. I have personal friendships, people who come to my house. It was a very magical thing. What I liked most about the stadium was the party, the fact that everyone was together. At the stadium, we would get angry together, at home we get sad, but there's nothing we can do. At the stadium it's everyone together in joy and sadness. It's a very crazy experience, because we've seen a lot of fights, a lot of running around. We have seen the bad parts, the fights, the internal fights. (FJV, 32 years old)

> The *Jovem* changed my life. The *Jovem* gave me a lot of things, a lot of emotion, a lot of love. I love the *Jovem*, but I love the *Jovem* that I lived through, not this one today. When we meet it's very funny. We look back and think it's funny, we have fun. Imagine if I didn't have these stories to tell? As with everything in life, it has its good and bad sides. The bad side is that I suffered too much. [...]. There were many things I gave up in life [...] But it was something I chose. But I do not regret it either, life has passed, several things served as learning, and I do not regret anything. (TJF, 44 years old)

Taking into account the statements above, it can be inferred that to be an organized supporter means to both collectively share the magical and crazy dimension of this passion and to know the good and the bad sides, to experience complicated phases, sadness, suffering, fears and internal conflicts.

One of the challenges, according to some of the interviewees, is to deal with the disqualification and undermining, as if they were dispensable, or tolerated and circumscribed to certain fields of action (such as women's subgroups and social departments). To what extent does this strategy not make their prominence invisible in the history of cheering? She says: "It is still an environment very much thought of for men, it is as if we were there by chance" (LPB, 34 years old).

Guacira Louro (1997) argues that the hierarchizations between femininity and masculinity are related to the way in which sexual characteristics are represented or valued. Thus, in order to understand the relations between men and women in a given society, it is necessary to pay attention to what has been socially constructed about the genders. For this very reason, the notion of gender becomes fundamental in the debate. It is a category of analysis that intends to unveil the inequalities between men and women (Scott, 1991). The relational perspective is central, since patterns of femininity and masculinity are reciprocally referenced.

In the fan clubs, certain moral expectations about women's behavior are based on naturalized conceptions that define them as fragile, sentimental, suitable for social and philanthropic actions, but with difficulties in exercising leadership positions. To act in a manner divergent from the conventionalized standards may result in discussions and recriminations. In the following excerpt, the female fan translates the fan club as "a meaning of life," reaffirms the pride she feels in her trajectory, her commitment and loyalty to the entity. However, she takes a critical position on those who depreciate her history:

> The fan club? Almost my whole life. It's a meaning of life really. Because I have lived, I live until today and I intend to live much longer. And if you give me strength, if you give me a voice to defend, I will defend like no one else. I want to see someone have a history within the fan club, to be recognized. I didn't do this to be recognized. I did it because I liked it, I went everywhere. I travelled to all sorts of places, I just didn't go to *Acre*. That's why I say, organized fan clubs depend on their phase. Nowadays, no way, "get out of here, you old woman, you don't understand anything about organized fan clubs." They curse at us, but those who know me don't. I've fought back, I've talked, I've pointed the finger. I've told them to respect me. What do you think? The organized crowd is for you to like the team, to fight when you don't like the team, now, don't fuck it up." (YF, 49 years old)

In her study on *Gaviãs da Fiel*, Andrade (2022, p. 90) exposes "that some women build their gender experiences from the experiences of masculinities imposed by men who make up and organise the fan clubs." Thus, the female fan's corporal performance is constituted and expressed in an environment marked by "masculine premises." There are codes that regulate the actions of men and women.

However, the rules that have been defined and agreed among men, have been questioned by women, who are increasingly "willing to face the difficulties in order to show the love for their team and the passion for their organized fan club" (Moraes, 2018, p. 114).

If the oppression of women remains constant over the years, this has not cooled their sense of belonging (Andrade, 2022, p. 17). To defend it, dialogues between female fans from different fan clubs have been developed. A milestone of this awareness was the *I Encontro Nacional de Mulheres de Arquibancada* (First National Gathering of Women from the Stands), an unprecedented event that brought together more than 300 female fans at the Football Museum in 2017.[9] Under the banner "Resistance and Empowerment," organized female fans from several states of Brazil shared experiences and formulated proposals to fight collectively, amplifying their voices to gain recognition and respect, inside and outside their groupings. From this meeting, debates and exchanges on the importance of uniting to transform dissatisfaction into collective action[10] gained strength.

> There were more than 300 women, from fan clubs all over Brazil and I was very impressed. I thought that no one would get involved, but to see that other women have the same thought as us of uniting, without vanity and doing something for the benefit of all, is what I said "the fight is not only mine, it is ours. (FJB, 32 years old)

Since the first decade of the 2000s, fan club association around professional football has undergone profound mutations. Collective mobilizations, constitution of broader coalitions to defend rights, preparation of documents, and activism in public arenas are among the initiatives that can be cited. In Brazil, a point of reference in this process was the foundation of the National Association of Organized Fan Clubs (2014).

The women's movements in the stands represent another important facet of fan clubs' mobilizations for rights today.

If the leaderships of the organized fan clubs aim to change the condemning view had of them and prove the legitimacy of their causes, why not include the demands of the female fans? Supporting the claims of women who actively

9. Available on the Football Museum channel at: https://www.youtube.com/user/museudofutebolspaulo/search?query=encontro+nacional+torcedores. Accessed on March 14, 2023.

10. Other meetings took place in the following years. The pandemic scenario interrupted these face-to-face actions; however, they are being resumed. On March 11, 2023, a seminar took place at the *Fiocruz* facilities in Rio de Janeiro, on the *Movimento Feminino de Arquibancada* (Female Stands Movement) founded on April 13, 2019. In this edition, public policies to fight against sexism in the stands were discussed under the motto "Rivals in the field, sisters in the fight."

collaborated/collaborate in the construction of this collective experience is part of their struggle for recognition. In contemporary discussions on the search for social recognition by collectives and entities, a basic assumption is that in the public sphere of law and politics, it expresses the longing for respect, consideration, and the desire to escape exclusion and stigmatization (Caillé, 2007).

In this direction, it is strategic not to lose sight of the fact that the ongoing battles of the women's movements in the stands can gain in breadth to the extent that they are understood and situated as a fundamental dimension of women's struggles in football.

REFERENCES

ANDRADE, Marianna Castellano Barcelos. **Para além da arquibancada: uma etnografia sobre as "Gaviãs" da Fiel (Beyond the stands: an ethnography on the "Gaviãs" da Fiel. Translated title)**. Dissertation (master's degree in social sciences), Graduate Program in Social Sciences, Universidade Federal de São Paulo (Federal University of São Paulo), Guarulhos Campus, 2022.

BENJAMIN, Walter. "O narrador: considerações sobre a obra de Nikolai Leskov" ("The narrator: considerations on the work of Nikolai Leskov." Translated title). **Magia e técnica, arte e política: ensaios sobre literatura e história da cultura (Magic and technique, art and politics: essays on literature and cultural history. Translated title)**. São Paulo: Brasiliense, 1994, pp. 197–221.

CAILLÉ, Alain. "Introduction." **La quête de reconnaissance**. Nouveau phénomène social total. Paris: Éditions La Découverte, 2007.

CAMPOS, Priscila A. F. **Mulheres Torcedoras do Cruzeiro Esporte Clube presentes no Mineirão (Women supporters of Cruzeiro Esporte Clube present at the Mineirão. Translated title)**. Dissertation (master's degree in Leisure), School of Physical Education, Physiotherapy and Occupational Therapy, Universidade Federal de Minas Gerais (Federal University of Minas Gerais), 2010.

COSTA, Leda M. "O que é uma torcedora? Notas sobre a representação e auto-representação do público feminino de futebol" ("What is a female fan? Notes on the representation and self-representation of the female football audience." Translated title). **Esporte e sociedade**, n. 4, 2007, pp. 1–31.

DAMO, Arlei. "Paixão partilhada e participativa—o caso do futebol" ("Shared and participatory passion—the case of football." Translated title). **História:**

Questões & Debates (History: Questions & Debates. Translated title), Curitiba, v. 57, n. 2, 2012, pp. 45–72.

HALBWACHS, Maurice. **A memória coletiva (Collective memory. Translated title).** Rio de Janeiro: Vértice, 1990.

HOLLANDA, Bernardo Buarque de, and TEIXEIRA, Rosana da Câmara. "Brazil's organized football supporter clubs and the construction of their public arenas through FTORJ and ANATORG." In **Football fans, rivalry and cooperation**, edited by Christian Brandt, Fabian Hertel, and Sean Huddleston. New York: Routledge, 2017, pp. 76–91.

LOURO, Guacira L. **Gênero, sexualidade e educação (Gender, sexuality and education. Translated title)** uma perspectiva pós-estruturalista (A post-structuralist perspective. Translated title). Petrópolis, RJ: Vozes, 1997.

MORAES, Carolina Faria. **As torcedoras (querem) poder torcer (Women fans (want) to be able to cheer. Translated title)**. Dissertation (Master in Culture and Society), Institute of Humanities, Arts and Sciences Professor Milton Santos, Universidade Federal da Bahia (Federal University of Bahia), Salvador, 2018. 157 pp.

POLLAK, Michael. "Memória e identidade social" ("Memory and social identity." Translated title). **Estudos Históricos (Historical Studies. Translated title)**, Rio de Janeiro, v. 5, n. 10, 1992, pp. 200–212.

SCOTT, Joan W. **Experience**. Translation by Ana Cecília Adoli Lima. Publication authorized by the author. (N.O.) A larger version of this essay was published in **Critical Inquiry**, v. 17, Summer 1991, pp. 773–797. Available at: https://historiacultural.mpbnet.com.br/feminismo/Joan_Scoot-Experiencia.pdf. Accessed on February 4, 2023.

SILVA, Carolina Fernandes da, et al. "As mulheres na torcida jovem do Grêmio Foot-ball Porto Alegrense" ("Women in the youth fan club of *Grêmio Foot-ball Porto Alegrense*." Translated title). **Revista Brasileira de Futsal e Futebol (Brazilian Futsal and Football Magazine. Translated title)**, São Paulo, v. 8. n. 29. March 2016, pp. 197–204.

TEIXEIRA, Rosana da Câmara. **Os perigos da paixão**. Visitando jovens torcidas cariocas. (**The dangers of passion**. Visiting young carioca fans. Translated title). São Paulo: AnnaBlume, 2004.

VELHO, Gilberto. "Unidade e fragmentação em sociedades complexas" ("Unity and fragmentation in complex societies." Translated title). In **Projeto e metamorfose (Project and metamorphosis. Translated title)**. Antropologia das sociedades complexas. RJ: Jorge Zahar, Ed. (Anthropology of complex societies. RJ: Jorge Zahar, Ed. Translated title), 1994, pp. 11–30.

CHAPTER 11

Football and Women in Brazil: A Weighing of Academic Production (1980–2022)

Luiza Aguiar dos Anjos and Marina de Mattos Dantas

Introduction

The 1980s is commonly considered, among researchers, as a milestone decade for the emergence of a systematized Brazilian production on football from a social science perspective,[1] a production that was effectively intensified from the 1990s (Alabarces, 2004; Giglio and Spaggiari, 2010; Silva et al., 2009; Toledo, 2001).

Alabarces (2004) points out that, in Latin America, until the 1980s, the near absence of football in the academic discourse is inversely proportional to its saturation in journalistic discourse, that is, football (practiced by men) appears and becomes established in newspapers and other mass media, while it was rejected as a theme in research centers.

It is not possible, however, to use this same logic when discussing football played by women. Its presence in the media did not have the same proportion in the newspapers during the early 20th century (nor in any other historical period). Besides, the reason for its absence in academia does not seem to have been the labeling of the practice as the "opium of the people," a common criticism of football played by men before the 1980s (Alabarces, 2004). It is worth remembering that Brazil was one of the countries in which the sport was forbidden to women, a restriction imposed during the period from 1941 to 1979 through Decree-Law 3.199 (Brasil, 1941).

Given this scenario, the fact is that football played by men was considered an academically pertinent topic before football played by women (and others

[1] It should be noted that the first productions on the subject date back to 1940 (Giglio and Spaggiari, 2010).

who do not fit into this binary division) became more consistently the object of attention of researchers.

It is necessary to acknowledge, however, that this is not specific to football studies. Goellner (2007) highlights how the history of men was for a long time treated as the history of humanity. Feminist movements and gender studies were fundamental to acknowledge women's participation and leading roles, and to think of new research issues, analytical instruments, and sources. In sport historiography, however, gender was late to be included (Goellner, 2013). For the author, a double marginality contributed to this delay: the feminist studies did not give more attention to the body practices, and the studies on sport (including those historiographical in nature) did not care much about its generified structure.

Other works endorse this argument. Analyzing the first eighteen editions of the Brazilian Congress of Sports Science (from 1979 to 2013), a recognized academic forum for Physical Education, Goellner and Macedo (2015) locate in 1999 the beginning of a more expressive production on gender. They also highlight that the category was used, for the first time, in a paper presented in 1996. In addition, despite the occurrence of a table discussion entitled "Participation of Brazilian Women in Sports," in 1979, only in 1995 was there again a lecture addressing women and gender.

In a complementary initiative, Andres and Anjos (2017) verified that, in 2006, the theme of sports stops being sporadic in the International Seminar Doing Gender, with its own thematic symposiums occurring, and an expressive number of papers presented. The authors mention that the theme most addressed in the papers is football, with 50% of them being about women, 30.5% about men, and 19.5% about the relations between girls/women and boys/men.

Despite the consensual perception of a theme still in the process of recognition, such publications also identified the expansion and diversification of research on women and sports, including those on football. With this in mind, we propose, in this chapter, to map and analyze this field, which is still in formation and development, focused on research about women[2] and football, from the Theses and Dissertations produced in Brazil and published from 1980 to 2022.

To accomplish this goal, we resorted to surveys and analyses of academic production on football in social science in Brazil. To situate ourselves in

[2] We recognize that the binary division between men and women is restrictive and open to criticism. However, given our objectives and the information we have found, we do not think it would be pertinent to address this issue in this text.

relation to what had already been surveyed and analyzed about football and women until then, we reviewed what there was on the subject in publications that, under different clippings and forms, wove a panorama of research on football, namely: Toledo (2001), Alabarces (2004), Silva et al. (2009), Giglio and Spaggiari (2010), Fensterseifer (2016), Souza et al. (2019), Salvini et al. (2014), and Cunha (2020), the last two being productions that, from different cuttings, illustrate the production of theses and dissertations dedicated to women's football[3] in Brazil.

To compose our body of analysis, we conducted a search in the *Catálogo de Teses e Dissertações da Coordenação de Aperfeiçoamento de Pessoal de Nível Superior* (Catalogue of Thesis and Dissertations of the Coordination Office for the Improvement of Higher Education Staff in English—*Capes*, translated text), with the keywords: women's football, football and women, football played by women, referees, coaches, women journalists, women managers. With the intention of getting as close as possible to the complete list of productions already defended, we compared this listing with previous surveys—Silva et al. (2009), Giglio and Spaggiari (2010), Salvini et al. (2014), Souza et al. (2019), and Cunha (2020), including works that met our criteria but had not been located in our searches. We found, in the end, a total of seventy-seven papers on women and football (fifty-eight academic master's dissertations, one professional master's dissertation, and eighteen doctoral theses).

From this scope, therefore, we present our considerations on the presence of the theme of football and women in the Brazilian academic field.

An Overview of Theses and Dissertations on Women and Football

As we have already anticipated, women's participation was not among the recurring themes of the first studies on football developed in Brazil. In the 1980s and 1990s, Giglio and Spaggiari (2010) list as the most frequent subjects:

3. We use the expressions "women's football" (*futebol de mulheres*) as opposed to the more recurrent "ladies' football" (*futebol feminino*). This conceptual and political change aims at rejecting the imposition of a hegemonic femininity on female footballers—especially for daring to occupy a so-called masculine terrain—as well as the commonly attributed understanding of femininity and masculinity as extensions of biological sex. Although in English-speaking countries this separation does not make much sense, in Portuguese, the mother tongue of the author's writing, there are sensitive differences between the two terms.

> the insertion and participation of black people in football; the relationship between football and national identity; discussions about football styles and schools, especially about "playing Brazilian style," better known as "art-football"; the circulation of Brazilian players in international football; the training of young players in football schools and youth categories; etc. Among the main themes, research on organised supporters (fans), and hooliganism, greatly influenced by the proliferation of conflicts and cases of violence in stadiums in the early 1990s, had a decisive impact on the expansion process of the scenario of sport studies in Brazil. (Giglio and Spaggiari, 2010, p. 296)

Nevertheless, when analyzing dossiers dedicated to football from the 1990s, the authors identify texts dedicated to the theme since 1994, the first year of publication.

The first survey of Brazilian production on football in the human and social science fields we found was produced by the Group of Studies on Football and Torcidas[4]—GEFuT (Silva et al., 2009). In it, the term "gender" is used to designate articles, books, theses, and dissertations "that addressed the category of analysis used to explain the image construction and the persistence of inequalities between men and women" (Silva et al., 2009, p. 10). In the researched material, the gender category appears among the articles (twelve of 133 articles), theses and dissertations (nine of 54 theses and 204 dissertations) and does not appear among the books, corresponding to 3% of the total production surveyed (twenty-one of 626 works).

In this research, we also verified that, in 1997, the first Brazilian postgraduate study was published focusing on women in football: the dissertation *Representations of women who play football*, by Lúcia da Costa Leite Reis. This work is part of a total of nine theses and dissertations included in the survey under the gender category, two of which were on masculinity and seven on football practiced by women (2.7% of the total production of postgraduate research studies). Thus, we noticed until that moment a preference for studies on women within gender studies.

This scenario is different from that found in Argentina, where, since the initial works on football, the discussion of masculinities appears as a theme of greater expression, mainly around the representation of the *aguante*[5] (Alabarces, 2004).

4. "Torcidas" is an expression in Brazilian Portuguese for which there is no equal equivalent in English, being similar to groups of supporters or firms.

5. In a broad vision, aguante is a value that can be associated with resistance, bravery, grit.

Thus, in Brazil, the discussions on gender—either masculinities or femininities—have a late start in relation to other themes. Besides, on a national level, women are the ones who, at first instance, are analyzed under the prism of gender in a more expressive way.

Another observation about the data set presented in the survey by Silva et al. (2009) is the absence of works that focus on the presence of women in other activities in football, other than that of being a player.

In the updated and expanded version of the previous survey, which considers the productions from 1980 to 2016, there are thirty-seven theses and dissertations that study themes related to women in football, of the thirty-eight on gender (Souza et al., 2019). The quantitative increase is also identified in terms of percentage, since these represent 3.8% of the total of 963 productions on football, as a whole.

In order to chronologically illustrate the production on women and football, we present Figure 12.1, which shows the number of theses and dissertations defended per year, already considering the total of seventy-seven productions that we gathered from the different surveys we consulted. We remind you that our section starts in 1980, but the first research identified was published in 1997.

We note that, since 2008, there has been at least one publication per year. Fensterseifer (2016), Campos et al. (2017), and Souza et al. (2019) also

Figure 12.1: Theses and dissertations on women and football between 1997 and 2022.

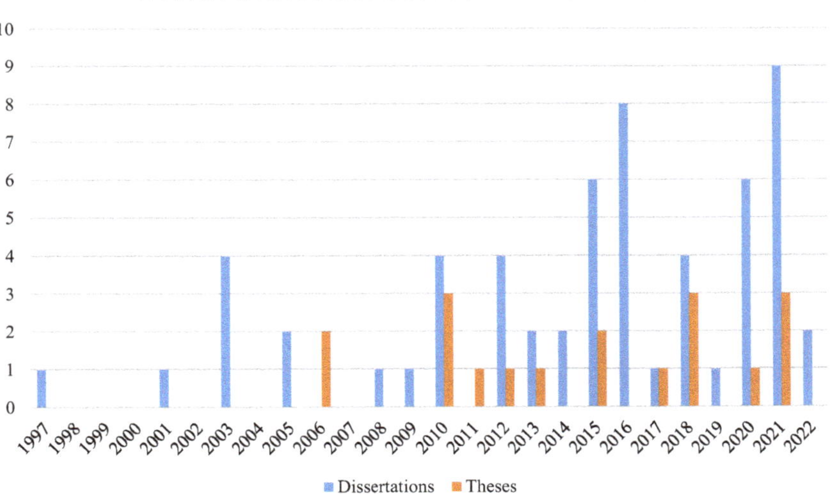

identify a gradual increase of production on football in general between 1980 and 2015. The authors of the last two papers draw attention to the increase of theses and dissertations on football from 2010 onward (three years after the announcement of the 2014 Men's Football World Cup in Brazil). According to them, the hosting of the World Cup and, subsequently, of the 2016 Olympic Games fostered this production. Although the World Cup in question is the one of football played by men, it is possible that the context of stimulus and attention to football has also influenced the productions about women. This justifies, although perhaps only in part, the increase in productions observed since 2010, although irregular.

Focusing on the places of production of these works, we identified that the Southeast region is the one that produced the most works about women during the established research period (thirty-nine papers, corresponding to 50.6%), followed by the South region (twenty-four works, 31.2%), Northeast (thirteen, 16.9%), and Center-West (one, 1.3%), with no productions from the North region. It is interesting to note that in the article by Salvini et al. (2014), whose research period goes until 2010, the predominance of the Southeast was greater, accounting for nine of the eleven productions (81.8%), while the others were from the Northeast (one) and the South (one). There has thus been a greater contribution from other Brazilian regions in recent years. We also verified that the growth in the contribution of the South region begins in the first years of the 2010s, while the Northeast region expands its production in the second half of this decade.

The evidence of a preponderance of the Southeast in the production of theses and dissertations, followed by the South region, is in line with what was detected in the two GEFuT surveys (Silva et al., 2009; Souza et al., 2019). Additionally, in the work of Fensterseifer (2016) and Giglio and Spaggiari (2010), it is indicated that these regions are the most frequent in the production of postgraduate research on football in general. Next, Figure 12.2 identifies, in each Brazilian state, the number of dissertations (D) and thesis (T) produced on football and women.

It is noted that, in the regions with a significant number of publications, there are contributions originating from those states. In relation to the division of productions by states, *São Paulo* (nineteen, 25%), *Rio Grande do Sul* (thirteen, 17%), and *Rio de Janeiro* (twelve, 16%) stand out, followed by *Minas Gerais* (eight, 10%); *Paraná* (six, 8%); *Santa Catarina* (five, 6%); *Bahia* (four, 5%); *Ceará*, *Paraíba*, and *Maranhão* (two, 3%); and *Sergipe*, *Pernambuco*, *Rio Grande do Norte*, and *Goiás* with one production each. As for the municipalities, *Rio de Janeiro—RJ* (ten) and *Porto Alegre—RS* (nine) are those with the largest number

Figure 12.2: Theses and dissertations on women and football per Brazilian state.

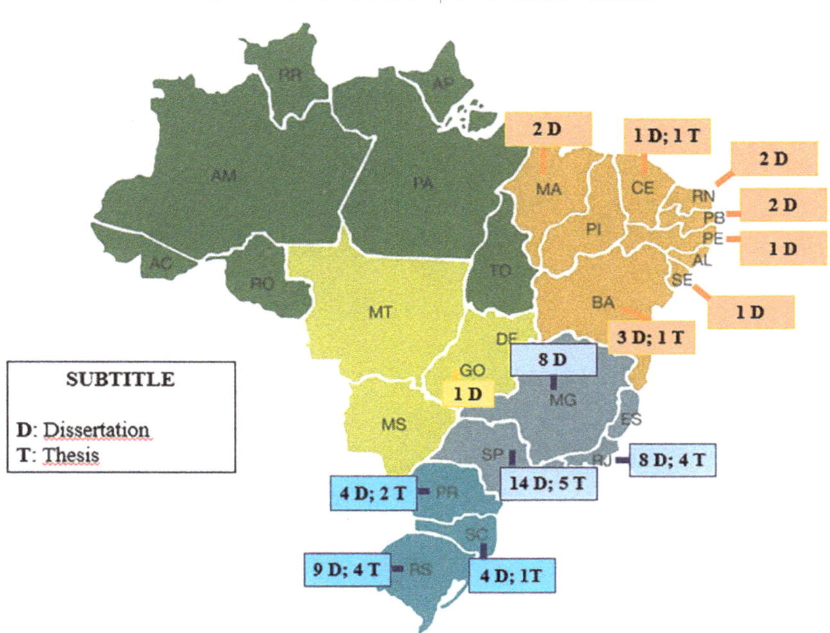

of productions, followed by *São Paulo—SP* (six), *Juiz de Fora—MG* (five), and *Florianópolis—SC* (four).

Regarding the Higher Education Institutions (HEI) in which the theses and dissertations on women and football were carried out, there is a spread in thirty-nine universities. Among them, the one with the most publications is the Federal University of Rio Grande do Sul (UFRGS) with eight productions; followed by the University of São Paulo (USP), with six; the Federal University of Juiz de Fora (UFMG) and Gama Filho University (UGF/RJ) with five; the Federal University of Santa Catarina (SC) and the State University of Campinas (Unicamp/SP) with four; the State University of Ponta Grossa (PR) and the *Paulista* State University of Júlio de Mesquita Filho (SP) with three; the State University of Rio de Janeiro (RJ), Federal University of Ceará (UFCE), Federal University of Minas Gerais (UFMG), Federal University of Maranhão (UFMA), Federal University of Paraíba (UFPB), Federal University of Paraná (UFPR), and Federal University of Santa Maria (UFSM/RS), with two each. Another twenty-five HEIs produced one paper each on women and football. Among these, USP, Unicamp, and UGF are also among the five HEIs that produced the most papers on football between the years 1990 and 2009 (Giglio and Spaggiari, 2010).

Additional evidence that endorses the development of research on women and football refers to the Research Groups. In previous research (Dantas and Anjos, 2020), we pointed out that, in 2016, out of seventy-four groups focused on football studies from a human and social science perspective, only six had women as one of their themes, and in two the interest in women's football is central to the production of the group at the time of the survey. These are: the Group of Studies on Sport, Culture and History (GRECCO/UFRGS), coordinated by Silvana Vilodre Goellner[6] and the Group of Studies and Research on the Pedagogical and Social Aspects of Football (ProFut/UFSCar), coordinated by Osmar Moreira de Souza Junior. Until 2010, there was no group dedicated to the theme (Salvini et al., 2014).[7]

As for the postgraduate programs from which the finalized theses and dissertations originated, the vast majority are linked to the area of Physical Education (twenty-nine), followed by interdisciplinary programs (nine), Anthropology (eight), Education (six), Communication (six), Social and Applied Sciences (six), and History (six), Psychology (four), Languages (two), and Administration (two).[8] The first two are also the most active areas in the production about football in general, according to the survey of Giglio and Spaggiari (2010) and Fensterseifer (2016).

We also noticed that Physical Education also started earlier to produce postgraduate research on this theme, being this area the only one responsible for the production of thesis and dissertations from 1997, date of the first publication, to 2005.

Authors and Advisors of the Theses and Dissertations on Women and Football

Perhaps due to the fact that the participation of women in football is still an emerging academic theme, we identified a great dispersion in the orientation

6. Since 2019, the leadership of this group has been shared with André Luiz dos Santos Silva.

7. Due to changes in the data made available by the Directory of Research Groups of the National Council for Scientific and Technological Development (DPG/CNPq), we were unable to update the data from this survey for the present text.

8. We also note that, in addition to these three productions in the area of History, a lot of research with a historiographical nature is produced in other postgraduate programs.

and supervision of the theses and dissertations analyzed: sixty people supervised the seventy-seven works surveyed. The person who supervised the most papers was Ludmila Mourão (seven, by UGF and UFJF), followed by Silvana Vilodre Goellner (five, UFRGS). Among others are Carmen Silvia Rial (UFSC) and Miguel Archanjo de Freitas Junior (UEPG), with three papers, and Heloísa Helena Baldy dos Reis (Unicamp), Roberto Ferreira dos Santos (UERJ), and Sebastião Josué Votre (UGF), all with two supervised research in the established period.

It is evident that all these researchers, despite having researched other themes in their dissertations and theses, or having other themes as central to their production, have various productions on football and women. Among these, it is worth highlighting the case of Silvana Goellner, who has made women's football her main investment in research and activism in recent years.

Among the authors of our survey, seven people worked on the theme both at master's and doctoral level. However, we also noticed that others, despite not having entered the doctorate or having dedicated themselves to other themes, produced texts published in books and periodicals and/or presented in events.

Still in the group of authors, we identified fifty-two women (72.9%) and eighteen men (27.1%), indicating that there is, also, interest from men to research about women. If many researchers are led to the subject of football by their personal experiences with the sport (whether playing it or in other ways), it is evident that the experience of the practice of the game (as a woman) is not the only mode of participation that generates interest in researching women in football.

Figure 12.3 illustrates the volume of productions, divided by the gender of the author, over the years. It is noted that the quantitative variation of authors and female authors occurs in similar periods, maintaining a greater production by women throughout the period, a difference amplified in recent years.

When we evaluate the authorship of papers about football, in general, the scenario regarding the distribution by gender is notably different. In Fensterseifer's (2016) survey, in the total of 1258 theses and dissertations on football, 955 are productions are of male authors (75.91%) and 303 of female authors (24.08%). Souza et al.'s (2019) study, which focuses on publications in humanities and social sciences, finds very close percentages: 74% of productions were by male authors and 26% by female authors. Through the published graphics, it was not possible to know what the productions of the female authors were about. However, an increase in the presence of female researchers in football studies in recent years was noted in the article by Silva et al. (2018), which analyzed the theses and dissertations on football (960) produced by women between the years 1980 and

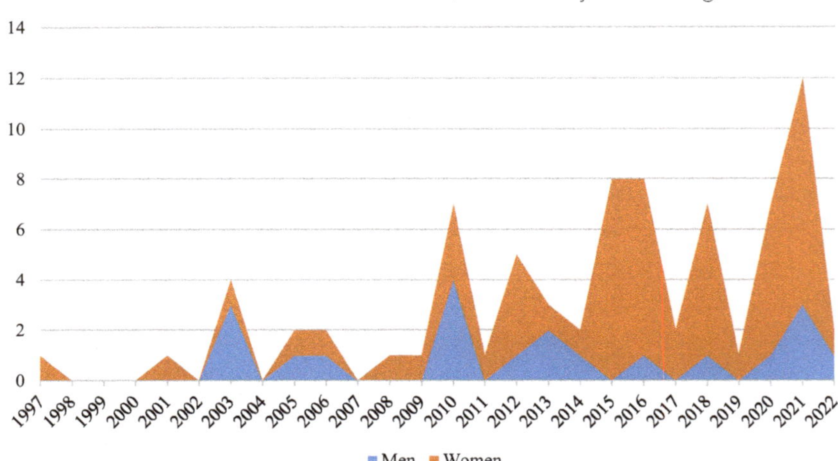

2016. The researchers identified 254 productions by female authors (26.5% of total productions) alongside 706 (73.5%) papers produced by men.

The authors also found that the production of theses and dissertations on football by women became constant from the year 1995, reaching its peak in the year 2016, with thirty-nine defended papers (Silva et al., 2018). The themes of interest found are diversified, among which gender[9] is the third with the most papers (nineteen, corresponding to 7.5%), behind media (twenty-six, 10.2%) and sporting spectacles (twenty-four, 9.4%). The greatest interest of female football researchers by themes that emerged from football practiced by men was also identified by Anjos and Dantas (2016).

The presence of women researchers is evident since the first years of a more systematized development of Brazilian research on football. We highlight the presence of Simoni Lahud Guedes as one of the four authors of *Universo do futebol* (Universe of football, translated title), a work organized by Roberto DaMatta and published in 1982, commonly identified as a milestone in the emergence period of these studies. In 1994, in turn, in *Dossiê Futebol* (Football Dossier, translated

9. The authors do not state whether the nineteen papers deal specifically with women and femininities, but they state that "gender studies also appears as a highlight, given that many women use this category of study to understand the place of women themselves in the practice of football, being related to the practice itself with the players, the techniques and the journalists" (Silva et al., 2018).

title), published by *Revista USP,* the first dedicated to the modality, there was a text by Fatima Martin Rodrigues Ferreira Antunes (Giglio and Spaggiari, 2010).

Furthermore, also in 1994, Maurício Murad created the elective discipline Sociology of Soccer, at UERJ (State University of Rio de Janeiro), possibly the first in Brazil dedicated specifically to reflections on this sport from the perspective of human and social sciences. Endorsing the evidence of an interest of women in the topic, he stated: "At the present date, in the second semester of 1998, we are concluding the ninth class, with a total of more than three hundred students, mostly women" (Murad, 1999, p. 2).

We note, thus, that there is a broad and diverse interest of women in football studies and that, as we have already stated, the gender theme is not the first preference of most of them (Anjos and Dantas, 2016; Silva et al., 2018). On the other hand, comparatively different to other themes, it is a subject in which the number of women researchers with completed works is higher than that of men.

The Content of Published Theses and Dissertations

Regarding the content of the theses and dissertations, we analyzed the titles, abstracts, and keywords of the productions to separate them by themes, approaches, and clippings.

It is clear that most of the studies on women and football are studies on football played by women. In total, we found fifty-nine works that, under different interests and focuses, address this universe, which represents more than half of the total productions.

There are eighteen articles that address women who perform other activities in the world of football, either exclusively or in combination with other activities. These include articles about female coaches (seven), female fans (six), female managers (four), female referees (two) and female workers (one). Among the papers on female fans, there are two papers on women in soccer fan clubs. In the management theme, we found papers on club management and two productions that presented the life stories of two female players that also focused on their period as managers.

Although numerically smaller, these papers that focus on other forms of women's participation, other than that of being a player, demonstrate the growing interest in such investigations. In order to illustrate the temporal distribution of these papers, Figure 12.4 shows the productions each year divided between those focused on football practiced by women and those in which the analysis approaches women's participation in activities other than that of being a player.[10]

Figure 12.4: Relationship between productions about football practiced by women and about women in other activities.

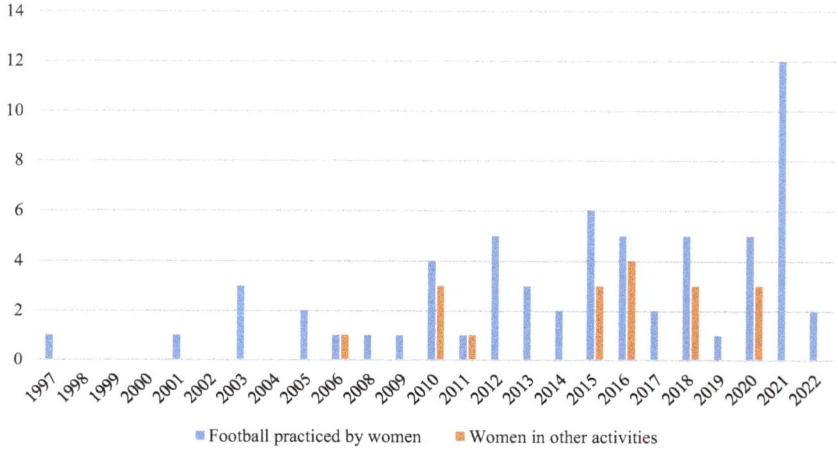

It is noted that seventeen of the eighteen papers were produced from 2010 onward, demonstrating the increased interest in this discussion in recent years.

Within the great theme of women's football, we found studies on both female players and teams formed exclusively by women. The Brazilian national team is the focus of six studies, either through life stories of female players (three), or on the national team itself (three). By portraying the trajectory of female players, the three studies also portray the continuity of their careers in the sporting environment. Seven productions focus on the main competitions between national teams in the category: World Cup and Olympic Games.

We found, with one occurrence each, papers on the exclusion of women in video game design, sports association activism, consumption, insertion, and permanence of women from a high socioeconomic class in football and analysis of academic production on women's football.

10. Five researchers address the participation of women in different functions, either as players, fans, managers, coaches and/or members of other positions in technical committees. Such productions were quantified both in the theme "football practiced by women" and "women in other activities." Similarly, the other three address women in more than one occupation in football, being quantified in the body of the text, in each one of them.

After the papers that have a gender discussion[11] as a central point (nineteen), the most addressed themes are the careers of female players, as well as the trajectory and memory of female players, referees, and coaches (fourteen), followed by the analysis of materials produced by the sports media (thirteen).

In the thirteen papers that addressed the discourse of print media, television, and web journalism on women's football, the national team and the players, the most used sources were: the *Globoesporte.com* portal (four productions), the *Placar* Magazine (three), and printed newspapers such as the sports section of *Folha de São Paulo* (two), *O Globo* (one), *Jornal dos Sports* (one), and *Jornal do Brasil* (one). Which leads us to understand that, in large part, these studies focus on narratives produced in the Rio–São Paulo axis.[12] In the online media, in addition to *Globoesporte.com*, the most analyzed portal, there was also productions by *ESPN Brasil* and *Dibradoras*, the latter being an independent media outlet produced by women, focusing on the coverage of sports played by women. In television, we found one paper on the discourse of *Rede Globo* (Globo Network, translated title).

Eight productions are centrally dedicated to the analysis of meanings, senses, and social representations about football played by women.

There are seven theses and dissertations on women and football in the school context. These studies focus on sport pedagogy or education in a broader sense and take into consideration the perspective or the representations of girls and boys on football played by women or the participation of women in football (in school or not) and also the perspective of physical education teachers on the subject.

Five papers focus on the institutional development, management, and/or structuring of the sports category.

In relation to other themes that appeared in the abstracts of the papers as central or important themes, we found leisure, identities (mainly gender identities), homosexuality, work relations, and *bullying*.

Regarding the fields of research and sources researched, we note that fifteen studies claim to have a national scope, including women and/or documents produced in various parts of Brazil in their analysis. Only four studies contemplate national and international sources. When we consider the states of the federation, twelve works are about women and football in *São Paulo*; seven in *Rio Grande*

11. Linked to these, discussions on race are much more timid and recent, appearing prominently in only two papers.

12. Term used to refer to the economic, political, and media influences concentrated in the two largest Brazilian metropolises.

do Sul; four in *Paraná*; four in *Rio de Janeiro*; four in *Minas Gerais*; two in *Paraíba*; two in *Bahia*; and *Ceará*, *Maranhão*, *Rio Grande do Norte*, *Goiás*, *Santa Catarina*, and *Sergipe* have one occurrence each. Therefore, the Southeast region of Brazil is the most investigated (twenty), followed by the South (twelve), Northeast (eight), and Center-West (one). Until this moment, we did not find in the clippings of this survey theses and dissertations about women and football in the North of the country.

Among the productions with a more local focus, *Porto Alegre* (five) is the most studied city, followed by *Rio de Janeiro* (three), *Belo Horizonte* (three), *São Paulo* (two), and *João Pessoa* (two). In seventeen dissertations and thesis the fieldwork was developed in cities in the interior of the states.[13]

Regarding the studied generation or the period in focus in the papers, one paper portrays the period from 1945 to 1941, one takes up the 1960s, three focus on the 1970s, seven on the 1980s, ten on the 1990s, twenty-two studies focus on the 2000s, forty-five on the 2010s, and twenty on the 2020s. This indicates that, although there is a large number of papers from a historiographical perspective, there are more papers dedicated to studies of the present time than focused on understanding women's football in the past. In three productions it was not possible to identify the period studied, because neither the papers nor their abstracts were available to the public.

Concluding Remarks

When Pablo Alabarces (2004) takes stock of the research on football in Latin America, he makes some considerations, presenting elements that he considers important for the continuity of research in this field. Among them is the perception that, "if in the Argentinean case, football organized the male imaginary, today it tends to expand its universes of representation to incorporate women" (Alabarces, 2004, p. 169, free translation from Spanish).[14]

13. Cities: Sobral (CE), Rio Claro (SP), Foz do Iguaçu (PR), São Luís (MA), Salvador (BA), Guanambi (BA), Londrina (PR), Criciúma (PR), Pelotas (RS), Campinas (SP), Santa Maria (RS), Macaíba (RN), Ribeirão Preto (SP), Goiânia (GO), Barbacena (MG), Campinas (SP), and Nova Iguaçu (RJ).

14. "Si en el caso argentino, el fútbol organizaba el imaginario masculino, hoy tiende a expandir sus universos de representación para incorporar a la mujer" (Alabarces, 2004, p. 169).

When we observe the Brazilian production about women and football that we exposed in this text, we realize that also in Brazil the statement, said in 2004, was pertinent, and a greater attention to it was becoming increasingly urgent.

However, almost twenty years after the speech, we can observe the result of a growing interest of many researchers to explore this universe of representation contemplating women. Contrasting the data we found, based on productions until 2022, with those of Salvini et al. (2014), whose period ends in 2010, we verified a series of indications that point to the intensification of the development of productions about women and football in recent years.

We list some points that had remarkable changes when compared to ours: (1) there was an increase in the number of productions per year; (2) there were no authors who had dedicated themselves to the theme in the master's and doctorate, while our search found seven; (3) four states had produced theses and dissertations, as opposed to the fourteen identified in our survey; (4) an institution had more than one paper, as opposed to the fifteen that we identified; (5) a researcher had supervised more than one study, as opposed to seven, from our research, with two or more supervisions.

It is also worth mentioning that we are aware that beyond the research resulting in theses and dissertations, there is much to be explored in articles, books, extension projects, and research groups dedicated to the subject. However, the increase in production, and the acceptance of new supervisors to the theme, already indicates that these studies are becoming increasingly recognized as necessary and relevant.

These changes in the academic field of football studies also seem to be accompanied by the development of women's football as a sport, an increase in its visibility in the media, as well as the achievements of women in other fields of action in this sport. Signs of this are: the maintenance of a Brazilian Championship with two leagues, in 2023 in its eleventh edition, with a better structuring of the participating clubs; the coverage of national teams and Brazilian Championship matches on television channels; and the increase in the number of women in sports media (both in the female and male categories). This includes female narrators, as well as in refereeing and other positions with historical underrepresentation, such as coaches and managers. We cite, as examples, Pia Sundhage as coach of the national team (after the pioneering work of Emily Lima); Leila Pereira, as president of *Sociedade Esportiva Palmeiras* (Sporting Society of Palmeiras, translated title), also after Patrícia Amorim's experience as president of Clube de Regatas do Flamengo; and Aline Pellegrino, as coordinator of the national and women's competitions in the CBF (Brazilian Football Confederation). The field of possibilities for new studies on women and football is proving to be increasingly fruitful.

REFERENCES

ALABARCES, Pablo. Veinte años de ciencias sociales y deporte en América Latina: un balance, una agenda (Twenty Years of Social Sciences and Sports in Latin America: An Assessment, an Agenda). **Revista Brasileira de Informação Bibliográfica em Ciências Sociais**, São Paulo, v. 58, pp. 159–179, 2004.

ANDRES, Suélen de Souza; ANJOS, Luiza Aguiar de. Práticas corporais e esportivas no Fazendo Gênero: primeiros apontamentos (Body and Sports Practices in Fazendo Gênero: Initial Notes). In: SEMINÁRIO INTERNACIONAL FAZENDO GÊNERO, 11, 2017, Florianópolis. **Anais** [...]. Florianópolis: UFSC, pp. 1–11, 2017.

ANJOS, Luiza Aguiar dos; DANTAS, Marina de Mattos. Pesquisadoras do futebol: discussões a partir de duas trajetórias (Women Football Researchers: Discussions Based on Two Trajectories). **Esporte e Sociedade**, v. 11, n. 28, pp. 1–28, set. 2016.

BRASIL. Decreto-Lei n. 3.199, de 14 de abril de 1941. Estabelece as bases de organização dos desportos em todo o país (Decree-Law No. 3,199, of April 14, 1941. Establishes the Foundations for the Organization of Sports Nationwide). Disponível em: https://www2.camara.leg.br/legin/fed/declei/1940-1949/decreto-lei-3199-14-abril-1941-413238-publicacaooriginal-1-pe.html.

CAMPOS, Priscila Augusta Ferreira et al. Pesquisas sobre futebol nas ciências humanas e sociais: um mapa a ser analisado (Research on Football in the Human and Social Sciences: A Map to Be Analyzed). In: CORNELSEN, Elcio Loureiro; CAMPOS, Priscila Augusta Ferreira; SILVA, Silvio Ricardo da (org.). **Futebol, linguagem, artes, cultura e lazer 2**: produção acadêmica sobre futebol, análises e perspectivas. Rio de Janeiro: Jaguatirica, 2017.

CUNHA, Andressa Caroline Portes da. Produção de dissertações e teses sobre os "futs" de mulheres no Brasil (2010–2016) (Production of Dissertations and Theses on Women's "Futs" in Brazil (2010–2016)). 235f. **Dissertação** (Mestrado em Educação Física). Setor de Ciências Biológicas, Universidade Federal do Paraná, Curitiba, 2020.

DANTAS, Marina de Mattos; ANJOS, Luiza Aguiar dos. Futebol e mulheres no Brasil: apontamentos sobre a produção acadêmica a partir de Teses e Dissertações (1980–2016) (Football and Women in Brazil: Notes on Academic Production Based on Theses and Dissertations (1980–2016)). In: KESSLER, Claudia Samuel; COSTA, Leda Maria da; PISANI, Mariane da Silva. **As mulheres no universo do futebol brasileiro**. Santa Maria: Editora UFSM, 2020.

FENSTERSEIFER, Alex Christiano Barreto. Produção científica sobre futebol: uma investigação do estado do conhecimento das dissertações e teses produzidas no Brasil (Scientific Production on Football: An Investigation of the State of Knowledge in Dissertations and Theses Produced in Brazil). 281f. **Tese** (Doutorado em Educação Física). Centro de Desportos, Universidade Federal de Santa Catarina, Florianópolis, 2016.

GIGLIO, Sérgio Settani; SPAGGIARI, Enrico. A produção das ciências humanas sobre futebol no Brasil: um panorama (1990–2009) (The Production of Human Sciences on Football in Brazil (1990–2009)). **Revista de História**, São Paulo, n. 163, pp. 293–350, Jul./dez. 2010.

GOELLNER, Silvana Vilodre. Feminismos, mulheres e esportes: questões epistemológicas sobre o fazer historiográfico (Feminisms, Women, and Sports: Epistemological Questions on Historiographical Practices). **Movimento**, v. 13, n. 2, pp. 171–196, 2007.

GOELLNER, Silvana Vilodre. Gênero e esporte na historiografia brasileira: balanços e potencialidades (Gender and Sport in Brazilian Historiography: Assessments and Potentialities). **Revista Tempo**, v. 19, n. 34, pp. 45–52, Jan./Jul. 2013.

GOELLNER, Silvana Vilodre; MACEDO, Christiane G. A categoria "gênero" nos Anais do Congresso Brasileiro de Ciências do Esporte e a constituição do Grupo de Trabalho Temático (The "Gender" Category in the Annals of the Brazilian Congress of Sport Sciences and the Constitution of the Thematic Working Group). In: RECCHIA, Simone et al. (org.). **Dilemas e desafios da pós-graduação em educação física**. Ijuí: Editora Unijuí, pp. 409–418, 2015.

MURAD, Maurício. Núcleo de Sociologia do Futebol—UERJ (Sociology of Football Research Group—UERJ). **Estudos Históricos**, Rio de Janeiro, v. 1, n. 23, pp. 207–208, 1999.

SALVINI, Leila; FERREIRA, Ana Letícia Padeski; MARCHI JÚNIOR, Wanderley. O futebol feminino no campo acadêmico brasileiro: mapeamento de teses e dissertações (1990–2010) (Women's Football in Brazilian Academia: Mapping Theses and Dissertations (1990–2010)). **Pensar a Prática**, Goiânia, v. 17, n. 4, pp. 1–14, out./dez. 2014.

SILVA, Indiamara Bárbara da; TAVARES, Marie Luce; SILVA, Silvio Ricardo da. **Levantamento e análise da produção de teses e dissertações realizadas por mulheres sobre o futebol (1980–2016)** (Survey and Analysis of Theses and Dissertations Produced by Women on Football (1980–2016)). 2018. 12 p. Artigo/Trabalho de Conclusão de Curso (Graduação em Educação Física)—Escola de Educação Física, Fisioterapia e Terapia Educacional, Universidade Federal de Minas Gerais, Belo Horizonte, 2018.

SILVA, Silvio R. et al. **Levantamento da produção sobre o futebol nas ciências humanas e sociais de 1980 a 2007** (Survey of Football-Related Research in Human and Social Sciences from 1980 to 2007). Belo Horizonte: Escola de Educação Física, Fisioterapia e Terapia Ocupacional/UFMG, 2009.

SOUZA, Adriano Lopes de et al. Levantamento e análise do desenvolvimento da produção e do estudo sobre futebol 1980–2016 (Public Policies on Sports and Leisure). In: COUTO, Ana Cláudia Porfírio et al. (orgs.). **Políticas públicas de esporte e lazer**: Centro MG da Rede CEDES. Belo Horizonte: Utopika Editorial, 2019.

TOLEDO, Luiz Henrique de. Futebol e teoria social: aspectos da produção científica brasileira (1982–2002) (Football and Social Theory: Aspects of Brazilian Scientific Production (1982–2002)). **BIB**, São Paulo, n. 52, pp. 133–165, 2° sem. 2001.

CHAPTER 12

A Small Feminist Revolution at the "Museu do Futebol"

Renata Maria Beltrão Lacerda

When the first museum dedicated to football in Brazil opened its doors in São Paulo in September 2008, women's football had little visibility in Brazilian media, but it was far from nonexistent. The women's Seleção had won gold medals at the Pan American Games in 2003 and 2007, silver medals at the 2004 and 2008 Olympic Games, and had been the runner-up in the 2007 FIFA Women's World Cup. Marta Vieira da Silva had already been a professional player for eight years; in 2007, she was the top scorer at the Pan American Games and the World Cup, and received the Ballon d'Or award as the best female player in the world.

However, the museum created to honor the epithet "the country of football" almost completely ignored women's football. Marta, and Marta alone, appeared on two monitors—in the first one, receiving the FIFA award, and in another, in a video compiling some of her incredible plays for the Seleção. She also had her name on a plaque that highlighted a quote from her speech at the Ballon d'Or ceremony: "You can be sure that I will work hard to come back here." No other female football player was represented throughout the exhibition, and this was not due to lack of space. The Museu do Futebol (Football Museum) occupies 6900 square meters in the existing rooms under the stands of the Pacaembu Stadium—a monumental 1940s *art deco* building, still one of the most beautiful stadiums in Brazil.

The press covered the opening extensively and mostly praised it, with little criticism focused on what would become the main characteristic of the Museu do Futebol: the lack of an object collection (Alfonsi, 2017). Along with the Museu da Língua Portuguesa (Museum of the Portuguese Language), inaugurated two years earlier also in São Paulo, the Museu do Futebol established a new typology in the Brazilian scene, that of the so-called experiential museums, aimed at the public, with a wealth of audiovisual resources, and with a heavy load of interactive installations, almost always involving digital technology. The absence of trophies, medals, and jerseys—relics and memorabilia in general—caused considerably more astonishment than the almost complete absence of women playing football among the over 1600 images on display.

It was not surprising, therefore, that the audience was predominantly composed of men: 70.1%, according to a survey conducted in early 2009. This number not only contradicted the traditional profile of museum visitors in Brazil—generally with a small majority of women—but also put the Museu do Futebol in the position of the Brazilian museum with the highest proportion of male visitors ever measured to that day (Lacerda and Bruno, 2022b).

This would change from 2015 onward, when a combination of internal and social factors led to a small feminist revolution within the institution, which is now—imagine that—a reference in terms of women's football in Brazil. This process was the subject of my study in *Chama as mina pro jogo: Museologia e Gênero no Museu do Futebol* (*Bring the girls to the game: Museology and Gender at the Football Museum*) (Lacerda, 2023), a master's thesis in museology defended in August 2023 at the University of São Paulo. Here, I provide a very brief summary of that work, highlighting mainly the practical results this trajectory had for the museum, its staff, the visiting public, and for the research field of the sport.

The Players

The Museu do Futebol was created during a bustling period in the São Paulo cultural scene. In the 2000s, the Government of the State of São Paulo made significant investments in establishing new museums in historic and protected buildings, under the premise that their use for culturally appealing purposes would ensure their sustainable preservation. Two of these projects—the Museu do Futebol and the aforementioned Museu da Língua Portuguesa—were coordinated by the Fundação Roberto Marinho—FRM (Roberto Marinho Foundation), a nonprofit private institution connected to the family that controls the Grupo Globo (Globo Group), the largest media conglomerate in Brazil, a leader in entertainment, journalism, and sports to this day. FRM has been involved in heritage preservation projects and distance learning television programs. This helps explain why these two projects, along with all others subsequently developed by the FRM in the museum field, focus heavily on audiovisual resources (Lupo, 2022).

In the specific case of the *Museu do Futebol*, it is important to note that for many years, Globo had the exclusive broadcasting rights of men's football matches in Brazil, both in the top category of the Brazilian championship and the FIFA World Cups. Since the early stages of the new museum project, it was established that the involvement of the FRM would mean easier access to Globo's archival images. Women's football, on the other hand, had been broadcast by other channels since the mid-1980s, but only sporadically, reflecting not only the disinterest of the broadcasters but also the lack of regularity and consistency in women's football tournaments.

Back in 2005, when the first steps were taken to establish the museum, the FRM organized two workshops with the aim of "determining what is truly important" for the new institution's narrative approach, as well as "discussing what representations should be included in the museum; [...] in fact, which memories this museum will transform into history," in excerpts from the statements of two professionals in charge of coordinating the meetings (Lacerda, 2023). In addition to the individuals directly involved in the project, external professionals from the municipal administration, as well as from the heritage and museum fields, researchers and football experts were invited.; for the second meeting, the external group was almost entirely composed of sports journalists who worked covering men's football. The idea was to establish a larger participatory process, which would provide a certain degree of social and political validation to the project.

There were over 6 hours' worth of debates, whose content I meticulously analyzed from a gender perspective based on the transcripts and, in the case of the first meeting, the video recording. The naturalized association between football and men becomes evident, and even more so, women's objective and symbolic exclusion. The word "woman" is mentioned eleven times in the two meetings, always as outsiders to football; they are objectified, stereotyped, or even seen as a barrier to the male experience—never as legitimate enthusiasts of the game. No female players are mentioned; the three athletes cited are from other sports (Hortência and Paula from basketball; Maria Esther Bueno from tennis). The only allusion made to a woman's professional involvement in football is to the referee Sílvia Regina (unnamed in the talks), who that year had been the first woman appointed to officiate a match in the men's Brazilian championship. It is even suggested that the primary target audience for the museum should be business*men* visiting São Paulo. Only one participant warns of the need for the future museum to also cater to a female audience, but this issue elicits no reaction from the other participants (Lacerda, 2023).

Much of what was discussed, raised, and validated in these two meetings did indeed materialize in the original configuration of the Museu do Futebol. Therefore, it is worth questioning the absence of dissenting voices that could have enriched the debate—and consequently, the project—from perspectives such as lived experience, regional diversity, alternative football variants (like amateur football, so present in the outskirts of São Paulo), and, of course, the gender perspective. At that time, important research on women's football in Brazil had already been published in various fields, such as the works of Suraya Cristina Darido (2002), Fábio Franzini (2005), Kátia Rubio, Silvana Goellner (2005), Jorge Dorfman Knijnik and Esdras Vasconcellos Guerreiro (2003), Eriberto Lessa Moura (2003), Ludmila Mourão and Marcia Morel (2005), Heloisa Helena Baldy dos Reis, and many others (Souza Júnior and Reis, 2018). This initial academic surge of interest in the topic was, however, overlooked in the formation of the museum.

What is also relevant in this process is the history and original vocation of the FRM in the preservation of built heritage and distance learning. Its entry into the world of museums was marked by a focus on architectural projects for the adaptation of buildings, and the development of lavish exhibitions (Lupo, 2022), as previously mentioned, emphasizing audiovisual material and multisensory installations. To display, however, is just one of the multiple functions of a museum. Museums have their operational framework anchored in a triad consisting of communication (including exhibitions as well as educational activities and cultural programming), preservation, and research.

The importance of these last two components were greatly diminished in the early museum projects carried out by the FRM. In the case of the Museu do Futebol, specialized museology consultancy was only integrated into the project in 2007 when all major decisions had already been made (Lacerda, 2023). When it set out the first museum plan for the institution, the consultancy suggested that the museum take on a preservationist approach anchored in the idea of cultural reference (rather than a collection of objects), thus assuming a "historical responsibility" to establish a somewhat kind of collection that was unusual for the time (Araújo et al., 2007). The plan already proposed, for instance, the mapping of sources about football and the creation of a reference database to streamline museum activities.

Then, in 2009, the first Museological Plan[1] for the Museu do Futebol was carried out, at a time when the institution was already open and fully operational. More emphatic than the previous document, this one highlighted the centrality of the long-term exhibition as a problem to be overcome because it limited the museum's potential (Bruno et al., 2010). The institution needed to look outward, engage with the world around it, and commit to social development. In sum, the Museu do Futebol was not yet a museum, despite its name. However, it would soon become one, precisely by way of women's football.

Why Does a Museum Matter?

The category of gender is still a subject of dispute. Among the many possible definitions, I deem that of historian Joan Scott (1995) to be more fruitful for the field of museology. Divided into two parts, it states: "gender is a constitutive element of social relationships based on perceived differences between the sexes, and gender is a primary way of signifying relationships of power." In fact, museum exhibitions operate precisely based on perceptions, instrumentalizing them in order to advance certain narratives.

Furthermore, historically, museums have been institutions developed as instruments to legitimize power—whether aristocratic, illuminist, colonialist, nationalist, socialist, or capitalist in nature—typically performing gender relations in a way that supports these same projects. Museums, like many other institutions, solidify an androcentric logic by considering male experience universal, that is, valid for both men and women (Audebert et al., 2019), as well as for people who do not identify within the binary spectrum.

Today, a discussion in museology has been taking place regarding the necessary critique of this state of affairs and the responsibility of museums toward other ways of existing. According to Aida Rechena (2011), museums can be analyzed using Serge Moscovici's Social Representation Theory, both for categorizing portions of reality to guide people in their relationship with cultural heritage—often corroborating commonsense views—and for their potential to formulate new kinds of representation, unlike those of the public when it comes into contact with an exhibition or collection.

1. The Museological Plan is the strategic planning of museums. In the Brazilian context, it became mandatory for institutions that wish to be recognized as museums following the promulgation of Federal Law No. 11,904 in January 2009, which established the Museum Statute.

While visiting museums is not a deeply ingrained habit among Brazilians—nearly 70% of the population has never set foot in one (Schiavinatto, 2011)—these institutions hold great credibility, and are seen as bearers of "truth" not only by those who visit them but also by those who do not. The Museu do Futebol has often taken center stage in over 3000 articles in Brazilian and international media outlets every year—I know this because, as I write this article, I am in charge of the institution's Communication and Marketing. In 2022 alone, during the FIFA World Cup in Qatar, there were nearly 38 hours' worth of broadcasts involving the museum on TV and radio news programs, mostly national, but also from other countries (Lacerda, 2023). Thus, the representations presented in the museum have had a reach that is much broader than its physical space or, with the advent of the internet, its digital properties.

"A museum that celebrates [...] Brazilian man"

What were these representations when the Museu do Futebol first opened? A publication from 2014, produced by the institution managing the space[2] to commemorate its first five years of operation, leaves little doubt:

> The Museu do Futebol is a museum of Brazilian history. A history that spans the 20th century, playful and captivating. It is a museum that celebrates the cultural expression of football. The gesture and the flair. Spontaneity. **It celebrates the Brazilian man. His ability to overcome adversity, as in football.** [...] In addition to the history of football and Brazil, the book proposes another story: **that of men and women who were able to conceive and carry out the project of the Museu do Futebol**, so contemporary with the early 21st century (Kaz, 2014, p. 11, emphasis mine).

In this case, "Brazilian man" is not just a figure of speech, a perception reinforced when it is admitted that women were involved in the project's conception. The long-term exhibition presented the history of Brazilian football intertwined with the history of the country itself from an exclusively male perspective. As

2. The Museum of Football, like other museums under the responsibility of the Secretariat of Culture, Economy, and Creative Industries of the Government of the State of São Paulo, is managed by a cultural social organization—a nonprofit private institution contracted by the Government for this purpose.

previously mentioned, among the more than 1600 images on display, only one female player appeared, Marta Vieira da Silva. Other female athletes or sports professionals represented could be counted on one hand: tennis player Maria Esther Bueno, gymnasts Daiane dos Santos and Daniele Hypólito, basketball players Hortência and Paula, and referee Sílvia Regina. In one of the exhibition rooms, writer Rachel de Queiroz, visual artist Tarsila do Amaral, and performer Carmen Miranda were credited as important figures in the shaping of a national identity, alongside a dozen male personalities—and this was the closest women came to playing a significant role in the entire exhibition.

All others represented in the Museu do Futebol at the time—including Marta—served as a backdrop to the stage where the glorious history of Brazilian men in football and their "ability to overcome adversity" unfolded. Interestingly, the 39-year ban on women's football in Brazil was not counted as an adversity that needed to be overcome. A reference to this episode appeared discreetly on an informational plaque that housed the TV screen showing a compilation of Marta's incredible plays. In a fourteen-line text, the information contained three errors.

The Dribble: *Visibility for Women's Football*

Though the media gave little importance to the absence of women in the exhibition, the same did not occur with the public. Complaints related to this issue began to appear from the very first visitor's profile and satisfaction survey in 2009. There were not many, but they were consistent, persistent, and drew the attention of the technical team, especially after the drafting of the institution's first Museological Plan. To establish a commitment to adopt a critical perspective and positively interfere in the reality in which it was inserted, as advocated by the Plan (Bruno et al., 2010), the Museu do Futebol needed to create relationship networks and engage with a community with which it could hold a dialogue.

This began in 2009 and 2010, by approaching academia, when the technical team started establishing contact with researchers on the subject, especially female researchers of women's football. It was in this context that the Museum created the International Symposium on Football Studies, held for the first time in 2010, and since then, every four years. Until that point, the Museum team, including women, had little or no information about the history of persecution of women's football (Alfonsi, 2023; Bonfim, 2019).

In 2014, the FIFA Men's World Cup was held in Brazil, and the Museum experienced its peak number of visitors, a record then.[3] The men's Seleção lost 7–1 to Germany, the country exploded with memes and entered a kind of football hangover, also because of the many protests against land expropriations and the astronomical investments made to build new stadiums. In terms of the economy, 2015 was a year of contraction, with heavy repercussions on cultural facilities maintained by the Government of São Paulo. The budget was cut, and part of the staff in many programs was dismissed. At the Museu do Futebol, part of the Educational Nucleus team left, and there was no budget for a temporary exhibition, a mandatory commitment according to the managing social organization's contract with the Government of São Paulo.

According to anthropologist Daniela Alfonsi, who had been a member of the Museu do Futebol staff since 2008 and had just taken over as technical director, in the midst of this situation, the team had already been made aware of the issue of women's football and questioned why the Women's World Cup was to be held in Canada when Brazil had a dozen brand new stadiums at its disposal. However, this questioning did not resonate in the public discussion or even among sectors of the Museum, who deemed women's football too niche of a subject, incapable of stirring interest in the audience. But paradoxically, the lack of money for a temporary exhibition helped leverage the first consistent project related to the theme. "When we brought a project that used the money we had and nothing more, no one was against it [...]. I noticed this: it passed. No one cared," recalls Alfonsi (2023).[4]

Visibility for Women's Football, which was launched in May 2015, was conceived as a series of interventions to include content about women's football in the long-term exhibition—an action that was later referred to by the team as "hacking"—while a series of events were held to discuss the history, reality, and prospects of the sport. The content to be included was curated by researcher Silvana Goellner, who authored one of the chapters in this book, with the active participation of the Museum's technical team. The panel discussions were coordinated by journalist and researcher Luciane Castro, researcher and former player Juliana Cabral, and René Simões, who had coached the Brazilian women's Seleção—the latter two were silver medalists at the Athens Olympics.

3. It was 419,201 people. Data from the internal visitor attendance spreadsheet of the Museum of Football.

4. The project cost, in current values, about $46,000. A temporary exhibition requires an investment at least five or six times higher.

The items included in the exhibition were primarily provided by players, former players, and researchers of the sport, as well as identified by the Museum staff in newspaper archives and periodical collections.

In the Penalty Area Room, consisting of 488 framed images of collectible items related to clubs and the Brazilian men's Seleção, twelve illustrations and photographs of objects related to women's football were included. In the Baroque Angels Room, where twenty-five idols from the Seleção are projected as holograms on screens, images of Marta and Formiga[5] were included.

The main intervention took place in the Origins Room, which consisted of 431 black-and-white photographs from the period between what is conventionally considered the arrival of football in Brazil (1894) and the professionalization of the sport (1933), with the regulation of the entry of Black athletes into clubs. The room displayed images of teams and players from the period as well as images providing social and historical context, with the aim of giving an overview of the time period. Among these photographs, 220 pictures represented women in their daily activities, socializing at parties and during Carnival, even performing on theater stages—but when it came to sports, there was only one image of a group of girls in white dresses playing basketball. With *Visibility*, thirty-eight images of women participating in sports, mainly playing football, were added.

Given the scarcity of Brazilian material from the period, the inclusions primarily involved photographs sourced from the collections of the United States' Library of Congress, France's National Library, the French periodical Fémina Sport, and the FIFA Museum. From Brazilian sources, three images taken in Rio de Janeiro in 1940 were found, as well as newspaper records, including an advertisement for a women's match to be held at a circus and a photograph of the players. The headline "Women's Football Prevented by Police"[6] was also included, and it became one of the images that drew the most attention from the public.

The inclusion of women as football players in the exhibition made it possible to offer a multifaceted narrative to the public, providing them with tools to construct different representations of the sport and women's participation. Beyond the content included in the exhibition, the research related to the *Visibility for Women's Football* project resulted in the digitization of 41 collections, involving

5. "Formiga" (Ant) is the alias of Miraildes Maciel Mota, a Brazilian footballer who played in seven Women's World Cups and seven Olympics. She retired from Seleção in 2021.

6. Newspaper A Batalha (RJ), June 1940. Fundação Biblioteca Nacional—Brazil.

over 5000 items related to women's football, most of which were provided by players. It also involved mapping 104 academic works on the subject, the production of 15 oral history videos of Brazilian players called up for that year's World Cup, and a significant increase in the influx of researchers to the Museum seeking sources on women's football (Museu do Futebol, 2016).

The parallel discussions held throughout the year served as a meeting point and exchange for this community. According to Luciane Castro's assessment at the closing event of the cycle in April 2016, the Museu do Futebol turned out to be responsible for bringing these people together and consolidating a network: "Without the Museum's involvement, maybe we would be scattered around" (Museu do Futebol, 2016).

Visibility was also important for the Museum's relationship with the community of female players and former players of football. It was the first time they felt honored by an institution of weight, even though it was outside the economic and sports ecosystem of football. Furthermore, the spontaneous audience satisfaction survey, which was conducted through an electronic tablet available at the museum's exit, showed a significant change in the gender profile: in the year of *Visibility*, 44.4% of respondents self-identified as women, and 55.6% self-identified as men—a significant variation from the 71% of men recorded just six years earlier (Lacerda and Bruno, 2022b).

The Public Responds to the Counterattack

The end of 2015 marked the beginning of what the press called "women's spring" in Brazil, which reflected the so-called fourth wave of feminism worldwide, yet mostly responded to local issues. The internet was taken over by the spontaneous campaign #MeuPrimeiroAssédio (#MyFirstHarassment) in response to the proliferation of comments by men on the internet sexualizing a preadolescent participant in the *MasterChef Brazil* show, as well as protests against a bill that aimed to further restrict the legal right to abortion for Brazilian women (Lacerda and Bruno, 2022a).[7]

In March 2016, FIFA amended its statute to include among its objectives that everyone should be able to play football, regardless of gender or age. It

[7] Abortion is prohibited in Brazil and considered a crime, punishable by a prison sentence of three to ten years, except in cases where pregnancy results from rape, when the fetus is diagnosed with anencephaly, or when the pregnancy poses a risk of death to the pregnant person. The bill in question aimed to eliminate even these exceptions.

also explicitly prohibited discrimination based on race or gender in the context of football and, more specifically, required confederations to include similar measures in their own statutes as well (Almeida, 2019). Starting in 2019, clubs participating in competitions organized by the Confederação Sul-Americana de Futebol—CONMEBOL (South American Football Confederation) and the Confederação Brasileira de Futebol—CBF (Brazilian Football Confederation) were required to maintain a professional women's team. It is true that most clubs did the bare minimum, for example, by "adopting" preexisting amateur teams and maintaining them without the necessary professional structure. However, this is the moment when women's football competitions began to gain a bit more visibility, and supporters of major teams, such as Corinthians, started to pay more attention to women's football.

The technical staff of the Museu do Futebol, much more knowledgeable about the subject after the *Visibility* project, proposed a major temporary exhibition focused on women's football. However, they did not find support from the Museum's executive management, which continued to find the subject too niche and without any appeal. It took the Itaú bank to show it intended to sponsor the initiative for the idea to come to fruition. This financial institution was already a sponsor of all Brazilian national teams (from youth to the men's senior team) and planned to strongly support the women's Seleção during the World Cup in France. Thus, with an approximate budget of $245,000, in current figures, the exhibition *COUNTERATTACK! The Football's Women* was held.

Inaugurated in May 2019, *COUNTERATTACK!* was once again curated by Silvana Goellner, and this time together with historian Aira Bonfim (author of the opening chapter of this book), the aforementioned Luciane Castro, and former player Aline Pellegrino. It was a politically charged exhibition that started from the period of the ban on women's football (1941–1979) and presented a narrative of Brazilian women's resistance, resilience, and disobedience.

The exhibition was, literally, a scream: the visual communication created by a Rio de Janeiro agency led by women used uppercase typography and the colors purple, orange, and red, which are complementary to the green, yellow, and blue of the Brazilian flag's color scale. As soon as visitors entered the museum, the first thing they saw was a huge LED panel sign with strong phrases like "Who's afraid of girls who play football?" and "Crazy, free, and skilled." There were tributes to women's football personalities in Brazil; a foosball table with women player figurines especially manufactured for the exhibition; and the display of uniforms worn by the women's Seleção, highlighting the disregard for their trajectory—2019 was the first year players had their own uniforms, and not borrowed from the men's team.[8]

During the research process for the exhibition, more than 1560 items were mapped out, of which 348 photographs, twenty videos, four illustrations, twenty-five documents, and sixty-six objects were displayed in the exhibition. In total, 449 women were portrayed in the exhibition, nearly all of them players, but also referees, journalists, coaches, and fans (Museu do Futebol, 2020). Even if temporarily, *COUNTERATTACK! The Football's Women* managed to represent the relationship of Brazilian women with the sport more justly. And though many male visitors refused to enter the temporary exhibition room as soon as they realized what it was about, according to reports from the museum's educators, for the first time, the spontaneous satisfaction and public's profile survey showed a balance between genders among respondents: from March to October 2019, while the exhibition was on display, the proportion remained at 50% each. As soon as it ended, in November, the proportion returned to 59% men to 41% women. The experience of *COUNTERATTACK!* proved, in practice, the validity of the expression repeated by activists: representation matters.

Moreover, interviews with female employees of the Museu do Futebol demonstrate that the process of incorporating women's football into museum practice also resulted in a consistent increase in the staff awareness of gender issues, and their connection with situations experienced at work and in their daily lives as women. In a patriarchal and highly sexist society, understanding the journey of women's football helped them understand how power relations operate in practice based on perceptions of gender. The process also provided them with tools to deal with their daily work, especially in the case of professionals who interact directly with the public, such as educators, who are often tested by male visitors and their colleagues regarding their knowledge of football.

This gain in awareness was not homogeneous, of course, and there are still enormous differences in how employees in the Museum environment understand the gender issue. However, as a Brazilian saying goes, it is undeniable that a goat has been placed in the room. And now, all—whether they like it or not—have to deal with it.

8. In the early years of the Brazilian Women's Seleção, the male uniforms were borrowed from the male players. The female players wore numbers much higher than their own, had to hand-sew their shorts to keep them from falling down, and were forced to return them to the CBF at the end of tournaments.

Final Thoughts

Visibility for Women's Football and *COUNTERATTACK! The Football's Women* demonstrated the potential of addressing gender inequality—a latent issue with significant consequences in Brazilian society—through the archetypal case of football, still considered a naturally male practice in Brazil. These experiences proved that including women in the narrative about the sport could bring about immediate changes in the profile of museum visitors, revealing a suppressed demand from women.

From the perspective of the museum institution, these experiences underscored how challenging it is to work based on a history that has deliberately been silenced and erased through state policy. The ban on women's football in Brazil not only hindered the development of the sport but also exiled its memories (Bruno cited in Wichers, 2017), necessitating alternative strategies to tell this story when its related documents and objects are scarce because of intentional processes.

REFERENCES

ALFONSI, Daniela.**Original replicas**: a study on football in museums. 187f. Tese (Doutorado)—Programa de Pós-Graduação em Antropologia Social, Universidade de São Paulo, São Paulo, 2017.

ALFONSI, Daniela. **Entrevista cedida a Renata Maria Beltrão Lacerda**. 2023.

ALMEIDA, Caroline Soares de. "O FIFA statute and gender equality in football: stories and contexts of women's football in Brazil" In: **Revista FuLiA** /UFMG, v. 4, n. 1, jun. 2019, pp. 72–87. Disponível em https://periodicos.ufmg.br/index.php/fulia/article/view/14658. Acesso em 8 jun. 2023.

ARAÚJO, Marcelo Mattos; BRUNO, Maria Cristina Oliveira; FELIPINI, Kátia. **Museological plan**: Museu do Futebol. São Paulo: ADM Museologia e Educação Ltda. Abr. 2007.

AUDEBERT, Ana; WICHERS, Camila A. M.; QUEIROZ, Marijara S. Critical interfaces between museology, museums and gender. In: ARAUJO, Bruno et al. (Orgs.). **Museology and its critical interfaces**: museum, society and heritage. Recife: Ed. UFPE, 2019. Disponível em: https://editora.ufpe.br/books/catalog/download/138/170/491?inline=1. Acesso em 12 abr. 2023.

BONFIM, Aira F. Visibility to the invisible? The formation of public collections about women's soccer in Brazil. In: LIMA, Cecília Almeida Rodrigues; BRAINER, Larissa; JANUÁRIO, Soraya Barreto (orgs.). **Women and football**. João Pessoa: Xeroca!, 2019. Disponível em: https://www.academia.edu/39520500/ELAS_E_O_FUTEBOL. Acesso em 27 mai. 2023.

BRUNO, Maria Cristina Oliveira; ARRUDA, Beatriz Cavalcanti de; FIGOLS, Francisca Ainda Barboza. **Museu do Futebol**: Museological Plan: diagnóstico institucional e linhas de ação. São Paulo, [s.n.], 2010.

KAZ, Leonel (Org.). **Museu do Futebol**: a museum-experience. São Paulo: IDBrasil Cultura, Educação e Esporte, 2014.

LACERDA, Renata Maria Beltrão. **Bring the girls to the game**: museology and gender at the Football Museum. 316f. Dissertação (Mestrado). Programa de Pós-Graduação Interunidades em Museologia, Universidade de São Paulo, São Paulo, 2023.

LACERDA, Renata Maria Beltrão; BRUNO, Maria Cristina Oliveira. Football, gender and guerrilla on Twitter: the case of the Museu do Futebol. In: **Anais do Seminário Brasileiro de Museologia**. 2022a. Disponível em: https://www.academia.edu/105262626/FUTEBOL_G%C3%8ANERO_E_GUERRILHA_NO_TWITTER_o_caso_do_Museu_do_Futebol. Acesso em 23 setembro 2023.

LACERDA, Renata Maria Beltrão; BRUNO, Maria Cristina Oliveira. Representativeness matters: presence of women in the public surveys of Museu do Futebol. In: **Simpósio Internacional de Estudos sobre Futebol**, n. 4, 2022, São Paulo. São Paulo: Museu do Futebol, 2022b. Disponível em: https://museudofutebol.org.br/crfb/acervo/774195/. Acesso em 1º maio 2023.

LUPO, Bianca Manzon. **The museum experience**: a Brazilian approach—the case of the Fundação Roberto Marinho. São Paulo. 456 f. Tese (Doutorado), Faculdade de Arquitetura e Urbanismo da Universidade de São Paulo (FAU-USP). São Paulo, 2022. Disponível em: https://www.academia.edu/96552503/O_museu_experi%C3%AAncia_uma_abordagem_brasileira_O_caso_da_Funda%C3%A7%C3%A3o_Roberto_Marinho. Acesso em 13 mai. 2023.

MUSEU DO FUTEBOL. **COUNTERATTACK!** The football's women: results of the temporary exhibition. 2020.

MUSEU DO FUTEBOL. **1980s:** regulation of Women's Football. YouTube, 2 abr. 2016. Disponível em: https://www.youtube.com/watch?v=s-wevOkGivs. Acesso em 25 jun. 2023.

RECHENA, Aida. Teoria das Representações Sociais: uma ferramenta para a análise de exposições museológicas [Social Representation Theory: a tool for the analysis of museum exhibitions]. Caderno de Sociomuseologia, nº 41, 2011. Disponível em: https://revistas.ulusofona.pt/index.php/cadernosociomuseologia/article/view/2651>. Acesso em 112 de abr. 2023.

SCHIAVINATTO, Fábio (Org.). **Social perception indicator system** (SIPS). Ipea, 2011. Disponível em https://repositorio.ipea.gov.br/handle/11058/3097. Acesso em 24 jun. 2023.

SCOTT, Joan. "Gender: a useful category of historical analyses" In: **Educação & Realidade**. Porto Alegre, v. 20, n. 2, jul./dez. 1995. Disponível em: https://seer.ufrgs.br/index.php/educacaoerealidade/article/download/71721/40667/297572. Acesso em: 9 abr. de 2023.

SOUZA JÚNIOR, Osmar Moreira de; REIS, Heloísa Helena Baldy. **Women's football:** the battle of all fields. Paulínia: Autoresporte, 2018.

WICHERS, Camila. Musealization of archaeology: feminist provocations and propositions. In: **Seminário Brasileiro de Museologia**. N. 3, 2017. Belém. [Anais...]. Brasília: Curso de Museologia da Universidade de Brasília; Projeto Museologia Virtual, 2017. Disponível em: http://sebramusrepositorio.unb.br/index.php/3sebramus/3Sebramus/paper/view/762. Acesso em 12 de abr. 2023.

Afterword: Brazil, the Country of Women's Soccer?

Silvana Goellner

The representation of Brazil as "the country of football" spans different temporalities and cultural contexts. Its widespread dissemination has favored the creation of countless narratives, including one that places in this sport one of, if not the greatest, national passion. A lot could be said about this social construction, but I want to emphasize one extremely important aspect: this self-identification has excluded women. The football seen, desired, and revered was and still is men's football, whose exacerbated valorization has historically overshadowed women's football.

There were many constraints, obstacles and prejudices directed at those who dared to enter a territory dominated by virile and toxic masculinities. From restrictions imposed by families to official bans, many impediments were used to keep them away from football, most of them supported by medical, pedagogical, legal and religious arguments. These discourses, even though they were widely endorsed by conservative sectors of society, were not enough to fulfil their purpose, because despite their widespread dissemination, women resisted and inscribed their stories in it. In other words, they played the game on and off the pitch. This statement may seem inadequate if we consider the gender inequalities that permeate this sport, but it makes sense when we consider that, despite everything, they persisted.

The abysmal differences that exist in terms of opportunities, structure, support and salaries when compared to men's football, although they need to be denounced on a daily basis, cannot justify erasing the actions undertaken by women past and present. By this I mean that the advances seen in football need to be analyzed with their intervention in mind, because nothing has been granted to them, everything has been achieved. They are not the result of changes in power structures but, fundamentally, of the individual and collective action of women who, in different professional fields, have broken down barriers and challenged hierarchical relationships that did not accept their competences and abilities.

The dispute over the right to play football has been going on since its first manifestations on Brazilian soil. The pleasure of playing football and enjoying what happens around it has led girls and women from the most varied regions of the country to use different strategies to circumvent the obstacles to this desire. Successful or not, it is worth noting that if football exists for women today, it is because some of them paved the way, created representation and did not allow it to disappear. This statement is not restricted to Brazil.

If we take the recently concluded World Cup in Australia and New Zealand as a milestone, we can celebrate a number of achievements, including the increase in the number of women in media coverage, in leadership and management positions, in technical committees, in refereeing, in stadium stands, in watching via streams and television channels, in infrastructure teams, in short, in everything that made the competition possible. Brazil's participation accompanied this movement and improvements were seen in terms of valuing women's football. The Brazilian Football Confederation (CBF) sent to Australia and New Zealand the largest delegation ever to take part in an international women's event, totaling thirty-seven people, including eighteen women on the coaching staff, in the medical department and in the support and logistics teams. The plane that carried the group was chartered exclusively for this purpose—something never seen since the national team was created in 1988—and its exterior was painted with the image of Masha Amini, an Iranian woman murdered in 2002 by the morality police for not wearing a veil. Next to the image was the phrase "No woman should be forced to cover her head," a clear message to the struggle of women.

In other areas, their presence was also amplified. Four Brazilian women were part of the refereeing team and in the most diverse sectors of the press we can see professionals in roles once reserved for men, such as narrators, commentators, reporters, photographers, editors, producers, *influencers,* etc.

In the run-up to the World Cup, there were also some new developments in terms of the flow of information circulating in Brazil because, as well as appearing more frequently, they included data that was little known to the lay public and those who follow the football circuit. I would also highlight the participation of players and former players in advertisements, newspaper and magazine editorials, radio and television programs, social networks, and streaming services. The market economy has not let this moment pass unnoticed either, creating products and services aimed at meeting the real and symbolic needs of old and new consumers. Even though this is an expected move in capitalist societies, the reference to the banning of the sport and the repression of former footballers was an innovation in terms of public loyalty, which was widely encouraged to watch the broadcasts and support their football. The "country of football" brand was activated and in a peculiar way mobilized appeals that resulted in both the amplification of the consumption of material goods and the dissemination of the idea that football is also for women.

It is precisely this theme that I would like to analyze. What made this reference possible? More than eighty years after the official ban on women's football in Brazil and more than forty years after its regulation, what brought these stories out of the shadows?

I have no doubt that women's agency and resistance have been decisive not only for some traces of the past to surface today but above all for football to remain on the horizon for those who wish to take part in it. Behind the scenes of the institutions that run it, such as federations, clubs, and sports associations, many female athletes confronted their bosses to demand rights and improvements, and for this reason suffered punishments to their careers. These disagreements remained private and were not echoed, leaving the insurgents with neglect and frustration, which for many was experienced alone. These stories remained restricted to the memories of those who lived them and began to be publicized very recently as a result of the increase in academic production and the choice of women's football as an object of research. Over the last four decades, football has emerged as a topic of interest in the social sciences and humanities, which has revealed how gendered its practice was and also the way its history was recorded. Female researchers, to a large extent those who focused on issues related to gender relations in the sporting environment, focused on the sport, analyzing it in its multiple dimensions and ways of happening. These productions have served as inputs for teaching activities and outreach activities that have gone beyond the walls of universities and reached diverse spaces, including those that promote policies, such as private organizations and government bodies.

In 2015, the year the Women's World Cup took place in Canada, there was an event that I consider relevant. I am referring to the "Visibility for Women's Football" exhibition held at the Football Museum in São Paulo, both because it brought women into this memory preservation space and because it had a major impact on the media and, to a certain extent, on the academic production that has grown since then. The execution of the exhibition was captained by a team of women, led by the institution's director, who implemented various actions to redress the erasure of women from the institutional scope. Until then, of the more than 1500 images that made up the Museum's permanent exhibition, not one depicted a female footballer. It was also curated by women, with the collaboration of athletes, coaches, journalists and referees who gave up their personal collections so that they could be shown to the public. The success of the exhibition led to further investment and in 2019 and 2023, the Museum organized two new temporary exhibitions called "Counterattack! The Women of Football" and "Queens of Cups," all curated by women and with a production and execution team made up mostly of women. In addition to these exhibitions, various other initiatives were carried out, such as digitizing the collection, producing an audio guide, holding events and providing information via the institutional website. I defend this position because I am convinced that the Football Museum, one of the most significant places of memory in the country, by showcasing women's football as one of its themes, has made a significant contribution to arousing curiosity about the subject. It is worth noting that the very organizations responsible for managing this sport do not have enough data to support analyses of the processes that structured it in the country.

In line with these actions, the work of women in the different media spaces was equally significant for the dissemination of news that prioritized their presence in the football universe. Despite facing an extremely hostile environment, several female journalists, narrators and commentators have destabilized hierarchies, including by making public a campaign denouncing the disrespect, aggression, sexual and moral harassment suffered in stadiums, on the streets and in newsrooms, the consequences of which have affected their careers and personal lives.

If female researchers and journalists have given rise to different visibilities, the inclusion of women in leadership positions has been no less significant. By taking on administrative, technical and management positions, they were able to access decision-making bodies to propose actions capable of minimizing certain disadvantages and inequities. Women managers, coaches, members of technical committees, referees and leaders of organized supporters have been indispensable both for the initiatives they have implemented and for the representativeness they have created by occupying such positions. Respecting the specificities of each role, being in these spaces, which are culturally assumed to be for men, made their abilities, competence, resistance and resilience public. In short, these women have created representativeness and led acts that have reverberated in different parts of Brazilian society, drawing attention to the subtle and explicit violence that is present in a society marked by many gender inequalities both inside and outside football.

In the specific context of the Brazilian Football Confederation, I would like to highlight a movement organized exclusively by women which, when publicized in the national and international press, exposed the treatment that women's football has historically received from the institution that governs it. Motivated by the dismissal of Emily Lima, the first woman to lead the senior national team, players and former players went public with their discontent with the organization, considering that the coach had not had enough time to consolidate the structure and execution of her plan. Her dismissal was announced on September 22, 2017 after a friendly tournament in Australia. Faced with rumors of Emily's possible dismissal, the players who were playing in the competition wrote a letter of support for the coach and her staff to the then president of the institution. The denial of this request sparked protests from five players who went public with their discontent and announced that they were quitting the national team. Their dissatisfaction with the interference of Brazilian football's governing body was transformed into an open letter written in Portuguese and English, highlighting the lack of support for women. Entitled "Brazilian legends call for reforms," the document, signed by eight female players and former players, called on the CBF to put into action a reform plan aimed at promoting the sport and building strategies that would value women and enable them to experience football with more dignity, respect, and opportunity.

More than analyzing the results of this demonstration, I want to show that women's struggle to enter and remain in football takes place in different areas and instances. Because of gender inequalities, they have to dedicate themselves every day to issues that go beyond the specific themes of their careers, and with that I proclaim loud and clear that, for them, football is not just football! Finally, I would like to point out that the "country of football" is definitely the "country of women's football"! Not because of the structure, support or visibility, but because of the resistance and resilience of the women who preserve and implement daily different ways of playing, cheering, working and experiencing football.

www.ingramcontent.com/pod-product-compliance
Lightning Source LLC
LaVergne TN
LVHW052350100826
845147LV00013B/804

* 9 7 8 1 9 6 6 2 1 4 0 4 5 *